Women and Fascism

Ever since it came into existence in 1919, fascism's relationship with women has been neither consistent nor predictable. Despite its male predominance and a popular perception of misogynist attitudes, the movement has, on several occasions, proved able to win large numbers of women both as voters and members. Martin Durham addresses this paradox by dispelling the myth that fascism uniformly upheld antifeminist policies which wanted women firmly kept in the home, breeding an endless stream of children for the master race.

Martin Durham analyses the role of women in fascist organisations across Europe from the early 1920s to the present, with examples from Germany, Italy and France. Unusually, however, he gives special attention to British Fascism, and in doing so he offers valuable new perspectives. The author investigates women's involvement as fundraisers and marchers, electoral candidates, branch officials and national leaders. Women were even involved as stewards at meetings and were trained in unarmed combat. The author also highlights women's relationship to fascist policies on the birth-rate, abortion and eugenics.

Women and Fascism breaks new ground by arguing that, in its efforts to recruit female members and increase its popularity, fascism has experienced serious internal conflicts regarding women's rights. Indeed, on a number of occasions, political expediency has forced fascism to oppose traditionalist patriarchy and put forward policies which were deliberately intended to be seen not as denying women's equality but as accepting and promoting it.

Martin Durham is Senior Lecturer in Politics at the University of Wolverhampton. He has published extensively on right-wing politics in Europe and the USA.

Women and Fascism

Martin Durham

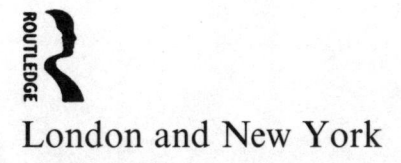

London and New York

For Stephanie and Nicholas

First published 1998
by Routledge
11 New Fetter Lane, London EC4P 4EE

Simultaneously published in the USA and Canada
by Routledge
29 West 35th Street, New York, NY 10001

© 1998 Martin Durham

Typeset in Times by
BC Typesetting, Bristol
Printed and bound in Great Britain by
Clays Ltd, St Ives PLC

All rights reserved. No part of this book may be reprinted or reproduced or utilised in any form or by any electronic, mechanical, or other means, now known or hereafter invented, including photocopying and recording, or in any information storage or retrieval system, without permission in writing from the publishers.

British Library Cataloguing in Publication Data
A catalogue record for this book is available from the British Library

Library of Congress Cataloging in Publication Data
Durham, Martin.
    Women and fascism/Martin Durham.
    Includes bibliographical references and index.
    1. Fascism and women – Great Britain – History – 20th century.
    2. Fascism and women – Europe, Western – History – 20th century.
    I. Title.
    HQ1236.5.G7D87   1998
    320.53'0820941 – dc21   98–4916

ISBN 0–415–12279–1 (hbk)
ISBN 0–415–12280–5 (pbk)

Contents

Acknowledgements vi

Introduction 1

1 Fascism, Nazism and women 5

2 Women in the Greater Britain 27

3 Blackshirt women 49

4 Patriots – and patriarchs? 74

5 For race and nation 95

6 Breeding more Britons 119

7 The home and the homeland 147

8 Fascism and gender 165

References 183
Index 195

Acknowledgements

During the years in which I have been engaged in this research, many people have helped me. I would like to thank Lynne Amidon, Janet Batsleer, Andy Bell, Lucy Bland, Sue Bruley, Erica Carter, Luciano Cheles, Mike Cronin, Stephen Cullen, Stephen Dorrell, Roger Eatwell, David Edgar, Chris Flood, Roger Griffin, Lyn Heath, Kerry Killin, Jill Liddington, Tom Linehan, Nick Mansfield, David Mayall, Larry O'Hara, Mark Phythian, Robin Ramsay, Richard Robinson, Stuart Rawnsley, Celia Shalom, Wendy Thomas, Richard Thurlow, Julie Wheelwright and Cornelia Usborne. I would like to give particular mention to four people. First, I am very grateful to Siobhan Cleary for allowing me access to material gathered for the television programme *Rise of a New Eve*. Second, I would like to thank Andrew Mitchell for his generosity in giving me access to the pamphlets he has gathered as part of his research on the British Union of Fascists. Third, I am indebted to Nick Toczek for his kindness in allowing me to draw on his research materials on the modern extreme right. Finally, for one of those defining moments when another researcher shares a vital document you would otherwise never have seen, my thanks to John Hope.

I would also like to thank *Searchlight* magazine for generously responding to an unreasonable number of pleas for help and Helen Hyde, Michelle Siddhu and Wolfgang Deicke for the vital work they did in translating material from Italy and Germany.

The material I have used in this study is scattered in many different locations. I would like to thank the British Library, the British Newspaper Library, the Bodleian Library, the Public Record Office, the British Library of Political and Economic Science, the Wiener Library, the Fawcett Library, the National Museum of Labour History, the Modern Records Centre at the University of Warwick, the Birmingham Central Reference Library and the libraries of the University of

Hull, the University of Sheffield and the University of Wolverhampton for allowing me access to much of the material that is discussed in this work.

Last, and most definitely not least, I would like to thank Stephanie, Nicholas and Alan, who contributed so much to the happiness of the circumstances under which this has been written, and without whom it would never have been finished.

Introduction

In the early twentieth century a new word and a new politics came into existence. The coming to power of Benito Mussolini, little over three years after the creation of the fascist movement, not only represented a fundamental shift in Italian politics but served as an inspiration to militant nationalists and anti-socialists elsewhere. Across Europe and beyond, groupings sprang up under the name of fascism and others consciously modelled themselves along similar lines. In France, Britain and other Western states, such organisations proved unable to break through liberal democracy's defensive fortifications. In some cases, as in Spain, they found themselves subordinated to ultra-conservatives who rejected democracy but saw little need for the popular mobilisation and social demagoguery which marked the organisations that can properly be called fascist. In Germany, however, where a myriad radical rightist, nationalist and anti-Marxist formations had already emerged before Mussolini marched on Rome, one such movement, Hitler's National Socialists, would eventually create a state that would overshadow its forebear in the ambition and brutality of the national transformation on which it embarked.

In characterising some movements as fascist, others not, we are already trapped in a thicket of competing definitions that have long troubled those who seek to understand the politics of our century. Neither nationalism nor anti-socialism is unique to fascism, and the latter term is itself a problem if it leads us to expect that what we call the extreme right always sees itself in that encapsulation. On the contrary, where some fascists might seem to be nothing more than particularly belligerent conservatives, others speak a language of social radicalism in which Marxism is attacked not only for cosmopolitanism but for being insufficiently revolutionary. To make matters yet more complicated, terms such as proto-fascism have been brought into play to categorise particular groupings, such as Action Française or the Russian Black Hundreds, which lacked what are taken to be the specifically modern features of fascism. Numerous attempts have been made to draw demarcation lines within the right and even, on occasion, to dispute whether fascism should be seen as being on the right at all. As we will see, this becomes even more problematic when we turn to a post-war political constellation in which militant nationalists often wish to emphasise their difference from pre-war movements. This study is not intended as an intervention into the debate on the boundaries of generic fascism. While rejecting certain arguments that have been put forward – most importantly, that National Socialism is too fundamentally different to be seen as a form of fascism – this work will not be concerned with the extended elaboration of criteria by which vexed questions about how we might define radical conservatives in inter-war Germany or the different anti-immigration parties of modern Western Europe can be settled once and for all. Instead, a variety of terms will be deployed to capture what is a complex and diverse family of political forces (family, of course, being a highly appropriate metaphor for the subject in hand). Within this study, I will be arguing that German National Socialism, Italian Fascism and the British Union of Fascists are all examples of fascism; in the post-war period, I will be arguing not that organisations such as the (French) Front National, the (German) Republikaner and the (British) National Front are the direct descendents of classical fascism, but that they share many of the concerns of the pre-war extreme right but in a context which is markedly different. The particular shape that Italian Fascism took was not pre-ordained and the movement both before and after coming to power contained different conservatising and radicalising strands. This was the case too with National Socialism and the multifaceted German anti-democratic right of which it formed a leading component. Over half a century later the division of Europe (and its supersession), the creation of Israel, the rise of the USA to global hegemony and, above all, large-scale immigration from other continents, have both revived age-old themes of the extreme right and reworked much of what it means to be occupying that particular political space. In some ways, the term fascism may not capture developments in the post-war period and the terms that extreme right activists themselves prefer – nationalists or racial nationalists – might be more useful. But, for better or worse, they have not achieved popular or academic currency. I have chosen not to follow the direction of some recent studies and adopt such categories as radical right or new right, more appropriately applied, I would suggest, to sections of the right with which the extreme right is in competition. Instead we are left with the other terms which I will use in tandem with nationalist – extreme right, racist and fascist.

For such movements, the nation is in danger. Threatened by external enemies, it is also under threat from enemies within. The enemies beyond the borders are sometimes to be found on the borders themselves, engaged in dispute over territory and the national identity of contested populations. At other times they are further away, threatening its position in the world and sometimes, as in the case of the Soviet state, the very ways of organising society it sees as sacred. In turn, the enemies within are seen as connected with those without. Communists are attacked as agents of a foreign power. The construction of a national mythology with its pantheon of heroes (and sometimes heroines) casts doubt on the loyalties of minorities, seen as owing allegiance not to the land in which they live but to the one from which they or their forebears came. For racial nationalists, such as Germany's National Socialists, the external foe and the domestic enemy have other connections. Politics is the conflict between races and for the nation to accept those of another race in its midst is to threaten its very survival. Not only are races the building blocks of history, they are organised in a hierarchy, with the white race at its apex. Other racial groups threaten that predominance but, for many of those who see events through a racial lens, one group represents the greatest enemy of all. Drawing on the resentments and fantasies of Christian anti-Semitism, National Socialists and similar groupings bring the medieval fear of the religious Other together with the modern dread of the racialised Other. The figure of the Jew becomes the spider at the centre of a web, the mysterious figure plotting in the darkness, deploying the unwitting as pawns on some giant chessboard. It is in this context, of nationalism, racism and anti-Semitism, that we will engage with the subject of this book.

In examining any political movement, we will find that it bears with it assumptions about the rightful place of men and women. In turn, this will impact upon a wide range of its policy concerns, from its stance on employment and on population to its views on crime and on sexual morality. The ways in which fascism has been influenced by such assumptions, sometimes implicit, sometimes consciously explicated and espoused, are our concern in the pages that follow. In discussing fascism and women, we need to examine two distinct although interrelated areas: first, fascism's policy stance towards women in society and, second, the role of women in the fascist movement. Much of the existing material on fascism has ignored both areas, in part because having recognised that both the membership and the electorate of fascist movements are disproportionately male, it is assumed that there is consequently no need to investigate why they should none the less still have some success in attracting women's support. This neglect of female support for fascism often comes side by side with a disinterest in what fascism actually says about women. In part, this work is an attempt to repair such an omission. But, more importantly, it is a challenge to what we could legitimately call a conventional wisdom on the relationship between women and fascism. This interpretation focuses on policy towards women rather than women as members or voters and, furthermore, is drawn overwhelmingly from one example – National Socialism. In the work that follows, we will be examining both policy and the role of women in the movement and extending our gaze beyond the Germany of the 1920s and 1930s. Not only, it will be argued, has the National Socialist case not always been well understood but it has been extended illegitimately to fascism in general. Conventional accounts see fascism as, by definition, an anti-feminist movement devoted to the removal of women from the labour market and their return to a life of domestic servitude and the unceasing production of children. But does such an approach accurately capture fascism's treatment of women, either as the objects of its political programme or as subjects in its political struggle? When we look at fascism's relationship to women, we think that we already understand it. In important ways, this study is intended to subvert that supposition.

1 Fascism, Nazism and women

In this chapter, we will examine the relationship between fascism and women in Germany and Italy in the early twentieth century. First, however, we will need to come to grips with the rise of fascism not only in those two countries, but as a movement across Europe. The term itself was first used by the movement that emerged in Italy after the First World War but many of the beliefs that this movement and its equivalents elsewhere championed had already long been in existence. It is possible to see such beliefs in different ways. If we were to focus on fascism's anti-liberalism or anti-Marxism, this would suggest that it emerged as a movement of negation. But if we were to emphasise instead the movement's fervent nationalism or its claim to represent a new civilisation, we would be more inclined to see it as innovative rather than merely reactive, a movement that believed itself to be forging a new order and, as it (not insignificantly) put it, a new man. Whether we approach fascism from the perspective of what it is against or what it is for, we will soon encounter the other aspect. If we see it as standing for what Roger Griffin calls palingenesis, 'a radically *new* beginning which follows a period of . . . perceived dissolution', it is also against movements it sees as antagonistic to that rebirth. If, with Roger Eatwell, we understand fascism as espousing a Third Way, distinct from both liberal capitalism and Marxist socialism, once again we are looking at the Janus face of a movement that has both a Utopia it seeks to establish and rivals it seeks to expunge. (Griffin 1993: 32–6; Eatwell 1996c: 313–14.) In addition to this alternation between the positive and the negative, we also encounter variation and contradiction. We experience the former when we compare the cultural vitalism of Italian Fascism to the racist nationalism of German National Socialism. We experience the latter when we see how fascism can be seen both as counter-revolutionary, the brutal defence of capitalism, and as, in its own way, a revolutionary challenge to bourgeois civilisation, a challenge that owes much to the leftist formation of some of its founding figures. It is undeniably important to recognise fascism's barbarism. But, destructive as it was, appealing to the irrational as it does, fascism is also a body of ideas. It is shaped by an array of nineteenth- and early-twentieth-century thinkers, ranging from elitists such as Vilfredo Pareto and Gustave Le Bon and race theorists such as Arthur de Gobineau and Houston Stewart Chamberlain to the proponent of the mobilising power of myth, Georges Sorel. Where elitism taught that democracy was a fraud, a disguise for the inevitable rule of the few over the many, it also emphasised that the exhaustion of a ruling group could be reversed by the infusion of new forces or even result in the emergence of a new elite. It simultaneously defended authority and legitimated attempts at radical renewal and, as such, although not itself fascist, would prove a powerful weapon in the hands of those who were. Elitism on its own would not have created a new mass politics. Alongside a radicalisation of sections of the right, dissident leftists such as Sorel were crucial in fusing faith in an elite with the belief that enormous powers lay latent within an as yet unawakened people. Long before the First World War, and the experience of comradeship under fire in the trenches and mobilisation for total war at home, the ideological elements of fascism were in place. Assumptions about the primacy of the nation and the superiority of the white race had considerable currency. Socialism already had a double meaning, as the international class movement which nationalists abhorred, and as the mobilisation of national resources for a common goal which nationalists espoused. But if the potential existed for a blurring of the boundaries between at least some on the right and some on the left, it would be preponderantly on right-wing terms. Socialism as it is usually understood would be the main enemy of the new movement, and established elites would find the new movement more of a reinforcement than a danger. Furthermore, the very currency of many of the beliefs so important to fascism made it possible for other forms of mass politics, particularly on the orthodox right, to retain control of the situation and keep challengers at bay. None the less, a new movement was to emerge across Europe and would come to power in two countries in the period following the First World War. Before we can turn our attention to the relationship between women and fascism, we will need to gain a fuller sense of the development of those movements and those regimes. It would be appropriate, then, to begin with the country in which fascism not only first emerged but first came to power. (For a fuller account of Italian Fascism, see

Lyttelton 1973; Roberts 1979; Forgacs 1986; Revelli 1987; Sternhell, Sznajder and Asheri 1994; for Germany see Mosse 1964; Herf 1984; Lane and Rupp 1978; Stachura 1983; Fischer 1995; for discussions of both in the context of international fascism, see Griffin 1993; Payne 1995; Eatwell 1996a.)

Following Italian unification in the 1860s, the new state had faced immense problems. Divided into a backward south and a modernising north, the country experienced both an insurgent labour movement in the cities and unrest among peasants and agricultural labourers in the countryside. Governments veered between repression and attempts at incorporation, and although some sections of the left would have been satisfied with reforms, large sections were intransigently revolutionary. Attempts at creating an Italian Empire in Africa were only partly successful, and already before the war a number of militant nationalist currents had emerged. The most important, the Nationalist Association, saw Italy as a 'proletarian nation' oppressed by the plutocratic powers of Britain and Germany. So too did some elements within syndicalism, the most militant wing of the labour movement, who were moving away from waging a class war against employers in favour of creating a new economic order based on an alliance of producers. Yet another strand of what might be considered proto-fascism was to be found in the artistic movement, the Futurists, with its celebration of technology, insurgent patriotism and war. When at last the First World War broke out the pressures on a reluctant government to enter the war and gain new territory were irresistible. The advocates of joining the war, so-called interventionists, varied from right-wing monarchists to republican radicals opposed to Austria, Italy's former occupier, but one component was to prove of particular importance. A former leading light of the left of the Socialist Party, Benito Mussolini, along with other renegade socialists and syndicalists, was to prove particularly adept at the politics of the street and, following Italy's disappointing share of the spoils after the Allied victory, was to create a new nationalist movement in 1919. It was not the only such force. In late 1919 the poet and war hero Gabriele D'Annunzio led an occupying force into the disputed Adriatic city of Fiume, claiming it for Italy. The Nationalist Association had also continued as a militant right-wing current but Mussolini's new group, the Fasci, would soon outstrip both. The radicalism of the Socialist Party and, from the beginning of 1921, the infant Italian Communist Party, and the militancy of unions and peasant leagues, threw large sections of the Italian upper and middle classes into disarray and, despite his initial denunciation of wartime profiteers and the monarchy, Mussolini soon became increasingly popular among the propertied. The fascist movement, which in 1921 became the Fascist Party, grew to over 80,000 in 1920 and over 200,000 the following year. The movement produced a flood of propaganda, denouncing socialism and promising social stability, sometimes arguing for freeing the economy from state controls, at other times calling for the creation of a corporate state in which employers, employees and the state would come together in the national interest. But more important than speeches or leaflets was the movement's physical destruction of its opponents' power-base. Claiming to speak in the name of the productive classes and those who had fought in the trenches, fascism unleashed its militants against those it portrayed as anti-national elements. The offices of socialist newspapers and the headquarters of unions were wrecked, left-wing councillors were beaten and driven from their positions, as fascist squads, sometimes in convoy, swept across the country. While the left was divided, conservatives and other anti-socialists were allied with fascists in elections, but it was ultimately by threatening to march on Rome that the fascists finally achieved power. In October 1922, in coalition with the Nationalists and other sections of the right, Mussolini became Italy's prime minister.

The coalition, and the existence of legal opposition, would last until 1925. The murder by fascist activists of the leader of the moderate wing of Italian socialism, Giacomo Matteotti, forced Mussolini to choose between his militants and his critics and, after some hesitation, he moved to centralise power in the hands of a one-party state. (He had already taken the Nationalists into the Fascist Party in 1923.) Opposition was driven underground and the government pursued a policy of economic nationalism, involving protectionism, state-aided agricultural development and, once the depression hit in the early 1930s, substantial state intervention in the economy. This economic nationalism went hand in hand with a sustained effort to deprive the left of its popular support through a state-controlled fascist union movement and the creation of twenty-two corporations to bring together employers and employees in different sectors of the economy. The party and its auxiliary organisations (for women, youth, students, etc.) attempted to organise the Italian population while the promotion of mass leisure activities through the state sought to bind the people to the regime. In the latter part of the 1920s, the government's ability to secure popular support was cemented also by the decision of the Vatican to reach agreement with the regime over the rights of the Church in Italy – something which had eluded all previous governments – and despite tensions over the rights of Catholic youth organisations, the regime made the most of its rapprochement with the Papacy. In 1935 the imperialist theme long present among Italian nationalists came to the fore in the decision to invade Ethiopia. By this time, however, the first fascist power had been joined by another, one that would soon come to overshadow it.

Only unified in the 1860s, Germany contained not only the largest Marxist party in the world (with over a million members at the outbreak of the First World War), but also a bitterly anti-Marxist ideology which harked back to medieval notions of estates and guilds. For many among the middle class, the German people, the *Volk*, was threatened by a Jewish enemy which at one and the same time controlled both international finance and the left. Bankers, it was argued, denied credit to shopkeepers and farmers, while Marxist agitators threatened to destroy them by socialisation. *Völkisch* ideology enjoyed a substantial following, and when the First World War ended in defeat, new *völkisch* groups sprang into life. The hated Russian Revolution, they believed, represented the alien tyranny foretold in the *Protocols of the Learned Elders of Zion*, supposedly the minutes of a meeting of Jewish conspirators, in fact a forgery by tsarist anti-Semites. *Völkisch* propagandists fulminated against both their internal enemies (particularly the emergent communists) and the victorious Allies who through the Versailles Treaty limited Germany's armed forces, deprived it of territory, occupied the Rhineland with colonial troops and forced the payment of massive reparations. What would prove to be the most important of the new groupings emerged in 1919, initially as the German Workers' Party. The following year, now the National Socialist German Workers' Party (NSDAP), it adopted a party programme, the Twenty-five Points, which made clear how it welded together the national and the 'socialist'. The party, it declared, stood for the abolition of the Treaty of Versailles and the union of all those of German blood in a Greater Germany. Wholesale businesses would be leased to small traders, trusts would be nationalised and all speculation in land would be stopped. Socialism was explicitly not the ending of private enterprise or the creation of social equality; instead it was the recognition of a common purpose in which all true Germans would find a meaning beyond the individual and beyond sectional interest.

Where historically *völkisch* ideology had expressed a reaction against modernity, National Socialism was Janus-faced. Denouncing both capitalism and urbanism, it none the less was enraptured by technology and embraced a mass politics which used the most modern means of communications to amplify and organise discontent. Communist attempts to seize power proved unsuccessful but persuaded many to look to the extreme right and despite involvement in a failed putsch in 1923 and a (brief) jail sentence, Hitler and the Nazis became the dominant force within the *völkisch* movement. At times this came under threat, particularly in the mid-1920s when some sections of the party, notably those around Otto and Gregor Strasser, accused Hitler of seeking to 'water down' the 'socialism' of the party. But the critics were defeated and when in the late 1920s Germany was to be hit by economic depression the party was in a position to benefit. The regime, Nazis claimed, had been imposed on Germany by the Allies and served the interests of Jewry. The impact of taxes on farmers, of chain-stores on shopkeepers and of unemployment on workers, could all be explained by the machinations of Germany's enemies, and the party's vote of 2.5 per cent in 1928 leapt to over 18 per cent in 1930. By late 1930 membership had grown to almost 130,000. That the Communist Party also grew in this period was of greater help to the extreme right than it was to the communists. First, communist growth was slower. Second, that it was none the less occurring was grist to the anti-communist mill. In an ambiguous alliance with the more upper-class Nationalists (DNVP), the Nazis campaigned against German reparation payments to the Allies, while, at the same time, they tried to win over communist supporters to the idea of a national revolution. Disagreements about the radicalism of the party again broke out and a small number followed Otto Strasser out of the party to create a more radical nationalist organisation. (The party was also criticised by more elitist elements of the nationalist right, notably the writer Oswald Spengler, and other adherents of the so-called conservative revolution. Both Strasser and Spengler, as we will have cause to note, would be influential on later extreme rightists.) But the Nazis continued to grow and in 1932 achieved 37.1 per cent (13.7 million votes), a higher vote than any other party.

A second election later that year saw a fall to 33 per cent, but key figures in the German establishment were being increasingly drawn to the idea of bringing Hitler into government. Of the main parties, the (moderate socialist) Social Democrats and the (Catholic) Centre remained strong but mutually antagonistic. The DNVP had lost some of its voters to the Nazis and the main middle-class parties (the German People's Party (DVP) and the German Democratic Party (DDP)) had lost nearly all their support. So too, even more dramatically, had an array of middle-class protest parties that had sprung up during the 1920s. Non-voters and new voters too had flocked to the Nazi banner. The Nazis had become the party of the nationalist (Protestant) middle class and had made inroads into other social groups. In January 1933, in coalition with the DNVP, the Nazis came to power.

The new regime moved far more quickly than Mussolini had done to destroy opposition. Both governments had begun to persecute opponents as soon as they came into existence, but in the German case legal opposition did not last beyond a few months. An attempt to burn the Reichstag, the German parliament building, was used as a pretext for creating a one-party state, and while the Nationalists were taken into the Nazi party, other parties were simply banned. This process took a stronger turn the following year when conflict between the party and some of its paramilitary wing (the SA) led to a bloody purge in which SA leaders, conservative critics of the regime and others (including Gregor Strasser) were murdered during the Night of the Long Knives. The anti-Semitism of the party increasingly shaped state policy and the budding alliance with Italy not only drew both regimes into the Spanish Civil War, and pushed Italy itself into an anti-Semitic stance, but it was to involve them ultimately in a war of far greater dimensions.

While in Spain, the fascists of the Falange joined forces with monarchists and the military to overthrow the republican government and create an authoritarian state, in Romania, the extreme nationalists of the Iron Guard, later an influence on sections of the post-war extreme right, were alternately suppressed and co-opted by the orthodox right. In France, the proto-fascist Action Française was challenged by newer organisations in an extreme right that achieved mass proportions while across the Channel, one such group, the British Fascists, had emerged in the 1920s, only to be effectively superseded by Sir Oswald Mosley's British Union of Fascists in the early 1930s. For each of these movements, women were significant for the future both of fascism and of the nation. Later, we will be devoting attention to the British example. First, however, we will discuss the most important cases – the Italian and the German. (For Spain, see e.g. Payne 1962: 203–4; for Romania, see e.g. Codreanu 1987: 9–10; for France, see e.g. Soucy 1986: 80–1; 1995: 198–9; Passmore 1997: 287–9.)

In 1919, at its founding meeting, the Italian fascist movement adopted a programme which included a call for women to have both the vote and the right to hold office. Nine women attended, some of whom were subsequently involved in the occupation of Fiume by D'Annunzio and his Legionnaires. One was an officer of an armed women's group while others organised an evacuation of many of the city's children. Some of the latter in turn joined with others to form a National Association of the Sisters of the Legionnaires of Fiume and

Dalmatia. The creation of the Association had been preceded by the emergence of the first women's groups within the fascist movement but D'Annunzian women continued to be important and would later agree to an electoral alliance with the fascists. The specifically fascist women's groups emerged independently of any official initiative and would prove troublesome for the movement's male hierarchy. In part, this concerned the involvement of some women in armed actions although the most famous example of such a woman, Ines Donati, had been a member of the Nationalist Association, who only became a fascist after the fusion of the two parties. (After her death, fascism both appropriated her militancy, falsifying when she had joined the party, and claimed that her last letter had declared that 'I wanted to be too manly, and forgot that, in the end, I was just a weak woman.' There was in fact a subsequent letter in which she had expressed her 'regret at not having died with a weapon in my hand'.) If, as we will see, there were problems over what fascist women should do, there were difficulties too over the 1919 pledge to extend the vote to women. (Detragiache 1983: 212–14, 218–27.)

By the end of 1921, some 2,000 women belonged to the movement and the Bologna party paper was already referring to 'Fascist feminism' in describing local militants. Attempts, however, were already being made to ensure that women's groups or branches were subordinated to male branch officers and some women, particularly those in the Rome women's group, were looked upon with favour for arguing that fascist women should engage in charitable work rather than political activity. The transformation of the movement into a party in late 1921 involved the issuance of a new constitution which declared women's groups to be subordinate and restricted to propaganda, welfare and charitable work and women's position in the movement became increasingly marginalised as conservative elements flowed into the party, both as it approached power and even more after it was achieved. Many fascist women, none the less, were hopeful that the new regime would enfranchise women and sought too to gain autonomy for the women's groups within the party. Both, indeed, appeared possible. Mussolini had indicated sympathy after meeting a women's deputation in 1924 and the previous year had even opened the Rome Congress of the International Alliance for Women's Suffrage, declaring that 'barring unforeseen developments, the Fascist government pledges to grant the vote to several categories of women, beginning at the local level'. Indeed, he appealed to an unsympathetic parliament to support reform, declaring that fascist women were calling for the vote and that fascist men should recognise that in the twentieth century women were no longer restricted to hearth and home. The proposed legislation, however, not only turned out to involve a strikingly limited number of women (notably the widows of veterans) but was also quickly followed by the abolition of local elections altogether. As for women fascists themselves, despite an attempt to argue that they deserved a greater say in the party in recognition of their support for the regime during the Matteotti crisis, this was to elude their grasp. Initially, Mussolini again appeared sympathetic and one leading woman was appointed to the seemingly significant role of inspector general of the women's branches. Soon after, however, the party hierarchy moved against both her and any notions of autonomy while those women members who disputed the failure to enfranchise women were expelled from the organisation. (Detragiache 1983: 231–4, 237–40, 243–51; De Grazia 1992: 36, 39; De Grand 1976: 954–5; Meyer 1989: 28.)

If Italian Fascism had not started as an anti-feminist movement, by the late 1920s it had become one. The regime's turn towards a campaign to raise the birth-rate combined with concern over rising male unemployment shaped the nature of its policy towards women. Speaking in 1927, Mussolini noted how the Italian birth-rate had fallen from 39 per 1,000 persons in 1886 to 27 by 1926. It would, he warned, fall yet further unless hedonism and moral cowardice were overcome. Italy already was outnumbered by the Germans, by the Slavs and by the population of the French and British Empires. What was needed was an increase in numbers. The following year, in a preface to a book by a German writer, Mussolini pictured a declining Europe threatened by a populous Russia and China. The book itself traced one of the causes of the falling birth-rate to women's emancipation. (Gregor 1979: 285; Meyer 1989: 30.)

Already in 1926 the sale of contraceptives had been banned as an offence against public decency, a move that was taken further in 1931 with the creation of a crime of inciting others to prevent births. (Abortion too was covered under both these measures, in the latter case punishing any woman who had consented to her abortion with up to five years' penal servitude.) In 1925 the Opera nazionale per la maternità ed infanzia (the National Agency for Maternity and Infancy), was set up in order 'to strengthen family ties to the greatest degree'. This involved the provision of maternity centres as part of an improvement of pre-natal and post-natal care, and also aid to unmarried women who might otherwise not carry their pregnancy to term. On Christmas Eve each year, designated by the regime as Mother and Child Day, the Agency gave monetary awards for marriages, for births 'and for the hygienic raising of children'. (Glass 1967: 231–4, 243; De Grazia 1992: 60–5.)

Other initiatives came from elsewhere in the complex state apparatus. Maternity insurance, which covered some women in pre-fascist days, was extended to others by a succession of decrees, married couples with children received preference in public housing, and family allowances were given to many state employees in 1929 and to workers in 1934. (In the latter case, however, this was less a matter of raising the birth-rate than of compensating workers with families for losses brought about by the decision to reduce working hours in an attempt to cut unemployment.) In 1928 large families were given tax concessions and the following year the married were given preference for state employment over the single (and those with children over the childless). In 1936 and 1937 family allowances were extended and were joined by loans to 'encourage the formation of Italian families and assure their development', awarded jointly to husband and wife, 10 per cent of the repayment to be cancelled in the event of the birth of a first child, a further 20 per cent for a second, 30 per cent for a third and the final 40 per cent for a fourth. Finally, in 1939 a system of marriage and birth grants was introduced. (Glass 1967: 241–4, 237–8, 248–52, 255–8, 260; De Grazia 1992: 86.)

Despite all its efforts, the regime did not succeed in raising the Italian birth-rate. Between 1931 and 1935, it averaged 24 births per 1,000, for 1936–1940 it had fallen yet further to 23.4. But if the regime had failed to secure increased births, what of its policy towards women at work? Despite opposition by some women supporters, the regime was increasingly opposed to women's presence in the labour force. Restrictions were placed on women's employment in the state sector soon after the regime came to power. Attempts were also made to stop women teachers from being responsible for boys and to channel girls into a specifically female education. Subsequently, the regime introduced restrictions on women's entry into the civil service and propagandised against women entering professions deemed unsuitable for them. In 1938, with over 5 million women still in the workforce the government declared that with the exception of what it defined as female occupations (typists, telephonists, the staff of dry cleaning establishments etc.), women's employment should be restricted to 10 per cent of any large or medium enterprise, and to none in small firms. This, it announced, would be implemented within three years (a time scale, of course, that was brought to an abrupt halt by the outbreak of war and the renewed need for women workers). (De Grand 1976: 953–6, 958–9, 962–3, 965; De Grazia 1992: 46, 179–80.)

This hostility to women's employment had already been anticipated in a striking article by Mussolini in 1934. Entitled 'Machine and Woman', it declared that women's work was a 'major aspect of the thorny problem of unemployment' and of the problem of population. Work, he claimed, distracted from reproduction, encouraging independence and 'habits that are incompatible with childbearing'. (As for the man, 'unemployed in every sense of the word', he would give up on family life.) What was needed, then, was the 'exodus of women from the work force' which would enable 'legions of men' to once again 'raise their heads high'. The same work that took away women's reproductive characteristics would, he declared, furnish 'man with an extremely powerful physical and moral virility'. (Bell and Offen 1983: 363, 369–70.)

Even this, however, was exceeded by a book, *The Politics of the Family*, which appeared in 1938, introduced by the minister of education. Written by Ferdinando Loffredo, the book argued that what the state needed was the full linking of wages and taxation to family responsibilities and the removal of women from the workforce and their subordination within the family. 'Women', he declared, 'must return under the absolute subjection of man – father or husband' while as for the 'abolition of women's jobs', this 'must follow from two convergent factors'. Far more than law, the woman 'who leaves the domestic enclosure to go to work' must become 'the object of public reproach'. (De Grazia 1992: 93–4; De Grand 1976: 965; Meyer 1989: 32.)

Loffredo's book represented the patriarchal fantasy of one particular strand of a movement which in its early days had called for women's suffrage and which, in power, included both supporters and opponents of women's role in the labour market. But if the movement did not speak with one voice, Mussolini's pronouncements on the contradiction between woman and machine and on population represented its dominant tendency. The movement came to adopt a misogynist stance, just as in a different tempo, it was to become racist. Nor did these processes develop without impacting on each other. In April 1937 intervention in Africa resulted in a decree-law prohibiting cohabitation between Italians and colonial subjects from Ethiopia, Eritrea or Somaliland, with a term of from one to five years' imprisonment. In November of the following year, marriages between Aryans and non-Aryans were forbidden. The increased strength of anti-Semitism within Italian Fascism was reflected in turn in the claim in the racist fascist journal, *La difesa della raza*, that feminism was a Jewish invention. Italian Fascism, we have argued, was not inscribed with anti-feminism from its beginnings. But what of National Socialism? (Preti 1974: 190; Noether 1982: 77, 80.)

For Hitler, writing in prison in 1924 following his unsuccessful putsch, National Socialists and a wider nationalist public needed to know what the movement stood for and how it had developed. The two volumes of *Mein Kampf* that resulted, although they sold few copies during the 1920s, were to gain increased sales in the early 1930s and, then, unsurprisingly, massive sales under the Third Reich. There is no chapter specifically devoted to the question of women's role in either the movement or the future state, but the work does, however, address the relationship of women and *Volk* at several points. In this, he shows the influence of two forces that were of importance not only in Germany and would have lasting influence on the extreme right as a whole. The first was moral conservatism, espoused in Germany by Protestant and Catholic organisations, in which the separation of sexuality and marriage was seen as emblematic of a decadence which threatened both family and nation. The second was eugenics, the scientific school founded in the late nineteenth century by Francis Galton for the improvement of human 'stock'. As we have seen in our discussion of Italy, nationalists were pro-natalists, concerned that their nation was not successfully keeping up with the birth-rate of potential rivals. Where eugenics differed from pro-natalism was in denying that an increase in numbers was sufficient. For eugenicists, what mattered was that only those they categorised as 'fit' should procreate. This was positive eugenics, alongside which was to be found negative eugenics, the discouragement of 'breeding' by those defined as 'unfit'. Neither moral conservatives nor eugenicists are necessarily fascists and, as we will see, we should not assume that fascists are necessarily proponents of 'traditional' morality or selective breeding. At this point, however, what is being argued is that both are important in the argument in *Mein Kampf* and, therefore, in understanding National Socialism. (For eugenics, see e.g. Soloway 1982, 1990; Weindling 1989; for moral conservatism, see Usborne 1992: 69–101.)

The most extended discussion, some ten pages in length, was developed from a diatribe against sexual disease. The populations of large cities were being increasingly affected by syphilis, it declared, with the inevitable consequence that 'the vices of the parents' were 'revealed in the sicknesses of the children'. What was needed was 'a fight against prostitution' and 'false prudery'. The young needed to be helped to marry early, not only so that prostitution could be curbed but because the purpose of marriage was to 'serve one higher goal, the increase and preservation of the species and the race'. For early marriage to be possible, housing shortages had to be dealt with as did the 'absurd way of regulating salaries, which concerns itself much too little with the question of the family and its sustenance'. But more than early marriage was required. Education had to guard against 'the emergence of sexual ideas at a much too early age' while parallel to this, 'a struggle against the poisoning of the soul' was called for.

> Our whole public life today is like a hothouse for sexual ideas and stimulations ... movies, vaudevilles and theatres ... shop windows and billboards ... This sensual, sultry atmosphere leads to ideas and stimulations at a time when the boy should have no understanding of such things.

To protect the young, the culture had to be transformed.

> Theatre, art, literature, cinema, press, posters, and window displays must be cleansed of all manifestations of our rotting world and placed in the service of a moral, political and cultural idea. Public life must be freed from the stifling perfume of our modern eroticism . . . The right of personal freedom recedes before the duty to preserve the race.
> (Hitler 1969: 224–34)

Only after such changes, Hitler argued, could the medical battle against disease hope to succeed. This would involve grave measures – 'defective people' should be 'prevented from propagating equally defective offspring' and, 'if necessary, the incurably sick will be pitilessly segregated'. The old Germany had failed to deal with the problem, Hitler declared, and what was needed was a gigantic 'struggle against syphilis and the prostitution which prepares the way for it'. (Hitler 1969: 232–3.)

Elsewhere in the book, Hitler linked women with the anti-Semitism and anti-black racism that suffused the German extreme right. In modern Germany, he declared, 'hundreds of thousands' were seduced by Jews who, with 'satanic joy' lurked 'in wait for the unsuspecting girl whom he defiles with his blood, thus stealing her from her own people'. This was a systematic attack on the white race and where the Jew did not ruin its women, then he brought black troops into the Rhineland with the same aim in mind. If Hitler was particularly exercised by sexuality, he was even more concerned about population. There was, he argued, only one sacred right, the right to preserve the purest blood, yet at present, 'every depraved degenerate' had 'the possibility of propagating' while street peddlers and 'every drug store' sold 'the means for the prevention of births . . . even to the healthiest of parents'. This availability of birth control facilitated the 'suppression of the procreative faculty in millions of the very best people' but the future state would set race at the centre, ensuring that only the healthy bore children. What would then be a disgrace would be for the unhealthy to bring children into the world or the healthy to withhold them. (Hitler 1969: 375, 295, 365–7.)

Hitler, of course, was not the only prominent Nazi to pronounce on the subject of women. One leading figure, Alfred Rosenberg, held that the state was based on male warriors and as such should not be influenced by women while a second, Gottfried Feder, declared that women should be rescued from Jewish notions of equality in order to be restored to their proper position of maid and servant. Another leading Nazi, Julius Streicher, achieved notoriety through the sensationalism of his paper, *Der Stürmer*, with its mixture of scandalous allegations and pornographic cartoons to present Jews as the enemy not only of Germany but of German womanhood. As for Hitler's eugenic enthusiasm, it was shared, in particular, by Walther Darré, who was to become the minister of agriculture and national peasant leader in the Third Reich. Darré did not join the party until 1930, when he had already written *The Peasantry as the Life-Source of the Nordic Race* and *A New Aristocracy out of Blood and Soil* but his work was to become particularly influential in the party during the 1930s. What was needed, he argued, was once again to recognise the centrality of selective breeding. As recently as 100 years before, an apprentice could not become a master without proving his descent nor retain that position 'if he chose a girl of unknown or undesired origin as his wife'. Nowadays, however, Germany was experiencing a 'proliferation of inferiors of all colours' and the road to recovery lay not only in population increase, but in increase of the right kind. By re-educating 'our girls', they could once again fulfil their responsibility to be mothers of 'a large number of children'. (Rupp 1978: 16; Showalter 1982: 64–5, 86–108; Lane and Rupp 1978: xx–xxi, 111–17.)

The NSDAP was clearly a party that saw women above all as mothers. This did not mean, however, that it did not want women as members, even though in January 1921 its first general meeting decided that no women would be allowed to run as candidates. In the very earliest period of the party, women may have reached 10 per cent of its membership (in Munich in 1921 the figure was almost 14 per cent) but this fell away to around 5 per cent by 1922. From early on, however, in addition to those women who belonged to the party, women's groups were also set up to help its work in particular localities. Among the activities these groups engaged in was the provision of canteens for SA men, the making and mending of uniforms, and bandaging the men after clashes with opponents. Women also went door to door collecting for less well off members and, during election time, canvassed for the party. (Boak 1990: 376, 393; Kater 1983: 149; Stephenson 1981: 26.)

There were also national organisations of pro-Nazi women. In 1923 Elsbeth Zander founded the Deutscher Frauenorden (German Women's Order) which the following year declared its support for Hitler. In 1926 Zander joined the party, which recognised the DFO as its women's auxiliary and in 1928 it made the Order an affiliated organisation with Zander as its national leader. The Order engaged in a variety of activities, ranging from providing aid to large families and imprisoned activists to training young girls in racial consciousness and women in nursing and welfare work. According to a police report, in August 1930 the DFO had 160 branches and some 4,000 members. Zander herself had claimed 13,000 members in the late 1920s. (Stephenson 1981: 28–30, 59; Koonz 1987: 76.)

Not all National Socialist women belonged to the DFO, however. Some local women's groups rebuffed approaches to join the Order while some women members, Stephenson notes, 'did not belong to any women's group at all'. To add to the complication, some women left the DFO and organised locally outside of its control. The result was the existence of more than one National Socialist women's group in some areas and a great deal of friction, not least between the DFO and local male leaders who preferred a local group to a national women's organisation which threatened their power. Ultimately the conflict was resolved by the amalgamation of the DFO and the local groups into one organisation, the Nationalsozialistische Frauenschaft (NSF), which came into existence in October 1931 under the leadership of Zander. But the NSF did not escape the problems that rival views on organising National Socialist women had long been causing, in part because of yet another women's organisation. (Stephenson 1981: 32–4, 38–58.)

In 1917, Guida Diehl had founded the Newland Movement for the religious and moral revival of Germany. Campaigning against both communism and moral decadence in the theatre, the dancehall and elsewhere, the movement claimed to have over 200,000 members in the late 1920s. Feminism, Diehl argued, had devalued motherhood and housework and women had succumbed to 'the search for pleasure'. In a future society, women would no longer have to work outside the home and either a family wage or state subsidy would ensure they could stay there. They could still vote, however, but for a women's chamber of the legislature where their (women) representatives could concern themselves with women's issues – the family, health, welfare, education and morality. Appealing to Protestant middle-class women, Diehl supported the Nationalists until 1930, when she joined the NSDAP. Having approached party organiser Gregor Strasser with proposals to reorganise National Socialist women's activity, she accepted an offer of a leading role within the party women's organisation. It was not, however, to be a successful move, for unable to accept subordination to other women and angry that rather than taking over women's work she was not even receiving much attention in the Nazi press, she abandoned her position in the National Socialist women's movement in late 1932. (Koonz 1987: 80–4, 112–13; Stephenson 1981: 77–81; Frevert 1989: 209.)

In late 1930 the party had 7,625 woman members, less than 6 per cent of the total membership, but this gives an artificially low picture of organised women's support for the movement, since we are unable to tell how many cases there were of a pro-Nazi couple only having enough money for the man's subscription. By the time the party came to power, female membership had increased to 64,011 (7.8 per cent of the total) while the NSF stood at some 110,000. (Stephenson 1981: 25, 148; Kater 1983: 150; Stephenson 1983: 41.)

If Nazi women made up a small percentage of a large membership, what of the party's electoral support? Women, enfranchised in 1918, outnumbered men in the electorate (although, conversely, the percentage of men who actually voted was higher than the percentage of women). The NSDAP was for most of the period noticeably weaker electorally among women than among men. In the 1930s, however, not only did Nazi support increase, the gender gap in electoral support declined substantially. (Indeed, in Protestant areas women overtook men, leading Evans to suggest that given the Protestant majority in Germany, women may even have formed a narrow majority of the Nazi electorate in 1932.) This rise of support among women was consciously sought by the Nazi leadership which decided to deploy women speakers prominently in the 1932 election campaigns. While the party had rejected a proposal by Zander that the party should run women candidates in the 1932 local elections, it did recognise that its relative weakness among women voters needed to be urgently addressed and one response, surprising as it may seem, was to energetically deny the charges of its critics that it opposed women's rights. In March 1932 the party paper reported on Gregor Strasser's call on party women's organisers to work to change popular impressions of the role of women in National Socialism. (The same issue also contained efforts by Rosenberg and Feder to 'clarify' their views on women.) Later in the year the party women's magazine declared that 'no woman who, out of personal preference wants to take up a profession, will be prevented from doing so'. (Farris 1975: 168–9; Evans 1987: 182–3; Stephenson 1983: 35–6, 40; 1981: 67; Rupp 1978: 23–4, 26.)

Such claims were undoubtedly a matter of electoral calculation. But the party was not uniformly misogynist. That differences on the question stretched quite widely is particularly evident in the debate that took place within the women's supplement of the party paper in early 1926. For Emma Hadlich, who initiated the debate in late January, Elsbeth Zander and other leading figures failed to recognise that women were equal to men and should fight alongside them. This was not alien feminism, Hadlich argued, but the order that had prevailed in ancient German society. Indeed, it was foreign values that had infected German society with belief in women's inferiority and a National Socialist state based on merit should recognise women's right to lead as much as men's. Neither Zander nor other National Socialists took kindly to this argument and the debate, which involved both genders (including Rosenberg, the paper's editor) raged on until April when Hadlich was allowed to reply to her critics and Rosenberg (who had insisted in January that ancient German society had been male-led) called for party members not to allow arguments about women's role to divert them from fighting against the enemies of the *Volk*. (Rupp 1978: 18–23.)

Similar views would be espoused after Hitler came to power, when in a collection of essays, *German Women Address Adolf Hitler*, women supporters of National Socialism argued that women in German society in the past had enjoyed equality and should do so in the German state of the future. This view was also argued in a dissident Nazi publication, *The German Woman Fighter*, which was banned in 1937. But contrary inclinations were clear before the party came to power, and a speech by the Führer soon after made clear which had been victorious. Speaking to the NSF in 1934, Hitler declared that opposition to women's participation in politics had attracted to National Socialism

> more women than all other parties combined . . . We do not envision our women's movement as one that inscribes a programme

for the battle of the sexes upon its banners; on the contrary, we ensure a women's movement that will struggle jointly with men.

It was on this basis, he declared, that the movement had gained 'millions of faithful, fanatical, female comrades-in-arms'. But what was it that Hitler believed these women to be supporting? According to him, 'man's world' was 'the state' while woman's was 'her husband, her family, her children, and her home'. But the bigger world of man, he went on, could not survive 'if there were none who considered the cares of the smaller world their life's work'. The slogan of women's emancipation, he claimed, was 'the product of Jewish intellect'. But German women had no more need of emancipation than a man need 'fear that woman would oust him from his position'. Only when men were unsure about their mission did women revolt, bringing about a situation 'that went against nature and that lasted until both sexes returned to the places assigned to them by eternal Providence'. (Rupp 1978: 18–25; Bell and Offen 1983: 373–7.)

One of the first measures introduced after the Nazis came to power was the June 1933 Law to Reduce Unemployment, under which a couple planning to marry would, providing the woman gave up employment, be eligible for an interest-free loan in the form of vouchers for household goods (paid to the husband) to be repaid at 1 per cent per month. Initially introduced to encourage marriage and discourage women's employment, the measure was changed later in the month to forbid the granting of loans to political opponents or people with hereditary defects and to allow for cancellation of 25 per cent of the repayment on the birth of a child (and the same percentage for any further children). It was subsequently estimated that by June 1938 nearly 1 million loans had been made and 840,000 children born to families receiving the loans. (Glass 1967: 287; Stephenson 1975: 46–7; Mason 1976a: 95.)

Both the birth-rate and the marriage rate rose during the Nazi regime (on the latter, Mason notes how the Nazis strengthened their 'pro-family' image by associating themselves 'with an unprecedented outbreak of domestic bliss'). In addition to marriage loans, the regime increased income tax allowances for children, introduced family allowances and added to the number of maternity clinics. In the mid-1930s the regime began to give financial support to large families, accompanied by a propaganda campaign against the common belief that such families were a sign of irresponsibility. On Mother's Day in 1939 Aryan mothers with four or more children for the first time received the Honour Cross of the German Mother, an honour which included the right to be saluted by members of the Hitler Youth. None the less, the regime could not gain the increased numbers it sought. Where in 1933 the birth-rate stood at 59 per 1,000 women of childbearing age, it had risen to 73 the following year, 77 for 1935, 1936 and 1937 and 81 and 85 for the last two years of the decade. While considerably higher than the figures in the late 1920s and early 1930s, this stood below that earlier in the century, when already concern about the German birth-rate was being expressed by conservative nationalists. The state, the Minister of the Interior declared in 1937:

> stands helpless before many things. The scornful smile, expressing the sentiments of the childless in regard to the 'stupid' people with large families, cannot be forbidden or restricted. The state cannot completely eliminate the manifold dangers of the large city and it cannot deprive mothers of their employment. At first it can only honour the mothers of children and remove from the fathers of large families part of their extra burden by reducing their tax rates.

(Mason 1976a: 95–9; Stephenson 1975: 48–51; Mason 1976b: 14, 30.)

If the regime used incentives, it also used repression, both to raise the birth-rate among the 'fit' and to depress it among those it did not favour. In May 1933 the regime strengthened the law against abortion (although, it should be noted, the Hereditary Health Court the following year ruled that abortion would not be against the law if it prevented the birth of an unfit child). Initially access to birth control was made more difficult (but, it should be noted, neither its use nor sale was forbidden), while during the war its production and distribution was banned and the death penalty introduced for abortionists. In June 1933 the Minister of the Interior, Wilhelm Frick, gave a speech on 'population and race policy' in which he claimed that over a million Germans were unfit to have children. 'We must', he declared, 'have the courage again to grade our people according to its genetic values.' The following month a law was passed to stop the propagation of 'lives unworthy of life'. During the following twelve years, it has been estimated, nearly 200,000 women were compulsorily sterilised as part of what the regime called 'a gradual cleansing of the body of the volk'. (Stephenson 1975: 62, 68–9; Glass 1967: 283–4; Kirkpatrick 1938: 169–71; Bock 1984: 276; 1991: 234–5.)

In September 1935 the Law for the Protection of German Blood and German Honour forbade both marriage and sex between an Aryan and a Jew, while the Marriage Health Law one month later decreed that before marriage a couple must obtain a certificate from a local health office confirming that they had been medically examined and found to be free of disease that might be transmitted to offspring. In the absence of such a certificate, they would be held not to be fit for marriage. (The tension between simple pro-natalism and eugenics is well illustrated by the relaxing of this restriction shortly before the outbreak of war in order to facilitate marriage by those about to go off to fight.) (Stephenson 1975: 41, 44; Bleuel 1973: 193.)

Population concerns affected not only marriage but divorce in Nazi Germany. In 1938 the divorce law was changed to allow for the dissolution of marriage after three years of separation. This liberalisation of divorce on the part of a nominally pro-family regime was partly defended on the grounds that remarriage would follow but another aspect of the new law, that grounds for divorce could include refusing to have children, points towards the central reason for the government's stance. New marriages could lead to more children. (Stephenson 1975: 42–4.)

There were also tensions over unmarried motherhood. The party had come to power claiming to be the champion of German morality against the decadence of Weimar Germany and one of its first measures had been an ordinance against obscene writings, pictures and performances. (Indeed, admirers were soon eulogising the new regime for its fight against 'Jewish' immorality.) Childbearing outside marriage was likewise initially denounced as immoral but the government eventually decided in favour of those leading functionaries who opposed the dismissal of women public employees for bearing illegitimate children. Single mothers were allowed to call themselves Frau rather than Fraulein if they wished and the head of the SS, Heinrich Himmler, was particularly vociferous that the most important thing about an unmarried mother was that she was a mother. The outbreak of war made a relaxing of what Hitler's deputy, Rudolf Hess, called 'bourgeois morality' particularly urgent. 'The highest service', he proclaimed, a woman could 'render to the community' was 'the gift of racially healthy children for the survival of the nation'. (Taylor 1983: 108; Bleuel 1973: 5; Kirkpatrick 1938: 103–4; Wolff 1986: 397–9; Stephenson 1975: 63–7.)

While we have concentrated on population, we began our discussion of the Nazi regime by considering the 1933 Law to Reduce Unemployment. What of the regime's policy towards women at work? As Rupp has emphasised, the regime's attitude to women in work was complex. That woman was above all things housewife and mother was much emphasised, but this said nothing of women before marriage or the large number of women who, due to the loss of men in the First World War, would never marry. The frequent suggestion that the world of work was the work of man cut across another idea, that some forms of work were manly, others womanly. Thus, it was suggested, girls would be taught by women teachers and women tended by women doctors. In some versions this went further, to see certain forms of work as appropriate to femininity, so that social work or education as such were seen as women's work. And, of course, there were the realities of the employers' demand for women workers and resistance on the part of individuals and families to the lowering of their standard of living by the removal of a vital wage. (Rupp 1978: 39–42; Mason 1976a: 93–4.)

The Nazis had been particularly vociferous against so-called double earners, women in the labour market whose husbands also worked, and in addition to seeking to encourage women to leave employment upon marriage, the new government also removed some married women from the civil service. Local initiatives to deprive married women of employment were sometimes supported, sometimes rejected by the party leadership, while other efforts to remove some women from employment came through the banning of women from certain forms of heavy work and, interestingly, the introduction of equal pay in some sectors with the intent of making women's employment less attractive to employers. If we examine industrial employment, for instance, the result of all these efforts was at first sight a fall in women's employment, from 29.3 per cent of the industrial labour force in 1933 to 25.5 per cent at the end of the following year. But overall employment was rising and these figures disguised a rise in the actual number of women in industrial employment. If we look more broadly, at the number of women in the insured labour force, in June 1933 this stood at 4.85 million. Three years later it was 5.63 million. As Stephenson notes, the decision in 1934 to create a Women's Section of the regime's organisation for employees, the Labour Front, was an acknowledgement 'that the employment of millions of women was a permanent fixture' even though its efforts to 'protect' women from particularly arduous jobs or to provide female volunteers so that some women could take time off work were undoubtedly motivated by the 'priority of ensuring that working women would bear healthy children'. The same year the NSF's leader, Gertrud Scholtz-Klink, told a party rally that it was not true that 'the factory spoils women'. A woman, she proclaimed, could 'remain womanly at the machine – so long as her strength and her work correspond harmoniously'. That women were not to be driven from the workplace as a result of National Socialism became even more clear once the regime began to experience labour shortages. From 1937 marriage loans no longer necessitated the woman giving up employment and by 1940 one Nazi woman official was observing 'It has been our chief article of faith that woman's place is in the home – but since the whole of Germany is our home we must serve her wherever we can best do so.' (Stephenson 1975: 88–90, 95–7, 99; Mason 1976a: 94; Newitt 1937: 101; Grunberger 1974: 328, 629.)

In comparing the two movements, we can already see some crucial commonalities and distinctions. Italian Fascism developed in an anti-feminist direction after it came to power. National Socialism, notorious for its anti-feminism, none the less denied it during its final bid for power. The National Socialists had pursued a racialist policy towards population. The Italian fascists, however, did so only under the influence of its ally. If the Germans were the pioneers of a eugenic racism, in opposing women's employment it was the Italian regime that was the more radical. In both countries hostility to women's rights was espoused by many, but not all, of those committed to fascism.

We have so far restricted ourselves to discussing the two most important examples of fascism in inter-war Europe. They were not, of course, the only examples. In Britain, too, fascism was highly visible for much of the 1930s. As we will see, both in its organisation of women and the place it envisaged for them in a future corporate state, it presents a particular challenging case to the conventional wisdom on the relationship between fascism and women.

2 Women in the Greater Britain

The Russian Revolution's impact on sections of the British left and the rise of the Labour Party profoundly disturbed important sections of the Conservative right and it was in these circles that British Fascism first came into existence in 1923, when Rotha Linton-Orman, who had served in the Women's Reserve Ambulance during the war, formed the British Fascisti, subsequently the British Fascists (BFs). Set up to oppose a feared communist uprising, the British Fascists organised in paramilitary units and was eventually to split during the 1926 General Strike over the government's insistence that the British Fascists would have to drop their military structure before their assistance could be accepted in breaking the strike. An earlier split had taken away some of the most militant members, while the 1926 split deprived it of elements who prioritised anti-socialism over any specifically fascist affiliation. Later in the 1920s, yet another group, the Imperial Fascist League, would bring together elements convinced that the BFs, rather than being truly fascist, had failed to break decisively with conservatism.

By the early 1930s the BFs had moved away from the Conservative right and were turning in a corporatist and anti-Semitic direction, but were in a very weak condition. British Fascism would enjoy a new lease of life, but in the very different form of Mosley's British Union of Fascists (BUF). Formed in October 1932, the BUF was from its inception committed to the ending of party politics in Britain and the creation of a corporate state. While the BFs, for most of their existence, had been associated with the orthodox right, the BUF had more complex roots. The leader, Sir Oswald Mosley, was a former Labour minister, and a small number of Labour activists (and even, as with the movement's theoretician, Alexander Raven Thomson, ex-communists) joined the infant organisation. Other figures had no previous experience, while some, such as leading propagandist William Joyce and one of the main organisers, Neil Francis Hawkins, had a background in the BFs. Mosley's original intent had been to swallow up the small fascist groups that had existed before the BUF, but this proved impossible, and while the BFs did not long survive, Arnold Leese's virulently racist Imperial Fascist League continued as a tiny rival through the eight years of the BUF's existence, while Joyce was to break away from the BUF later in the decade to create the even smaller National Socialist League. (Other anti-Semitic groups, such as the Britons, the Militant Christian Patriots and the Right Club were also active outside the overtly fascist movement.)

At the core of the BUF's appeal was the belief that the 'old gang' politicians had failed the nation and that deepening economic problems called for a fundamentally new policy. The economy, while still functioning on private enterprise lines, needed to be organised along corporate lines both to maximise its efficiency and to raise the living standards of the British people. A high wage economy would provide a buoyant home market, and the erection of barriers against foreign goods and the reaching of mutually beneficial arrangements with the other countries of the Empire would ensure that British industry would not be undercut. This emphasis on economic revival, elaborated in Mosley's 1932 book, *The Greater Britain*, drew in part on proposals made by Mosley when still in the Labour Party. It also drew on the protectionist traditions of sections of the British right and when, in early 1934, thousands flocked to the movement, it was particularly thanks to the vociferous support of the *Daily Mail* and other papers owned by the Conservative magnate Lord Rothermere. But where Rothermere believed the BUF would bring new forces to the Conservative Party, Mosley envisaged shattering the party system altogether. Expressing admiration for Italy and Germany (and in receipt of funds from the former), the BUF organised meetings marked by the violent removal of anti-fascists by blackshirted stewards. Claims that the British economy was under attack from international Jewish finance and the BUF from Jewish communism had already begun to appear in the movement's propaganda, and by July 1934 the alliance between the BUF and Rothermere was at an end. The organisation's membership fell away rapidly from a peak of over 40,000 in mid-1934 to perhaps 5,000 a year later. Clashes between the BUF and its opponents continued, notably in Cable Street in East London in October 1936, shortly after which the government passed a Public Order Act forbidding the wearing of political uniforms. None the less, membership revived, particularly in what became its heartland in the East End of London, where anti-Semitic feeling was especially virulent. (The organisation did not field any candidates in the 1935 general election but did take part in some later council elections in a number of localities. Amid generally poor results, it achieved a significant level of support in East London, particularly in Bethnal Green and Limehouse.) The organisation's increased numbers can also be attributed to the general atmosphere of appeasement, with Mosley arguing that only a sympathetic response to Hitler's demands could keep the peace. But while its membership was rising as war approached, the outbreak of hostilities with Germany would lead to an escalation of suspicions as to the movement's loyalty. Nor was this simply a matter of establishing whether the BUF, or some elements within it, were actively working for German victory. While it had dropped the 'of Fascists' from its name in the latter part of the decade, the movement was insistent that what it espoused was a British national socialism and, indeed, it had briefly called itself the British Union of Fascists and National Socialists. The movement's continued advocacy of negotiations with Germany and the intelligence service's concerns over secret meetings bringing together key members with other sections of the extreme right destroyed any possibility that the government would continue to tolerate its existence. In early 1940, amid fears of a German fifth column, hundreds of its members were interned and the British Union was subsequently declared a proscribed organisation. (For a fuller account of British Fascism, see Cross 1961; Mandle 1966, 1968; Benewick 1972; Skidelsky 1975; Lunn and Thurlow 1980; Webber 1984; Cullen 1987; Lewis 1987; Thurlow 1987; Kushner and Lunn 1990; Linehan 1996.)

During the BUF's short existence, its Leader, as he was known, expressed himself on the subject of women on a number of occasions, two of which deserve special attention. Writing in 1932, he had declared that '*we want men who are men, and women who are women*' (emphasis in original). For 'the great majority', for 'normal women', he went on, women's sphere was that of motherhood. Yet, eight years later, following his arrest, he was to declare that the British Union believed in the complete equality of men and women. The earlier views would appear to be classically patriarchal. (As the feminist writer Winifred Holtby commented in 1934, Mosley's words appeared 'characteristic' of the 'Fascist inclination to dream of an . . . Olympus of virile he-men . . . separated sharply from all lower forms of being'.) (Mosley 1932: 41–2; PRO HO283/14/101; Berry and Bishop 1985: 84–6.) They are, we might conclude, what we would expect of fascism and the later statement, delivered under the constraining circumstances of internment, should therefore be judged to be simply false. Furthermore, the BUF, like its German counterpart, had emerged in a society in which women were already enfranchised. While the militant Suffragette movement had long since ceased to exist, organisations descended both from it and from the less militant wing of the suffrage movement were active in the 1930s and forcefully argued that fascism represented a threat to women's rights. So too did the different liberal, socialist and communist organisations that mobilised against the BUF during the decade. Surely, if, in order to achieve election, National Socialism in Germany had felt forced to pretend that it would not deprive women of their rights, we should see any such claims by the BUF in the same way? (On feminist opposition to fascism in the 1930s, see e.g. Harrison 1978: 233; 1987: 195–6, 198–9; Bruley 1986: 229–30, 249–53, 275–9; Eglin 1987: 226–7, 231–2; Liddington 1984; Alberti 1994: 111–22; for contemporary anti-fascists on fascism and women, see e.g. Strachey 1933: 64–5; Dutt 1934: 218–22; *New Statesman* 28 April 1934.)

A closer examination, however, suggests a more complex picture. In understanding why Mosley emphasised women's difference from men in 1932 and their equality in 1940, we need to turn first of all to the BUF's somewhat disconcerting view that corporate organisation, rightly understood, should be seen as conducive to women's rights. Writing in an early BUF pamphlet, *The Corporate State*, Alexander Raven Thomson argued that the failure of democracy to end economic distress necessitated its replacement by a form of government that would be effective. This would recognise the nation as an organism above and beyond the individuals within it. Rather than being based on geographical units, the Corporate State would be based on occupational groups which would bring together representatives of employers, workers and consumers. Each corporation would reach decisions on such subjects as prices, wages and new investment and could appeal to government for arbitration in the event of an inability to agree. Thomson envisaged that these corporations would total twenty-three in number, ranging from agriculture and engineering to wholesale and retail trades and the civil service. The 23rd and last corporation would be for married women. As part of the representation of consumers, this corporation would, where appropriate, provide representatives to sit on other corporations 'where their interests as housewives' were involved. In the case of agriculture, for instance, it was unacceptable that 'the housewife' should have no say in the supply of milk and bacon,

considering that the well-being of her children, and the good temper of her husband at the breakfast table, depend so directly on these products. The Fascist Corporate System will rectify this intolerable defect of the present system, and women, through their own corporation, will . . . have a large measure of influence over the supply and prices of all agricultural products.
(Thomson n.d. (c. 1934): 4–11, 30)

Married women, housewives, women; the 23rd Corporation had been described as representing each of these overlapping but not identical groups, and in a chapter towards the end of the pamphlet Thomson tried to set out exactly how women would be represented in what he now termed the domestic corporation. Denying that fascism saw women 'purely as breeders of "cannon fodder"', and expressing regret that 'many feminists' had become anti-fascists, Thomson insisted that women in industry would be represented by women and that equal pay would 'lead to a more truly functional discrimination between the sexes, women doing the work for which they are best suited'. But what of women in the home? Fascism was 'convinced that many women to-day are forced into industry by economic conditions' and that they would 'prefer married life'. The Corporate State, by enabling men to earn more, would enable women to leave employment and in order to give them 'a status at least equivalent to that of women in industry', a domestic corporation would be formed, in which 'all married women, and women acting as housekeepers, will be represented as employers, while female domestic servants would be represented as employees'. In addition to providing consumer representation on relevant corporations, the domestic corporation would also enable married women, in 'their capacity as mothers', to be consulted on matters concerning children, would provide facilities for expectant mothers and would give 'training in hygiene and infant welfare'. Contrary to anti-fascist claims, Thomson argued, women would not be deprived of their hard-won vote but either as an employer or a worker in industry or a member of the domestic corporation would be represented by women within parliament. Fascism insisted upon 'occupational differentiation' between the sexes but would not deny women 'the right of entry . . . into all professions and occupations, which they are physically capable of undertaking' and would insist on equality with men both within employment and within the state.
(Thomson n.d. (c. 1934): 43–4.)

In a later pamphlet, *The Coming Corporate State*, the number of corporations had grown by one and references to a specific representation for married women had vanished, to be replaced by a corporation for 'house-wives' and domestic servants. A Charter of Labour would be introduced, its provisions to include equal pay, 'no dismissal upon marriage' and 'holidays on full pay for mothers upon birth of a child (probably four months)'. The cotton and woollen industries, it was argued, would have 'seats especially reserved for women to represent the women operatives so prominent in these industries' and women were promised equal rights as candidates and voters and women-only representation where women had a large enough block. 'By this means', Thomson observed, 'women will be guaranteed a much larger permanent representation' than they had obtained under democracy. (Thomson n.d. (c. 1937): 7, 25–6, 29, 30, 32.)

Reviewing the new publication, the BUF's magazine claimed that the 23rd Corporation's change of name from Married Women's to Domestic was 'certainly an improvement. Since male servants will presumably be included, it disposes of the contention that Fascism is anti-Feminist.' This was curious. In the earlier publication, the corporation had been called *both* Married Women's and Domestic, and considerably greater effort had been made to refute allegations of anti-feminism. A subsequent review (by the same writer) of the second impression of the pamphlet suggested that women members would 'find great propaganda value' in the Labour Charter 'which prohibits differentiation on the grounds of sex or marriage' and in the treatment of women's corporate representation. 'Only the extreme feminist, who demands that women shall be forced into industry, can criticise British Union policy on this subject.' The writer did not, however, note that in this second impression, a new shift in the argument had occurred. In the first impression, as in *The Corporate State*, the state had been viewed first, as 'a united nation; second, as a functional expression of occupational groups; and finally, as a mass of individual citizens'. In the second impression, rather than as a mass of individuals, the state was now seen 'finally, as a multitude of reproductive family units'. But nor did he comment on another development. In the original pamphlet, as we have seen, Thomson had suggested that one of the effects of equal pay would be an occupational differentiation between the sexes. Indeed, in 1934 he had even stated this in reply to an inquiry from the feminist London and National Society for Women's Service, suggesting that by taking posts for 'which they are best fitted', women and men could find their rightful place. Now, however, no such claim for the effects of equal pay was made. (*British Union Quarterly* April–July 1937; *Action* 14 January 1939; Thomson n.d. (c. 1934): 5; n.d. (c. 1937): 4; n.d. (c. 1938): 2; Harrison 1978: 231; 1987: 112.)

In its literature, the BUF was at pains to portray a future in which women's lives would be improved. In a 1935 pamphlet, *Women and Fascism*, one leading activist, Anne Brock Griggs, argued that women would vote by trade or profession and that where they ran a home or were employed in domestic work they would be represented in a home corporation. Women would be 'free to follow the career which their talents and the national need indicate'. Fascism recognised 'the need for more women in such professions as medicine, architecture, engineering, nursing, law and domestic science' and conditions would be improved so that domestic workers and nurses would be properly trained and 'women architects and engineers will help in planning the homes and cities of the future'. At the moment women worked for sweated wages but equal pay would end the situation where married women worked to support their unemployed husbands, girls were forced into immorality and future mothers were undermined in health. Married women would not be compelled by economic pressures 'to work to maintain the home' but there would be no marriage bar and no discrimination against women. The corporate organisation of women workers would secure better lighting and ventilation, recreational facilities would be developed and paid holidays would be compulsory. Health would be improved as would housing and schooling while the failure of democracy to reduce maternal mortality since the ending of the First World War would be dealt with by better antenatal education, more clinics and women doctors, better conditions for midwives, legislation enabling working women to rest for at least six weeks before and after birth and convalescent homes and home helps to enable mothers to recuperate. Food would be cheaper and more plentiful and family nutrition better under the Corporate System, the system which would enable women 'to advise and assist in carrying through the great Fascist programme of social reform'. (Griggs n.d., 1935.)

Writing in the BUF's magazine the same year, Griggs further eulogised the Corporate State. It would, she wrote, empower women to carry through social reforms. 'As the theory of relativity enables one to visualize the universe as the size of an orange or extending to infinity, so woman's "sphere" may lie within the four walls of her home, or may embrace the Nation's destiny.' Fascism, she claimed, would provide enough ante-natal care, maternity hospital beds and home helps to significantly reduce maternal mortality. Women should be educated to seek advice, clinics made more attractive and midwives given better training and conditions. There should be better obstetric training for doctors and to help remedy a situation where 60,000 mothers were 'more or less crippled' every year, convalescent homes would give 'a few weeks' rest and quiet where the mother can recuperate and start her work when she leaves with fresh hope and courage'. Better urban and rural planning could lower the infant mortality rate while the mental and physical development of children necessitated nursery schools. 'When the family is reunited at tea-time, the mother has had time to rest from household labours and appreciate the companionship of her youngsters. The children on their part show greater affection and loyalty.' But before all such reforms stood the need for planning – accommodation standards, access to schools without dangerous road crossings, reserved land for parks and playgrounds, the protection of agricultural land from speculative building. 'No woman would allow the nation's food-supply to be jeopardized in this manner.' A well housed and healthy population would form the 'stable background against which will rise the mighty creation of the Fascist State'. (*Fascist Quarterly* October 1935.)

As we have noted, the organisation in the later 1930s described itself as National Socialist. But this did not mean that it adopted a more misogynist stance. A pamphlet published in 1939, Olive Hawks' *Women Fight for Britain and for Britain Alone*, presented a picture of a movement in which 'the factory girl' worked 'side by side with the clerk, the nurse and the housewife'. In the future, it declared, a secure home market would allow many women to leave industry and instead 'serve their families and strengthen the nation' at home. 'In return, the Domestic Corporation' would 'give them real power in government', social services would be extended and maternity and infant welfare 'receive particular attention'. It noted, however, that many women would, 'of course, prefer to remain in industrial and professional life . . . No barrier of sex discrimination will prevent their full service to the nation.' Equal pay would ensure both elementary justice and the protection of 'male labour from unfair competition'. Corporate institutions would improve women's working conditions while allied social organisations would provide cheap holidays and an extended pension scheme. Nurses would be given proper conditions of employment, both girls and boys would give a year's service after their education had finished and exceptional young men 'and women' would receive 'special executive training to fit them to lead the nation'. (Hawks n.d. (1939): 2–6.)

Amid such a widely ranging policy stance towards women, one of the most striking characteristics is the movement's apparent defence of women's right to work and its support for equal pay. But how committed was the movement to women's participation in the workplace?

Here evidence is contradictory. In an early pronouncement, one of the BUF's weekly papers suggested that nothing was 'more fatal to the well-being of the nation than a system which keeps men unemployed and drives women into industry for cheap wages'. It was false, it went on, to claim that fascism would 'drive women out of industry and the professions'. Instead, in a system where men had good earnings, it would be 'possible for women who so desire to marry and to keep a decent home'. Writing shortly after, one BUF writer, Elizabeth Winch, argued that for fascism to want women to return to the home was no matter for condemnation. Manufacturers employed women at lower rates than they would pay men. This meant 'not only that more men are put out of work, but that the women whom they would normally have married are now forced to earn their own livings because the men cannot keep them'. Fascism would instead secure equal pay, 'and this would place men in a position to marry, without penalising the woman who has no interest outside her trade or profession'. Fascism would recognise the married state as a profession for women who run 'their homes cheaply and efficiently, look after their children, and administer to their husbands'. (*Fascist Week* 17–23 November 1933, 29 December 1933–4 January 1934.)

The question was discussed elsewhere in the fascist press. In the summer of 1933, the *Blackshirt* published an imaginary conversation between a male BUF member and another man which dealt with what the latter called 'the women who have done men out of their jobs'. This, the BUF member replied, was an unfair comment for, 'A single girl to-day has a very poor prospect of carrying out her natural destiny: many a married woman is at work to keep her unemployed husband.' Equal pay, the fascist solution to the problem, would probably result in a 'lot of women displaced from situations of work; but in the long run this would cancel itself out' because the greater employment of men on an ample wage would encourage them to marry 'and the need of the woman to "go out to work" would be removed. No married woman should find it necessary to go to work, any more than any man desires it . . . woman's birthright is to be a wife and mother, not a breadwinner' and unless the BUF's policy was implemented, the country would suffer 'the end of home-life', a declining birth-rate and 'the Suicide of a Race'. Another article lamented that in the Cheshire silk industry, 'The women-folk go off on their daily tasks while the men have to stop at home, look after breakfast, nurse the baby, and do other domestic duties.' Returning to the theme, the BUF weekly subsequently claimed it was 'a stupid system which takes the mothers and daughters from the home and pays the father unemployed benefit to become housekeeper' for them. Under fascism, it was claimed, women who had 'been forced into the position of bread-winners for their families while their husbands grow bitter in enforced idleness, will see again balance restored to their home life'. (*Action* 28 February, 7 May 1936, 11 February 1939.)

Compared with views such as these, those expressed by Mosley himself appeared considerably more sympathetic to women's employment. Fascism, he declared, would

> care for motherhood but women who care to pursue other lives, will not only be free to pursue them, but for the first time will do so in conditions which make possible for women a happy and prosperous industrial or professional career.

The emphasis was on choice:

> Women who elect to pursue industrial or professional careers will be free to follow those avocations without disability . . . On the other hand, women who desire to follow the great career of Home and children will be among the first cares of the Fascist State.

An attempt to summarise the BUF's beliefs, the 'Ten Points of Fascism', included a pledge that 'Women will not be compelled to retire from industry, but the high wages of their husbands under the Corporate system will make it possible for them to retire if they wish.' This position was reformulated the following year in one of the points of 'Blackshirt Policy', another attempt to explain the BUF's stance: 'Married women will not be compelled to retire from industry. All women will be paid wages on an equitable basis with those of men. But the higher wages paid to husbands under the Corporate system will not necessitate women working to maintain the home.' (*Fascist Week* 12–18 January, 30 March–5 April 1934; *Blackshirt* 1 February 1935.)

This was a remarkably ambiguous policy. Writing in the BUF's paper in 1936, Olive Hawks showed how it could be presented in seeking to appeal to women. There were, she wrote, many girls in factories who were 'counting the time, perhaps years', to their wedding day. But the young man was not earning enough to support both of them and all that the old parties offered was 'the freedom to go on waiting . . . till the joy of it has almost gone'. Fascism would bring higher wages, 'and in that way many a girl will no doubt happily leave the workshop for the home'. At present girls often had to return to work after marriage, leaving their children with 'Grannie'.

> I cannot believe they wish to do so – indeed, I've the word of several of them that it's almost the last thing they like to do. If the husband was earning enough, they say, it would be goodbye to the time clock and the supervisor, and the grudged few shillings a week. The Blackshirts offer you this – security for the jobs of your menfolk, so that you can live at home if you wish; 'Equal pay for equal work', so that if you prefer to work, you are employed on your own merits and not because you're cheaper, giving you complete equality in the labour market; and the organisation of the Corporate State to protect your interests both as worker and as married woman.
> (*Blackshirt* 10 October 1936)

Another woman activist, Agnes Booth, insisting that fascism did not stand for 'a back to the kitchen stunt', claimed that starvation wages or 'the meagre pittance paid to the unemployed girl' meant that democracy left 'women to become the prey of any prowling beast with the price of a meal in his pocket'. National Socialism, however, offered women equal pay and 'free choice as to whether she shall or shall not go out to work when married'. Not every woman was

> a born home-maker, but we would not deny the companionship of the man she loves by saying either you stay at home or remain unmarried; we say to her by all means go to the work you like, and by the combined wages of yourself and husband, employ some woman who does love home-making, but who for some reason has never had a home of her own, thereby satisfying not the hopes of two but of three people.
> (*Action* 26 March 1938)

Of the different views expressed in the movement's press, one that particularly showed the ambiguities of its stance appeared at the beginning of 1937. In 'The Problem of the Woman Worker. National Socialism Will Solve It', both modern industrialism and feminists were criticised for failing to recognise that the question was not whether a woman should work but 'what work she should perform in the dual interests of herself and the community'. At present she was being taken away from the home and thus the family was being undermined. National Socialism did 'not deny women the right to work' but it did not go to the other extreme of complete equality, which was 'anti-social and contrary to the dictates of Nature itself'. National Socialism would 'encourage women to choose careers and occupations more in harmony with their natural abilities and qualities' and once more make it possible, 'if she so desires', for her 'to exercise her natural vocation of wifehood and motherhood'. Rising wages would 'obviate the necessity for women to supplement family incomes, and the single woman who enters industry will do so because she desires such work or wishes for complete independence'. A woman would be 'at liberty either to accept or reject the glorious heritage of her sex', able to enter the labour market but 'more especially will the Greater Britain of National Socialism make it possible for her to make her peculiar contribution to society in the sphere of the home, leaving gainful occupation and the support of the family to her man'. (*Blackshirt* 23 January 1937.)

This view, in the name of National Socialism, emphasised women's role in the domestic sphere. Yet the following year, in an extended discussion of British Union policy, Mosley was again at pains to declare that women were not to be driven from industry nor confined to the home in the Corporate State (Mosley 1938: 16). The exact implications of British Fascism's policy on women and work remained unclear, and when we turn to its stance on population, yet more ambiguities come to the surface.

In 1936 the BUF issued *Fascism: 100 Questions Asked and Answered*, in which Mosley dealt with a wide range of policy questions. Question 76 concerned the movement's stance towards birth control, and he replied that like all modern scientific knowledge, an understanding of birth control 'should be available to all who desire it'. But if Mosley was surprisingly sympathetic to birth control, he also had eugenicist and pro-natalist considerations. At the present, he held, the very poor did not know of birth control while the relatively prosperous did. 'The result is exactly the reverse of national interest.' The social responsibility and economic security which fascism would facilitate, however, would lead to 'larger families among those who at present practise restriction', and those who 'rightly oppose present tendencies of birth control', he suggested, would only achieve success with fascism. (Mosley 1936: Question 76, n.p.)

In Italy, if not in Germany, fascists had forged a close relationship with the Catholic Church which at the time not only championed anti-communism but inclined towards a corporate organisation of society. In commenting as he did on birth control, Mosley was attempting in part to steer a path that minimised criticism from Catholic circles which he hoped might be sympathetic to fascism. As early as 1934, one

Catholic paper, the *Universe*, had expressed concern over reports that the BUF favoured 'legislation in the name of eugenics which would be obnoxious to Catholics'. The following month, the paper published the text of a BUF statement (which also appeared in the *Fascist Week*) declaring that only when the more important problem of how to 'feed, clothe and house the people' had been dealt with would the movement turn to 'consider whether there be a case for such interference with individual liberty as might be calculated to promote or discourage contraception or sterilisation'. Another publication, the *Catholic Times*, declined to publish the BUF statement, in part because of its attitude to contraception. It did, however, publish an extract from a letter to a clerical inquirer by the deputy director of policy, Alexander Raven Thomson, in which he declared that 'the question of race suicide has been given our very earnest attention'. The BUF, he continued, rejected the pessimistic view that population should be restricted and held that a 'frequent incentive behind birth-control' was 'the self-seeking impulse of modern democracy towards personal enjoyment and gratification, which can be more easily realised when the duty of parenthood may be evaded'. Discussing the issue in an editorial, the *Catholic Times* declared that it had been concerned that the BUF's original statement had not seen birth control as a crucial question. This, it suggested, was to misrepresent fascism, which in both Italy and Germany had 'been sound on the question of contraception from the beginning'. (*Universe* 6 April, 4 May 1934; *Fascist Week* 4–10 May 1934; *Catholic Times* 11 May 1934.)

The *Catholic Times* was not the only publication concerned that the BUF might not be taking an uncompromisingly pro-natalist stance. The Catholic social critic G. K. Chesterton had long opposed birth control, and his journal, *G. K.'s Weekly*, expressed grave doubts at a statement that, while declaring that a policy on contraception or sterilisation would not be decided upon 'without due reference to Catholic theory', had gone on to add that 'no sect whatever can seek to have our ruling upon a problem of *secondary* importance which we have not had time to consider'. If Chesterton was sceptical about the BUF's intentions, so too was the League for National Life, which had come into existence in 1926 to oppose contraception. In March 1934, the League published the text of Thomson's letter under the heading 'Fascism Supports the League'. The following year, however, under the heading, 'Hedging', it noted that the BUF director of policy had declared that contraception and sterilisation were not matters 'on which the Fascist movement is prepared to be dogmatic' and that it would 'be submitted after we come to power to the full consideration of medical and moral authorities'. This, the League made clear, was unacceptable. Why should fascism wait until after they had come to power and to which authorities would the new government turn? 'Be it understood from the beginning that we are not willing to take Oswald Mosley for our authority in matters of morals.' (*G. K.'s Weekly* 10, 24 May 1934; Soloway 1982: 250–1; *National Life* March 1934, 2 December 1935.)

In 1936 the BUF went so far as to tell a Catholic inquirer that birth control was 'entirely a matter for the private conscience of the individual' and that the fascist state, while encouraging a higher birth-rate, would 'not interfere with the private and intimate concerns of the family'. But if there was tension between the BUF and Catholicism over birth control, there was even more difficulty over eugenics. Question 76 of *Fascism:100 Questions* had included a reference to 'compulsory sterilization of the unfit' as well as to birth control, and Mosley had replied that those who should not have children would be given the choice of segregation or voluntary sterilisation. As we have seen, the issue had played a part in the 1934 statement, in which it had been argued that only after economic problems had been solved would there be time to consider the appropriateness or otherwise of sterilisation. *G. K.'s Weekly* had responded to this by remarking that if British fascists had 'not been able to spare the time to consider sterilisation, their German brethren have dealt with the question remarkably soon after their accession to power'. The question continued to cause trouble and in 1939 the *Catholic Herald* published an interview with Mosley in which he acknowledged a difficulty between Church and state over 'the breeding of the diseased or unfit' and argued that while the Church opposed sterilisation it would accept the possibility of segregation. In the interview, however, he continued to advocate voluntary sterilisation, unacceptable to Catholic doctrine, and in the correspondence that followed, one former member wrote in to decry the widespread advocacy of contraception and sterilisation within the British Union, a claim that another correspondent, still a member, was at pains to deny. (*Action* 23 July 1936; Mosley, 1936: Question 76, n.p.; *G. K.'s Weekly* 10 May 1934; *Catholic Herald* 21, 28 July, 11 August 1939.)

While unwilling to ban contraception, the movement, as we have seen, was not indifferent to the declining birth-rate and the threat of 'racial suicide'. Mosley told the *Catholic Herald* that 'The British race' was 'dying out' and that only by encouraging a sense of social duty could 'the people . . . be induced to make large families'. Crucial to this, he argued, were family allowances. One of the final issues of

Action carried an article on the State Endowment of Motherhood as a key step towards reversing the fall in the birth-rate. 'Motherhood', the article declared, was 'the country's most important industry, but also the one most neglected by the State'. Was the nation, it went on, to follow France's example 'in inviting immigrants from every other country in Europe?' That the government had introduced income tax allowances for children was far from enough when so many did not pay income tax and when poverty caused much child mortality. Weekly allowances for each child, 'paid to the mother as a natural right' and graduated so that more would be paid for each further child were the answer. Contraception, 'that policy of despair' would 'no longer threaten the future of the nation'. Under Britain's present political masters, there was no hope – 'Financial Bonds are more sacred to them than family bonds!' But under National Socialism, family life would enjoy a renaissance. (*Catholic Herald* 21 July 1939; *Action* 7 March 1940.)

Nor were these the only occasions on which BUF writers had considered the issue. In 1937, for instance, one article in the movement's quarterly had contrasted Italy's distribution of family allowances with the situation in Britain, where men and women had 'to embark on unnatural practices in order to restrict the number of children'. Another article had suggested that the 'instability of our homes' and 'the destruction of the family by the use of contraceptives' had 'originated from the Jews'. The year before, writing in *Action*, a leading activist, A. K. Chesterton, had attacked attempts to 'destroy the means of life by birth-control' while a woman writer, lamenting population decline in Britain and among whites in general, urged reduced taxation for parents. 'A natural return', she declared, 'almost to the Victorian ideal of a large family might well ensue from a system which made a family of five or six a burden no greater than one upon the parents' resources.' But such concern had not been espoused in Anne Brock Griggs' *Women and Fascism* or Mosley's *The Greater Britain*. Instead, it was the approach of war and the haemorrhage of British lives that it portended that turned the British Union in the populationist direction that its German and Italian comrades had long espoused. (*British Union Quarterly* July–September 1937; *Action* 25 June, 26 December 1936.)

If the BUF was to prove somewhat unpredictable on women's employment or on the centrality of the birth-rate, in one area it was to echo the Nazis' sexual politics. As we have seen, the movement was no stranger to anti-Semitism, and both in its magazine and elsewhere, it accused Jews of promoting and profiting from sexual immorality. This had long been a concern of anti-Semites and the BUF sold *Jews and the White Slave Traffic*, a pamphlet originally published in the early 1920s by the Britons, an anti-Jewish society which had been set up at the end of the First World War. The Britons had also published an English-language edition of the supposed evidence of the Jewish conspiracy, the *Protocols of the Learned Elders of Zion*, and the author of *Jews and the White Slave Traffic* quoted from it ('In countries known as progressive and enlightened we have created a senseless, filthy, abominable literature') in claiming that the Jews had 'a practical monopoly' of the white slave traffic 'in the western world', enriching themselves, facilitating blackmail, providing a 'lucrative practice for Jew doctors' and undermining Christianity. In a second pamphlet, produced by the BUF itself, Jews were seen as especially associated with white slavery, while in a third, again from the BUF, the author claimed that the nation suffered 'the decadence of excess' involving the toleration of 'any exotic depravity, and of every kind of vice which Jews or aliens think it worth while to commercialise'. (*Blackshirt* 4 April 1936; Banister n.d. (c. 1923): 1–2; Anon. n.d. (c. 1938): 5; Freeman 1936: 58–9.)

The theme continued elsewhere. In 1935 a BUF writer was claiming that Jews controlled most white slavery and encouraged immorality through the press and cinema. Two years later, Jewish influence was blamed for 'the discontent occasioned in British families by the falsity of Hollywood sex-filled entertainment', while in one of its last issues, *Action* attacked British democracy as 'a system which allows millions of our decent English girls to be fooled by Jewish films and advertisements into believing that erotic sex-appeal and so-called glamour are more desirable than motherhood and family life'. Yet, even here, the situation is more complicated, with the BUF's attitude towards censorship being considerably less illiberal than might be expected. One *Fascist Quarterly* article, 'This Freedom', lambasted the censorship of films and plays and the finding of such works as *Ulysses* or *Lady Chatterley's Lover* as obscene despite their literary merit. 'The mania for interfering in the purely private affairs of the individual, in cases where his conduct cannot possibly injure the State', the article proclaimed, was 'endemic among democratic politicians', and in a pamphlet, *We Fight for Freedom*, published by the BUF the following year, it was argued that while in a fascist Britain trafficking in pornography ('largely in Jewish hands') would be stopped, work by Shaw, Wilde and Lawrence would be left untouched. Censorship, it was declared, 'would be directed, not against the legs of chorus-girls, but against . . .

subversive propaganda'. (*Fascist Quarterly* January, April 1935; *British Union Quarterly* July–September 1937; *Action* 28 March 1940; *Fascist Quarterly* July 1935; Freeman 1936: 46–9.)

But if the BUF was not as censorious as might be expected, it certainly contained, as we have seen, puritanical strands. This was most strikingly demonstrated in early 1940, following the announcement that 'Commandant Mary Allen, head of the Women's Auxiliary Service' had agreed to write a series of articles for *Action* on the development of 'the vice racket . . . under the influence of refugees from the Continent'. Recently, it reported, she had written to the *Daily Telegraph*, as part of a correspondence on the subject of nudity on the stage, pointing out that strip-tease (as it was then known) was a 'national disgrace . . . deliberately designed . . . to cater to all the worst in human nature', and would now be dealing with the points that had been raised by the large number of letters she had received. This announcement followed *Action*'s publication the previous week of horrified reports of strip-tease in London and Northampton and two letters on the subject, both of which compared Britain with pre-Nazi Germany. One, by E. G. M., 'the mother of three grown-up daughters and two sons', declared her outrage at the daily exposure of the young 'to the most hideous temptations and depravities. The vice-racket that was such a feature of Germany under the Weimar Republic . . . distinctly traceable to Jewish influence, has laid its stranglehold upon us.' The 'Mothers of England', she declared, lived only for the day when the British Union would sweep away the 'reign of unchecked vice and sexual perversion'. The second letter, reprinted from the *Telegraph*'s correspondence on the issue, declared that what was happening in Britain was reminiscent of the 'commercialised obscenity' which had flourished in post-war Berlin. Such shows, the writer remarked, did not come about because young girls wanted to take part in them but because of economic pressure, and patriotism demanded that youth be protected from abuse. This letter, *Action* commented, had not made clear that what it described had not been ended until 'the famous Nazi "clean-up" in 1933'. If the authorities looked into the situation in London today, it claimed, they would find it run by refugees who had previously operated in Weimar Berlin. (*Action* 11, 18 April 1940.)

In the series that followed, Mary Allen was insistent in rebutting letters she had received arguing that 'opposition to suggestive and indecent shows . . . is necessarily an attack upon perfectly legitimate performances'. On the contrary, commercial interests were exploiting sex and threatening to pervert young people who 'all unknowing, chant the catchwords of their ultimate destroyers'. It was 'sentimental nonsense', she wrote, to allow large numbers of refugee women and girls into the country 'whose knowledge and practice of vice is gradually permeating our underworld'. In other countries the degradation of youth had been 'drastically dealt with', but 'in our country' what she termed the 'Hidden Hand' was using the methods it had used elsewhere and the only answer was 'the total elimination of all foreigners engaged in this abominable trade'. Allen's concerns stretched widely. Objectionable photographs too had to be dealt with and nudist camps should be closed down. It was women's role to protect the family and care for the welfare of children; and women police, in patrolling parks and streets, could protect children. 'The world today', she concluded, 'is not suffering from the feminine principle, but from the crude, undisciplined female' and if women took 'their responsibilities seriously, men will be forced to in far greater numbers'. (*Action* 25 April, 2, 9, 16, 23 May 1940.)

This denunciation of metropolitan depravity raises a number of questions. One, which we have already raised in our discussion of National Socialism in Germany and to which we will return, is the relationship between fascism and moral conservatism. Two others, however, are worth addressing here. One, which flows from Allen's enthusiasm for Nazi policy towards 'vice', concerns the extent to which the BUF identified with already existing fascist regimes. First, however, we need to consider another aspect of Allen's – and the BUF's – concern with women. Mary Allen's Women's Auxiliary Service was an important part of the long fight to gain access for women to the police force, and Allen herself was both a former Suffragette and, it would later be revealed, a member of the BUF. Nor was she the only BUF member with a background in the Women's Social and Political Union, the leading organisation on the militant wing of the movement for women's votes. How was it possible for an overtly fascist organisation to encompass women who had earlier fought for women's suffrage, and at the very time that feminist organisations were actively involved in opposing fascism? (Allen and Heyneman 1934: 53–63, 79, 83–91; PRO HO/144/21933/467.)

In 1935, as we will discuss in the next chapter, a local women's organiser left the BUF, declaring that fascism would reduce women to 'where they were before the days of the Suffragettes'. The response of the BUF was to publish an anonymous article by 'an Old Suffragette', arguing that fascism would do no such thing. Having 'suffered imprisonment, and the horrors of the hunger and thirst strike', the *Blackshirt* writer insisted that women had engaged in suffrage militancy 'to have the means of helping to lift their country to a higher standard of economics', greater standing in the world and a higher civilisation. While many such women, she declared, had succumbed to the party system, 'such women as myself have turned to Fascism' which would bring plenty in place of poverty. 'No woman who loves her country, her sex or her liberty, need fear the coming victory of Fascism'. (*Blackshirt* 22 February 1935.)

Articles shortly after by Norah Elam, described in *Action* as a 'prominent Suffragette leader', reiterated this argument and, in using several of the same turns of phrase, probably revealed the identity of 'an Old Suffragette'. In one, Elam argued that democracy had rendered the efforts for women's suffrage meaningless. From the moment women gained the vote, she claimed, they had with few exceptions aligned themselves with the very parties that 'had treated them with such unprecedented contempt . . . they have turned again as handmaidens to the hewing of wood and drawing of water for the Party wirepullers'. But it was in another article, 'Fascism, Women and Democracy', that we can best see how she connected her critique of democracy to her part in the suffrage movement before the war and in the BUF a little over twenty years later. Opening her article with Sorel's claim that 'Democracy is the land of plenty dreamt of by unscrupulous financiers', she criticised those 'whose one obsession seems to be the alleged danger to enfranchized women in a Fascist Britain'. This, she claimed, was to entirely misunderstand the meaning of the suffrage struggle and to construe 'the demand for political liberty as a desire for personal licence'. The women's struggle, on the contrary, had arisen from a recognition that to exclude women from decision making was to deprive the nation of a vital contribution. Both men and women, the suffrage movement had understood, suffered from bad housing, from economic insecurity and from government policies at home and abroad. Women had demanded an equal role with men in saving the nation, a 'conception of practical citizenship', she declared, that was akin to fascism. 'Indeed, Fascism is the logical, if much grander, conception of the momentous issues raised by the militant women of a generation ago.' Nor should this be seen as the only connection. Both movements were disciplined, cross-class and above party. Both ascended beyond self-interest, gave absolute authority to the leader and faced brutality and slander. The vote, Elam argued, had only been a symbol and only 'the unintelligent woman' could believe that democracy was anything else than 'the careful and organized exploitation of men and women'. Women MPs and women voters alike were merely cogs in this system and had no power to end the despair of derelict areas or the decay of agriculture or 'the disintegration of the Empire'. In the end the only choice was between fascism and communism, the latter 'the negation of the natural instincts of womanhood', the former a system which offered 'real freedom' and an equal status within the Corporate State. Through equal pay, the removal of class barriers and the ending of the financiers' power to bring about war, fascism would ensure co-operation between the sexes in the creation of 'an ordered State . . . Fascism alone will complete the work begun on their behalf by the militant women from 1906 to 1914'. (*Action* 26 March 1936; *Fascist Quarterly* July 1935; for Elam's Suffragette past, see PRO HO/144/21933/417.)

In deliberately (and provocatively) comparing the BUF and the charismatic leadership of Mosley with the Women's Social and Political Union and Christabel Pankhurst twenty years earlier, Elam was not alone. Another BUF activist, Mary Richardson, replying to an attack on fascism by the former Suffragette, Sylvia Pankhurst, was to make a similar point. She had first been attracted to the BUF, Richardson wrote, 'because she saw in them the courage, the action, the loyalty, the gift of service, and the ability to serve which I had known in the Suffragette movement'. But if some former Suffragettes could see British Fascism as a continuation, not a contradiction, of their earlier commitments, Sylvia Pankhurst was one of many who followed a different trajectory. Nor was that necessarily one that lay on the left of the political spectrum. Thus in one article, Elam attacked Flora Drummond, formerly a leading Suffragette and now the head of the Women's Guild of Empire, a pro-Conservative (and feminist) grouping that opposed both communism and fascism. But if the gravitation of a handful of former Suffragettes to the extreme right need not lead us to conclude that the WSPU and the BUF enjoyed an elective affinity, it should certainly make us hesitate at drawing the seemingly obvious opposite conclusion – that fascism is always anti-feminist and feminism anti-fascist. (*Blackshirt* 29 June 1934, 25 September 1937; for Richardson's memoirs of her life as a Suffragette, see Richardson 1953.)

In her exchange with Sylvia Pankhurst, Mary Richardson had contended that it was wrong to use events in Italy to attack British Fascism because 'the position of women in Italy has never been on a par with that of British women', a point which takes us to our last concern in this chapter. Repeatedly during the 1930s, the BUF was to come under attack for supporting regimes which denied women's rights. In so fervently defending Hitler and Mussolini, anti-fascists argued, the BUF was revealing what it too would do to women should it come to power. The BUF continued to defend the governments in Germany and Italy, but it was never able to find a consistent response to its opponents' arguments. One approach was to portray Italian and German women as the beneficiaries of the new regimes. Women in Italy, one article claimed, were not denied equal rights. In contrast to frequent practice in Britain, they were not dismissed from their jobs upon marriage. As for feminist criticisms of the failure to give women the vote, this, it was suggested, was irrelevant since the Italian government was likely to abolish parliamentary elections altogether! Likewise, for one woman activist, Eileen Lyons, German women were happy with the new regime. They had not been 'forced into the home' and 'all classes of women' had been brought together 'to make life easier for their own sex', with expectant mothers receiving paid holidays from work while 'volunteers, usually girl students', took their place in 'a fine example of real sisterhood'. Whatever feminists claimed, and 'the writer is one', Lyons declared, the majority of women were wives and mothers, and National Socialists in Germany, as would occur in a fascist Britain, devoted their greatest efforts to 'the motherhood of the race'. (*Blackshirt* 29, 1 June 1934, 13 June 1936.)

If part of BUF strategy was to eulogise Hitler's or Mussolini's policies towards women, another element was to argue that they had been misrepresented. Thus in 1937 the BUF published an article by a Nazi woman, Anne Seelig-Thomann, who declared that it was not true that working women were forcibly removed from employment and their jobs given to men. Instead, the Labour Front had removed women from factory work which was 'unsuitable for the female physique' but they had been found work elsewhere. 'German women are still employed in all the trades concerned with clothing ... millions besides are teachers, nurses and domestic servants' and millions more were in general industry with a special section of the Labour Front. (*British Union Quarterly* October–December 1937.)

But the BUF did not always simply defend the measures introduced by Hitler or Mussolini. It was possible to argue both that policy elsewhere had been misrepresented by anti-fascists and that opponents had failed to recognise that fascism would take different forms in different countries. Thus, in 1936, again in debate with Sylvia Pankhurst, Anne Brock Griggs had claimed that her opponent was misinformed about both German and Italian policy while also suggesting that Pankhurst had ignored 'the difference in outlook between the Latin and Anglo-Saxon'. There was one final possibility, in which it could be contended that fascist policy in Europe was undergoing a fundamental change. Thus in reply to a letter from a woman BUF member concerned at reports that the Nazis were removing women from teaching, Griggs argued that 'a differing racial tradition' in the Italian and German 'attitude towards women' made comparison with British Fascism impossible. None the less, she went on, while initially after the Nazi accession to power the pendulum had swung too far against women's employment, this had proved temporary. Similarly, in 1938 *Action* reported that five years after the removal of 'double earners' there was no longer unemployment and married women had been invited back to work. To create jobs for men, it declared, women had been moved to lighter occupations or removed from employment altogether if a husband or son could gain a job. Now, with a shortage of workers in Germany, this was no longer necessary. (*Hibbert Journal* April 1936; *Fascist Quarterly* January 1936; *Action* 27 August, 3 September 1938.)

Contrary to conventional wisdom, the BUF, rather than denouncing feminism, claimed to be compatible with it. It called for equal pay, promised that women would not be sacked and even sought to present policy in Germany and Italy as favourable to women's position not only in the home but in the workplace. As we have already had cause to note, it contained a number of enthusiastic women propagandists, some with a feminist background, who debated with anti-fascist feminists as part of the movement's unceasing attempt to persuade women of the virtues of its position. Fascism is famously seen as a male movement, and Mosley himself described it as 'the organized revolt of the young manhood of Britain' (Billig 1978: 255). But no more than Italian Fascism or German National Socialism was British Fascism exclusively male. Indeed, as we will now turn to discuss, it was a movement in which women were highly active, and in ways that could be very different from what we would expect.

3 Blackshirt women

During the interrogation that followed his arrest in 1940, Mosley declared that the British Union had a higher percentage of women candidates than any other party. His movement, he went on, had 'been largely built up by the fanaticism of women . . . Without the women I could not have got a quarter of the way . . . ' (PRO HO 283/14/101). This was a somewhat remarkable claim for a movement that has so often been seen as essentially male. We have already discussed one of Mosley's other statements to his interrogators, that his movement was committed to complete equality between the sexes. But what of his claim that women were crucial to the movement? While one account has suggested that probably over 20 per cent and perhaps as many as a third of the BUF's membership were women, another has proposed a similar figure of between a quarter and a third (Thurlow 1987: caption to photograph opposite 142; Cullen 1987: 47). In chapter 2, we made extensive use of the BUF's own publications to establish how it saw women's role in society. In using the same body of work in exploring women's role in the movement, we need to be especially aware of two problems. First, if we should be aware that what a movement's propagandists say is likely to be influenced by electoral, factional and other considerations (indeed, this is part of our argument about why there is no single view of women on the extreme right) we also need to be sceptical about how a movement describes its activities – and its activists. If its publications are likely to enthuse over the commitment of its militants and the size of its meetings (and, equally, to fail to admit the inactivity of many members or to reveal that hitherto leading figures have left the organisation), there is also another problem in considering the BUF. At least two former activists, one the editor of *Action*, the other the woman district leader for Nelson, have claimed that BUF officials painted a false picture of the movement's progress. District reports were falsified, the latter stated, and 'meetings that were flops were written up as highly successful' (Thurlow 1987: 133; Driver n.d.: 44–5). BUF publications, while they include considerable material on women's activities, are fortunately not the only source that has proved useful and where appropriate other sources – not least the valuable Special Branch reports on the movement – have been drawn on. But no more than with BUF publications, should other sources be always taken at face value. We cannot claim to have a complete picture of what BUF women did between 1932 and 1940. But in examining the BUF's view of women's place in society, we have already found that fascism can be considerably different from what we might expect. Does the BUF's conception of women's place in the movement also diverge from our expectations?

Writing in 1932, Mosley noted that it had been suggested that 'in our organisation, too little attention has been made to the position of women'. What followed was a discussion of women in the Corporate State, rather than in the BUF itself, but preceded by an acknowledgement that the movement had so far concentrated on organising men, believing it was they who should deal with violent opposition. But if Mosley was initially little interested in recruiting women, the BUF soon began to set about doing so. Writing in the *Fascist Week* in early 1934, Esther Makgill (or Lady Makgill, as she was more accurately described in another version of the article) wrote that she had started the Women's Section of the BUF in March 1933. 'We had then a few dozen women scattered about the country.' Such had been the response, however, that 'to-day we occupy a whole building as Women's National Headquarters at 12, Lower Grosvenor Place, London, S.W.1, and have Women's Branches in seventy-five per cent. of the districts where the Men's Branches are established'. A 'small squad of women stewards . . . all trained in ju-jitsu' had been set up for use in public meetings but 'the main women's activities are propaganda, speaking to women audiences, and the organisation of a political section'. (Mosley 1932: 40–1; *Fascist Week* 23–29 March 1934; *Age of Plenty* II.1, 1934.)

Another account shortly after described the original number of Women's Section members as seventeen. Both at headquarters and locally, it declared, the most important class was 'the Study Circle or the Speakers' Class (some branches hold both these)'. The first involved discussion of BUF policy, the second training of 'young speakers who will later address meetings in every part of the country . . . The class director criticises their delivery and elocution, while they make speeches of five or ten minutes' duration, on subjects chosen either by themselves or the director.' Such classes, it observed, were held 'in addition to . . . First Aid, Physical Training, Fencing and other classes' because a sound understanding of fascism was needed 'for women to undertake what is essentially *their* work for the Movement – that of canvassing'. This involved women members typing up index cards, dividing them into streets and blocks, and then being assigned a block whose houses they would call at regularly, distributing free literature, announcing local meetings and answering questions. There was, the article declared, 'work of every kind' for women members. 'We want speakers, canteen helpers, women who can paint posters and placards; girls who will sell literature and join in our classes; we want women who can entertain and women to run our children's clubs. Whatever your talent, there is a place for you in the Fascist Movement!' (*Blackshirt* 1 June 1934.)

As these articles suggest, women were involved in a number of ways within the BUF. Some were of particular importance. 'Considerable interest', it was claimed in 1934, had 'been aroused in many quarters at the sight of Women Blackshirts holding street corner meetings, and handling hecklers with a skill which would not disgrace a seasoned Hyde Park orator'. Nor were speakers only used to address street meetings. In the same issue the *Blackshirt* announced a series of meetings for women only to be held in the Gloucestershire area. 'The Blackshirt speaker will be a woman, and the meeting will be stewarded entirely by women members . . . Halls in all parts of the area are being booked.' (*Blackshirt* 29 June 1934.)

The following year the *Blackshirt* declared that the approaching general election made the work of women members

> increasingly important. It cannot be too strongly urged that women Fascists should take every opportunity offered both at Headquarters and at the local centres, to train as speakers, while the effectiveness of canvassers, as well as those who spread Fascism privately among friends and acquaintances, is enormously increased if they have practised stating their case clearly and impressively in a speakers' class.

Such classes, the article claimed, would enable women to deal with both genuine queries and points made by hostile questioners.

> Daily, from every part of London, requests for women speakers pour in to Headquarters. They are sorely needed, not only for outdoor work, but for afternoon and evening branch meetings. There are also countless opportunities constantly presenting themselves

for women to talk to groups of their own sex in private houses. To meet these ever-increasing demands, the Movement must have an increasing corps of competent trained speakers upon which it can call at any time.

A class took place at 8.30 p.m. every Wednesday at Women's Headquarters, 'and women are urged to take advantage of this opportunity to learn to express themselves convincingly in the furtherance of the Fascist cause'. (*Blackshirt* 1 February 1935.)

Such training was not restricted to London. In May 1935, for instance, Mosley's mother, Maud Lady Mosley (who had become director of organisation of the Women's Section shortly after its formation) visited Manchester where several 'potential women speakers' had 'shown promise' in the speakers' class. Following her visit, a Women's Propaganda Section was organised, led by the Manchester women's officer, Ursula Corderey, and, the *Blackshirt* reported, an

> experiment made by getting women speakers to open the ordinary Blackshirt meetings in Stevenson-square, Manchester and the surrounding districts, is causing much interest . . . Women's speakers' classes are being held regularly in Manchester, and before long it is hoped to send the ladies to Blackburn, Bolton, Preston, and elsewhere.
> (*Blackshirt* 23 February–1 March 1934, 7, 21 June 1935)

'I am glad', the BUF's woman propaganda officer, Anne Brock Griggs, declared the following year, to report 'steady progress in the training of women speakers . . . at our Central Schools of training and at local classes'. The old parties 'could not produce speakers like these. I have heard one propagandist after another, the majority young, courageous, yet level-headed, giving speeches which in their simplicity of language and sincerity could not fail to convince.' Such speakers, she held, were crucial for building an electoral machine and all 'women in Fascism' should come forward. 'Let us remember that every one of us who goes out to speak the word of Fascism, whether on the doorstep, on the street corner, public platform, or in private argument, is representative of the great Leader whom it is our pride to serve.' (*Blackshirt* 3 January 1936, 25 October 1935.)

As such accounts would suggest, it was not only in street corner meetings that BUF women speakers were to be found. In 1938 *Action* announced that the British Union had a large number of experienced women speakers who are available to address meetings. Districts who can utilise the services of these women speakers should make application to N.H.Q. . . . They are available for meetings organised by Districts and also . . . are available to address meetings of various women's organisations at the invitation of those organisations.

District leaders, it noted, 'should see that no opportunities are missed in the above connection'. The BUF had long been interested in making contact with women's organisations. In early 1934, for instance, its director of propaganda had defended the BUF's policy towards women in a debate with the prominent anti-fascist Ellen Wilkinson at a meeting organised by the Women Clerks and Secretaries Association. Likewise, later in the year a woman BUF speaker had debated 'Democracy v. Fascism' at a meeting organised by a branch of the feminist National Women Citizens' Association. But if the BUF sought to win over support in organisations which women already supported (in one article in 1939, women were urged to make propaganda in Parents' Groups, Co-operative Societies, Women Citizens' Associations or whatever organisation they belonged to), there were other ways too in which women could be reached. (*Action* 18 June 1938, 28 January 1939; *Fascist Week* 2 March 1934; *Blackshirt* 7 December 1934.)

In 1934, women in Hull organised Fascist Teas on Saturday afternoons, preceded and followed by sales drives of the *Fascist Week* while, earlier that year, the *Blackshirt* had suggested that in rural districts women should organise cottage meetings (with 'sandwiches, cakes, etc.') for their friends to hear an address on such subjects as 'The position of women in the Fascist State'. It was meetings such as these that figured when, in 1936, the *Blackshirt* found itself 'ticked off something awful' for having 'put the ladies last' in its weekly report of BUF activity. Chastened, it begrudgingly decided to place them first. At Bethnal Green, it announced, 'Mrs. Thomas addressed women's afternoon meeting. Yes! You guessed it: tea was served! The Green are holding one of these tea-meetings every month. Women District Leaders mark this down as AN IDEA WORTH USING.' The following week, it returned to this theme: 'It's ladies first again this week, and from the women comes another great idea. Private house Fascist meetings. On Thursday, April 23, Mrs. Ann Brock Griggs addressed a dozen ladies', gaining increased support for Muswell Hill District. Members should 'GIVE AFTERNOON TEA MEETINGS

A TRIAL. Reports tell us that they are a great success.' (*Blackshirt* 4–10 May, 9–15 February 1934, 25 April, 2 May 1936.)

Given the degree of anti-fascist activity, the organisation of meetings was not an easy matter, and in February 1934 the *Blackshirt* announced that Women's Section 'special Propaganda Patrol squads' had been set up 'under the leadership of Miss Phyllis Davies and Miss Marjorie Aitken'. They would be responsible for the sale of literature and would also 'undertake other propaganda work as necessity arises'. In May the *Fascist Week* reported that women Blackshirts were now holding 'their own outdoor meetings with women speakers and women stewards, the ban originally placed on women members of the British Union of Fascists holding outdoor meetings having been lifted'. The chief speaker was Mary Richardson and many requests for women speakers had been turned down due to a shortage of speakers. 'The first meeting was recently held at Bromley. Mrs. Perry, Women's Organiser for the South East London area, was in charge of the Defence Force recruited from the local Women's Section.' Meetings were being held every Sunday afternoon, usually in South London, and stewarded 'by the Women's Defence Force, under the control of Miss M. Aitken'. (In January, the *Sunday Dispatch*, one of the Rothermere papers then sympathetic to the movement, had reported on the 'rapid headway in the principal branches' of women's ju-jitsu and first aid squads, publishing a photo of Aitken and two other members of what it described as the headquarters squad.) As we have noted, there was inevitable controversy as to the extent to which Blackshirts were the initiators of violence, and this did not always apply only to the men in the movement. Following the particularly violent meeting in Olympia in June 1934 which was to precipitate the withdrawal of the *Daily Mail*'s support for Mosley, fascists and anti-fascists were both to claim that women had been attacked by the other side. A letter published by the anti-fascist *Daily Herald* described a woman heckler being brutally treated by both male and female Blackshirts while Mosley himself was to claim that 'not only were our male Blackshirts kicked in the stomach and slashed with razors but our women Fascists were terribly assaulted'. Clashes were to continue throughout the decade and one incident, for instance, led to the Women's Defence Force's Marjorie Aitken appearing in court. Following a fracas at a meeting in Manchester, six anti-fascists were summoned. Giving evidence against one of the accused, Aitken claimed that 'she warned Miss Taylor who, however, refused to be quiet and seized a steward by the hair and spat at him. She also seized witness by the hair and kicked her. Witness added that she had to strike defendant in self-defence.' Taylor, however, claimed Aitken 'went for her first'. (*Blackshirt* 23 February–1 March 1934; *Fascist Week* 25 May 1934; *Sunday Dispatch* 21 January 1934; Lewis 1987: 79–80, 88, 119; *Manchester Guardian* 6 December 1934.)

As such accounts would suggest, Mosley's belief that physical clashes precluded women's participation in the movement had been superseded. 'Many women members of the Richmond branch', it was reported in 1934, had gained the St John's Ambulance Certificate, and were now eligible for 'the coveted fencing jacket after they have passed the additional P.T. and ju-jitsu tests'. In Kilburn, it was noted the same year, ju-jitsu proved popular, 'the ladies especially showing remarkable aptitude in this splendid form of defence so suitable to members of the "weaker sex"'. Later in the decade, Griggs reported that women members in Kingston were developing physical fitness by hiking and, she went on, not only could this be emulated elsewhere but 'The idea of rambling foreshadows the possibility of a Summer Seaside Camp for women and girls' which, if there was enough interest, would occur that August. (*Blackshirt* 20 July, 9–15 March 1934, 17 April 1937.)

Encouraging a feeling of camaraderie was crucial for women in the BUF as it was for men and, three months later, the *Blackshirt* announced that the annual Blackshirt camp would be open a week longer, from 29 August to 4 September, for the women members of the British Union. The following month it called for women Blackshirts to 'Take Advantage of the Opportunity' to 'Make History!' Cost would be 30*s*. a week and full details could be obtained from the women's camp commandant at National Headquarters. The first two issues for September were to carry enthusiastic reports of the camp. The first described how 'with great hustle and bustle the National Socialist women took over the camp . . . from the men. Within a few moments of their arrival they were busy under the direction of Miss Doreen Bell settling themselves at home.' There was, the writer went on, 'Nothing silly or soft about these women . . . and the happy carefree way in which they made themselves at home, was so refreshing after one has had their fill of the simpering little brats that democracy and Jewish films have produced.' Having so effectively reminded the reader why the British Union described itself as National Socialist, the following week the *Blackshirt*'s publication of a photograph of a 'jolly group' of women members at the camp was accompanied by a fuller report of days that began with cold showers, bacon and eggs and inspection of tents before the breaking of the flag 'while the camp stands tensely at the salute'. There followed horse-riding or shopping or swimming (interspersed with 'an excellent lunch') before 'Tea – then perhaps a well earned rest, or for the more energetic, table tennis in the main marquee.' At sundown the flag is lowered and then the women spend time in the nearby village before coming home to 'a substantial, truly English supper of bread, cheese and pickles' and dispersing to their tents. (*Blackshirt* 17 July, 14 August, 4, 11 September 1937.)

Only some women members would have even considered attending such a gathering. The focus of BUF activity was the branch, and these varied greatly in level and types of activity. In Manchester in the mid-1930s, sales drives, ju-jitsu and first-aid classes reportedly kept women members 'active four and five nights a week' while in 1938 Anne Brock Griggs attended a local Women's Section meeting to outline a scheme to create a women's sports and athletic section for both members and non-members. 'Mrs. Simpson, of Manchester, who is responsible for the scheme, and Mrs. Faulkner, of Platting, who will be in charge of the hiking and camping sections also addressed the meeting, which was followed by a demonstration of fencing by Miss Renwick and Miss Thomas.' In Shoreditch in the same period women were described as being engaged in a summer campaign that entailed sales drives and canvassing. 'One night a week it is proposed to relax from the ordinary district activities when they will drill, play table tennis, and be happy together in the true National Socialist spirit.' (*Blackshirt* 8 March 1935; *Action* 12 March, 2 July 1938.)

While physical fitness was clearly considered of great importance, sales drives of BUF material, as we have seen, were also of particular significance. In mid-1934 women Blackshirts in Leicester were described as 'selling literature on the streets daily' and in Manchester, the *Blackshirt* reported, the Women's Section's first sales drive in Didsbury had taken place despite rain. Similarly, in Streatham a little later in the year, women members were reported to be 'taking a keen interest in the activities of the women's propaganda section, which is organising to co-operate with the men in increasing the sale of the *Blackshirt*'. (*Blackshirt* 15 June, 11–17 May, 28 September 1934.)

Propaganda could also be made in other ways, and in September 1934, women members took part in a march to Hyde Park, Lady Mosley subsequently declaring that 'the Leader' had told her that 'the women were splendid and had more than justified his decision that they should be allowed to join in the march'. In May 1936 the first Women's Propaganda March took place, in which 'the women Blackshirts of London' marched from Bethnal Green to Victoria Park under the leadership of their women's executive officer, Olga

Shore. Many who had intended to march, the *Blackshirt* claimed, had been unable to do so but those who were able came from

> shops, offices, and their own homes ... and marched through one of the most poverty-stricken districts of London ... And how they marched! It was a revelation to many who had doubted the ability of women to march properly. They marched in perfect step, with commendable order and discipline, the more praiseworthy because they had no bands or drums to lead them.

More marches took place and by September the paper was claiming that, 'In London streets, the smart disciplined columns of uniformed Blackshirt women are becoming a familiar sight.' The same month, Yorkshire Blackshirt women marched from Mosley House, the Central Leeds British Union Headquarters, to Woodhouse Moor. On the previous day, 'the streets of Lower Belgravia and Pimlico resounded with the tramp of marching feet' as women, 'led by Miss Jackson', carried 'their Union Flag and District Standard through the streets in which they have worked so hard to further the cause of Fascism'. The next month it was Manchester's turn, women marching from Old Trafford to Stretford, while at the famous confrontation at Cable Street, the *Daily Herald* described 'a column of 3,000 ... with over 200 black-bloused women in the centre'. (*Blackshirt* 14 September 1934, 23 May, 19, 26 September, 10 October 1936; *Daily Herald* 5 October 1936.)

Despite the mass opposition the BUF experienced at Cable Street, it continued such activities, and the following year *Action* claimed a 'fine contingent of nearly a thousand women' on the march to Bermondsey. Led by the woman administrative officer, Anne Brock Griggs, the 'women were carrying their own colours that day for the first time. Later the leader officially presented them at the Victoria Grill and right well had they been earned.' But marching behind their own colours was not to be the only innovation in women's marches. Shortly after, the women's district leader for Westminster (Abbey) District appealed for any women members of London area who wished to learn the drums to get in touch. Practice was scheduled for every Thursday at 8.30 p.m. at National Headquarters and a fund opened to pay for the purchase of drums and the hire of practice halls. In November, *Action*, announcing that the 4th London Area Women's Propaganda March would assemble on the 27th at Central Hackney District Headquarters, urged: 'Women of London roll up and have the honour of being the first to march behind the Women's Drums.' As a later report indicated, however, the drums actually appeared on a Central Hackney District march one week earlier. 'On both occasions,' *Action* claimed, 'the marching columns and the highly efficient Drum Corps made a deep impression on the watching crowds'. (*Action* 9 October 1937, 2 July, 19 November, 3 December 1938.)

If women marched, stewarded meetings and spoke in public, they also raised money for the movement. In Leicester West in 1938, women were reported to have raised over £65, while a whist drive in Edinburgh the previous year was said to have been very successful in raising money. Women could play a key part, Mosley declared, in organising fund-raising events in order to build up the election fund. According to the organisation's 1938 constitution, 'Bazaars, jumble sales, whist drives, dances, etc.' run by women members would result in 70 per cent of the proceeds going to the election fund and the remainder being earmarked for use by the Women's Section, and a leaflet issued by the two BUF candidates for NE Bethnal Green the previous year noted: 'Our women members have already raised £200 for the L.C.C. elections.' (*Blackshirt* March 1938, 10 April 1937, 29 November 1935; PRO HO144/21281/47; BUF leaflet 1937.)

The BUF engaged in cultural activities too. In 1934, for instance, women in the Streatham branch were involved in the production of plays which, it was hoped, would 'prove a great attraction throughout the winter months'. In Ilford, they had formed 'a small orchestra' while at National Headquarters a women's choir gathered for 'community singing'. Some women were involved in work among youth. In 1934 in Plymouth, women members organised games for children and 'gave them brief and simple talks on loyalty to King and Country to counteract the teachings of the Communist organisations' while two years later Mrs James of the Shoreditch branch was organising 'Fascist boys and girls' in the BUF's Youth Movement. Articles in the BUF press proposed other areas in which the cause could be advanced. In 1939, as war with Nazi Germany approached and Europe's Jews came increasingly under threat, it was even suggested that women could write letters to the local press protesting against 'the flow of Jewish refugee children'. Or they could simply talk to their neighbours, and then report the conversations to their woman district leader who could make use of such reports to gain a better sense of popular opinion. Another article, the year before, calling on women to join, urged the younger ones to sell papers and the older to make a room available for meetings or to check details of voters. In addition, it suggested, women could make goods for sale, carry out clerical work or ensure 'the keeping clean and in order of District Headquarters

Premises'. As one woman district leader noted, women members, among other activities, 'kept the H.Q. clean and tidy' and 'brewed tea for the men as they came in from active duty'; another former member recalled 'Serving in canteens, scrubbing floors, as well as paper sales . . . meetings . . . looking after newer women members . . . propaganda marches . . . leaflet distribution etc.' (*Blackshirt* 28 September, 12 October, 7 December, 6 July 1934, 30 May 1936; *Action* 28 January 1939, 25 June 1938; Driver n.d.: 29, 46; Cullen 1996: 55.)

From some even more was expected, and of the eighty prospective parliamentary candidates chosen by Mosley between 1936 and 1938, eleven were women. The BUF press published biographical details of its candidates and made sure that readers were aware that the former Suffragette Norah Elam, the prospective parliamentary candidate for Northampton, had been imprisoned three times and 'endured several hunger strikes'. She had also, it noted, been involved in recruiting, had worked in a munitions factory and sat on several government committees before standing as an Independent candidate, then joining the Conservatives and finally joining British Union shortly after its creation. Her Suffragette past was also praised by Mosley himself. Speaking at a meeting to introduce her to her prospective constituents, he declared that 'it killed for all time the suggestion that National Socialism proposed putting British women back in the home'. (Cross 1961: 179; *Blackshirt* 21, 28 November 1937.)

Selection as a candidate could involve considerable effort on the part of the woman chosen. Thus, in May 1937, one was described as 'very busy getting known to her constituents; she has been touring local factories and addressing the workers and holding afternoon meetings at local cafes, and in the evenings calling on contacts'. In October, another was likewise described as 'getting down to the task of calling upon her constituents with a view to winning support for the forthcoming Parliamentary Election Campaign'. For others, however, selection as a BUF candidate was a more short-lived honour. Following the launch of William Joyce's National Socialist League in 1937, the second issue of its paper announced the formation of a Women's Special Propaganda Section. It already possessed a Canvass Corps, it noted, led by 'Miss Barrington', the British Union's former prospective parliamentary candidate for Fulham West. Nor was she the only woman defector to Joyce. Holland-with-Boston's branch leader was Sylvia Morris, the former BUF candidate for that locality. (*Blackshirt* 8 May, 9 October 1937; *Helmsman* 1.2, n.d.)

Since the 1940 general election was never to take place, none of the BUF's prospective parliamentary candidates were ever to face the electorate. Some BUF women, however, did stand at local level. In 1938 Margaret Pye, standing in Manchester, declared in her election leaflet that 'you can make a start to clean up Local Government by sending a woman of action to the Council Chamber' (she was to gain a total of twenty-three votes). The previous year there were women candidates in municipal elections in Shoreditch, Bethnal Green North and St Pancras and, most importantly, Anne Brock Griggs's London County Council candidature. Reporting on the bitterly anti-Semitic campaign, *Action* claimed that Griggs 'by now is known to thousands of Limehouse electors as "Our Annie"'. At one of her public meetings, it described her urging the audience to vote British Union. 'She pointed out how the L.C.C. elections in East London could force Jewry to show a clean pair of heels. She added that it would be the first clean thing they had shown.' The eve of poll message by Griggs and her fellow candidate, Charles Wegg Prosser, included a call for the defence of the family. It was 'only by attacking the corrupting forces of Jewish Communism', they declared, 'that we can restore the Christian basis of family life'. Griggs, the BUF declared, had 'made a tremendous effort with results which have amazed the old gangs'. She gained just over 2,000 votes, some 6,000 behind the victorious Labour candidates. (Rawnsley 1981: 185, 385, 195; *Blackshirt* 30 October, 20 March 1937; *Action* 27 February 1937; *East London Pioneer* 24 February 1937; Benewick 1972: 282.)

If such effort on the part of candidates was to bear fruit, it was vital that members worked to secure voters' support, and for the BUF, as we have already seen, this was considered a crucial part of women's work. Speaking in mid-1934 at a cabaret ball held in aid of the Women's Section, Mosley declared:

> We are now entering into a phase in our work when the activities of the women are vital. That phase is the building up of an electoral machine, and when it comes to electoral work, the canvass on the door-step and the persuasion of the voter, I think we men have to give first place to the women.

The *Blackshirt* had reported earlier in the year that, following an appeal by Lady Makgill, canvassing of the Abbey Division of Westminster had been begun by Women's Headquarters and now, in response to Mosley's call, a canvassing drive in the district was announced.

To carry this out successfully we need fifty women at least, and are offering to train any desirous of taking up this very necessary work. No one need be diffident in applying ... and any member who can devote two evenings a week to attend the training classes should apply. There are many women who have leisure in the daytime, and to them a very special appeal is made.
(*Blackshirt* 26 January–1 February, 9–15 February, 6 July 1934)

It was canvassing, indeed, that was to present particular difficulties for the organisation of women in the BUF. In January 1935, in an effort to build a well-organised electoral machine while retaining a uniformed elite, plans to restructure the whole movement were announced, whereby Blackshirts, who would be expected to devote at least two evenings a week to the movement, were to be organised separately from a political organisation. In part this would involve the political organisation taking over all 'existing women's organisations' which were expected to begin to develop constituency work immediately. Blackshirt organisation, however, would 'control women who are prepared to operate as Women Blackshirt Units under the same conditions as the men'. All the proposals, it was announced, would be finalised after consultation. For some women, the take-over of women's organisation was seen as a threat, restricting women to electoral work, and following a flow of letters to Mosley on a number of questions raised by the proposals, he announced in February that women officers would retain their posts, that all women could, if they wished, continue to wear the black shirt and 'Any application to form units of women under special conditions of Blackshirt Command will be forwarded to Blackshirt Organisation for consideration between Blackshirt Command and Women's Organisation.' (*Blackshirt* 18 January, 1 February 1935.)

In March still more effort had to be made to put women members' anxieties at rest. 'Women's organisation', Mosley wrote, 'gave us perhaps the most difficulty under the new scheme. A mistaken idea was current that women were to have their Black shirts taken away and to be treated as if they were in the Old Parties.' The relationship between women's organisation and men's in the new scheme, he declared, did not differ from that in the Conservative and Labour Parties but this was 'in order to dispel the absurd charge by our opponents that women are placed in an inferior position by Fascism'. Women were eligible to be both candidates and agents and could work in teams which if they gave 'the requisite high standard of special service' could be attached permanently to Blackshirt Command. The 'great majority' of women, however, should be organised in teams 'for the vital work of canvass'. In the event, however, plans for a separate political organisation were abandoned, and in May the movement was reorganised into three divisions, in which the conditions were the same for men and women. Members of No. 1 Division were to devote five nights a week to the movement, No. 2 Division two nights, and No. 3 Division, who were not entitled to wear uniform, had no obligation other than the payment of a regular membership subscription. (*Blackshirt* 22 March, 24 May 1935; PRO HO144/20145/274–5.)

In early 1937 Anne Brock Griggs set down 'the next stage in women's organisation'. The electoral work in East London, she declared, had demonstrated 'that the pull in the home is greater than the enthusiasm of the street meeting, which must be backed and followed up by canvass and the selling of papers, not only on the street corner but door to door'. The objective now was a street block system with two teams of five women each in each polling district. Each woman district leader should organise her members along these lines, and the ultimate aim was that every member would have responsibility for some 300 houses. The primary purpose of the teams was 'to complete the canvass, i.e. to spread our propaganda as widely as possible in every ward'. (*Blackshirt* 27 March 1937.)

The following year, a fuller account was given of what this new phase in women's organisation would mean. According to the British Union's 1938 Constitution and Rules, the woman district leader's first responsibility was to train women for Ward Teams, each of whose members would be responsible for a particular block of houses, selling papers, canvassing, obtaining donations, collecting subscriptions from No. 3 Division members and recruiting to the organisation. (Such teams would be 'composed both of men and women' and could be led by women.) The woman district leader's second responsibility was to organise and train Women's Action Teams for 'propaganda marches, street sales, literature distribution, mass canvass, street collections for election fund at open air meetings, etc.' Meetings for all women members in a ward had to be held at least monthly, particularly to bring together No. 3 Division members and their 'friends and sympathisers'. A talk on policy would be given but 'the main purpose of this meeting will be to engender the spirit of the Movement to which end community singing of the Movement's song is particularly valuable'. (PRO HO144/21281/46.)

As the Constitution also made clear, women district leaders were subordinate to male district leaders. Power in the movement ultimately lay with a male hierarchy, and the authority that women enjoyed had very definite limits. Women themselves disagreed about what role women should play in the BUF, and if the arguments over canvassing were eventually weathered, they represented but one of the problems that troubled the BUF women's organisation. In early 1934, for instance, a Special Branch report noted that Mary Richardson had replaced Lady Makgill as 'chief organiser of the Women's Section', Makgill having resigned during the current month, after being suspended in consequence of 'serious deficiencies in the funds of the Women's Section'. In one woman member's recollection, Richardson was 'a fiery speaker' at street corner meetings and 'a magnet to us young people'. Yet she would prove a controversial figure, and was not to last long. A former socialist parliamentary candidate as well as a ex-Suffragette, she had joined the BUF in late 1933, declaring in the light of her 'previous political experience, I feel certain that women will play a large part in establishing Fascism in this country'. In the months that followed her appointment as organising secretary of the Women's Section, the BUF press carried a number of reports of her activities, ranging from addressing a 'rough crowd' in Chiswick to attending, with Lady Mosley, a 'garden meeting held in the grounds of the Richmond Branch'. On 5 October 1934, the *Blackshirt* reported that she had been slightly injured in a motor accident while returning from a meeting and would 'not be able to carry out her speaking engagements, or attend to correspondence, during the next fortnight'. Two weeks later she was reported to be making progress, 'but it is still not yet possible to say definitely when she will be resuming her propaganda work'. By 29 October, she had sufficiently recovered to represent the BUF in a debate organised by Hampstead Garden Liberal Women's Association. Her future, however, was now in doubt and in January the following year, a Special Branch report noted that she had been sent to work for the BUF in Lancashire. This was, it said, despite the objections of Lady Mosley, with whom she had been in conflict for some time. (PRO HO 144/21281/46; PRO HO 144/20140/112; Cullen 1996: 57; *Fascist Week* 22–28 December 1933; Kean 1994: 67; *Blackshirt* 1 June, 10 August, 5, 19 October, 16 November 1934; PRO HO144/20144/183.)

She had already, by then, vanished from the pages of the *Blackshirt*. What had happened? In November 1935 a trade union official, the defendant in a court case brought by Mosley, received a letter from a former union member offering to provide him with evidence. 'I was Chief Propaganda Officer for the Women's Section of the B.U.F.', the correspondent wrote, and had been 'expelled for daring, with other women, to put forward demands to the great Mosley, whereby women would receive *some* measure of fair play. All the best women left when I was expelled.' She could be contacted, the writer noted, at an address in Welwyn Garden City where she would be 'until after the election'. An examination of the local paper for the period of the 1935 general election does indeed record Mary Richardson's appearance in the area, addressing a meeting of Welwyn War Resisters. In an account of the 'well attended' meeting, the paper reported that Richardson, the new honorary secretary of the anti-war group, had told the meeting that she had joined the BUF believing that it opposed class distinction and stood for 'equality of opportunity and pay for men and women'. She had found, however, that the organisation was riddled with hypocrisy and had been expelled in February for 'attempting to organise a protest'. (MSS 127/NU/GS/3/5D; *Welwyn Times* 12, 19 December 1935.)

In an angry letter the following month, Anne Brock Griggs defended the BUF's stance. Richardson, she suggested, had misrepresented fascism and descended to 'personal criticism of our Leader'. Replying, Richardson was to make more detailed allegations of the unequal remuneration of women employed by the movement, something Griggs would deny in the final contribution to the exchange. In Richardson's account, interestingly, Griggs's attack on her was particularly 'surprising' since Griggs had been 'one of the forty Fascist women who met in my home in London last spring', and had been 'one of the most vehement in demanding that a deputation' be sent to Mosley 'to demand a fair deal for women'. (*Welwyn Times* 2, 16, 30 January 1936.)

While Richardson had raised the question of disparities of pay within the movement, it is likely that the protests of her and her supporters related to other aspects of the BUF's organisation of women. In part, this may have concerned the plans to reorganise the movement discussed earlier, plans which seem to have led to a more publicised resignation at the time. In February 1935 a London paper, the *Star*, reported that a north-west London area organiser, Mrs H. Carrington Wood, had resigned from the BUF. She had 'fought unavailingly for the equality of women within the Blackshirt movement', she told the *Star*, and sent Mosley a memorandum declaring: 'The promises made on Fascist platforms and in Fascist literature' did not convince women, 'who naturally do not want to risk going back to where they were before the days of the Suffragettes'. Mosley, in reply, had thanked her for her letter 'in response to my request for suggestions on the new organisation scheme' and promised that her proposals would be 'carefully studied during the preparation of the final scheme'. She left and, two months after the appearance of the report, spoke at a meeting of the feminist organisation, the Six Point Group, during which, it reported, she 'described her experience as an organiser of the British Union of Fascists and clearly showed the anti-feminist trend of that movement'. If the departure of Richardson and other women may have been connected with plans to reorganise the movement, it may also have concerned another change in the BUF's approach to women. In March 1934 the first issue of *The Woman Fascist* had seen the light of day. Appearing fortnightly and edited by Elizabeth Winch, it was described in the *Blackshirt* as intended to 'deal with news and problems peculiar to women members. The first issue contains an article on Fascism and Religion, branch news and some practical hints for women Fascists.' In June, it was reported to have over 700 subscribers. In September, however, the *Blackshirt* initiated 'a page of direct interest to all women readers', promising that every week in future it would devote a section to articles by or about women along with news of women Blackshirt activities. This would, Maud Lady Mosley declared, replace *The Woman Fascist* which, as it stood, did not represent the importance of the Women's Section. A separate publication, she suggested, was incompatible with co-operation between men and women. (*Star* 11 February 1935; Six Point Group 1934–5: 7; *Blackshirt* 23–9 March, 7 September 1934; *Sunday Dispatch* 17 June 1934.)

Other women, however, were to eclipse both Richardson and Lady Mosley. Anne Brock Griggs, whom we have already encountered, was the subject of an admiring profile in *Action* towards the end of 1936. Then the women administrative officer (southern), she was described as 'one of the most popular officers in the British Union', combining 'a keen and active brain, a gift for speaking, and able powers of administration with an attractive physique'. Having held many outdoor meetings in London and the Home Counties, it noted, she had joined the British Union staff in early 1935 as woman propaganda officer. With the growth of the women's section, she had taken 'complete charge of the administration of women's activities' in the south, a position in which she had demonstrated 'infinite tact and patience'. Despite many demands, it was claimed, she was none the less 'never so busy that she cannot spare a few moments to give helpful advice to women officers and members on the many difficulties which arise in running the women's section of the Movement, and that advice has been instrumental in smoothing out friction on many occasions'. (*Action* 21 November 1936.)

The following year, another leading woman, the women's administrative officer (north), Olga F. C. Shore, received similar treatment, portrayed as 'an excellent example of the generation of women who have turned from the ties of Victorianism to the wider world of business'. Having engaged in a varied commercial career including 'world travels in the course of her duties in the shipping and marketing worlds', she had, *Action* reported, learned several foreign languages and, while seemingly 'flippant in some respects', had developed great powers of assessing character. 'In her selection of women officers to work under her she displays a fine sense of discretion, and in her interviews a tact which is unrivalled.' (*Action* 13 February 1937.)

Lady Mosley, writing to her son in early 1935, had had doubts about one of the rising stars in the movement ('It remains to be seen if Miss Shore is superwoman enough to do all she has undertaken') and had been decidedly critical of other leading women in the movement's early years ('Lady Makgill did nothing but use the premises for her own business . . . Then came Miss R—— with her dishonest inefficiency'). As for Griggs, she too, as we will see, was to fall from favour. When war broke out, however, she was still very much a central figure in the BUF's work among women. In October 1939 *Action* published her call for more women speakers.

> The past few weeks have shown that some of the most effective of our meetings have been held during shopping hours. Sales and enrolments at such meetings are very high. We want still more meetings in the afternoons, mornings or during the lunch hour . . . At such meetings we reach mothers and housewives.

Griggs and the increasingly important Olive Hawks turned to training more women speakers ('As propaganda work is bound to fall more and more upon the women members we must be trained and ready to give vital service when it is most needed'), and women members were called upon to take advantage of Christmas shopping to sell *Action*. 'Make arrangements to cover last minute shoppers, and to concentrate on railway stations from which people will be travelling during the holidays.' (Mosley 1983: 92; *Action* 19 October, 7, 21 December 1939.)

If women were becoming more important, this was particularly significant for the BUF's stance towards foreign policy. As a fascist movement, the BUF was very far from being a pacifist organisation. But its opposition to conflict with fascist powers meant that much of its energies were expended on campaigning against war, and in doing so it was far from averse to drawing connections between women and peace that we might more usually associate with certain strands of feminism. (Women, one activist later claimed, were drawn to the movement because they were 'naturally more concerned with cradles than with graves'.) As early as 1935, in an effort to avert war over the Italian invasion of Ethiopia, men and women Blackshirts had marched with sandwich boards in the West End, and 'Parties of girls distributed handbills', while as part of what it called its National Peace Campaign a women's meeting had been held in Leicester. Similarly, in September 1938, women members took part in poster parades in the West End as part of the movement's efforts to stop Britain from going to war over Czechoslovakia. (Bellamy n.d.: 753–4; *Blackshirt* 6, 13 September 1935; *Times* 7 October 1935; *Southern Blackshirt* October 1938; *Action* 1 October 1938.)

Once war broke out, BUF women became increasingly prominent in anti-war activity. In Bournemouth, a November issue of *Action* reported, 'Miss Hayes addressed an indoor audience . . . [which] was very much enlightened on the Peace Policy' while in Manchester 'Miss Hadaway . . . and Miss Booth' had been part of 'a fine team of speakers, conveying the message of Peace to large audiences'. In late October, Anne Brock Griggs was arrested while addressing a meeting in Limehouse. She was charged with using insulting words likely to lead to a breach of the peace, unlawful obstruction of the police and endeavouring to influence public opinion in a manner likely to be prejudicial to the Defence of the Realm. The last charge, the most serious, was dropped but on the other two charges she was found guilty and bound over for a year. Such attempts to break the spirit of British Union speakers would not succeed, the BUF declared, and it would 'continue throughout the land to advance the cause of Britain, Peace and People'. (*Action* 16 November 1939.)

In January 1940 *Action* announced plans for a Women's Peace Campaign. The call up of men up to thirty years old, it declared, meant that women members had to

> take up the burden . . . The aim, therefore, of the women of the Movement at this time should be two-fold: to fit themselves to shoulder the sternest tasks of District organisation and propaganda, and to mobilize the women of the country for Peace.

In order both to train women members for the work that lay ahead and to take the peace message to the women of Britain, the paper declared, the campaign would start with a large indoor meeting at the end of February followed by the deployment of women speakers across

London during March. Other districts would be 'asked to run parallel campaigns' and in order to finance all this activity a fund had been set up. 'Although this is essentially a women's campaign, we shall certainly not refuse contributions from men!' (*Action* 18 January 1940.)

The opening rally was to take place in the Holborn Hall at 8.15 p.m. on Wednesday, 28 February. Two weeks before, *Action* reported that three-quarters of the tickets had already been sold and districts were planning their own campaign weeks. 'Foremost in this great effort are the women of Shoreditch, Tottenham, Central Hackney, St Pancras and many other London districts, which have already submitted their programme of meetings, leaflet distribution, paper sales and poster parades.' Meetings were scheduled for St Pancras, Tooting and Dalston

> where well-known British Union women speakers will put forward the message of Mosley to the women of London. From the Provinces comes news of districts who are organising their own Women's Peace Campaigns to run parallel with the great effort of the women of London. From Hampshire, from Sussex, from Kent, from Lancashire, from Wales, come campaign plans which will make the race with London a close one.
>
> (*Action* 1, 15 February 1940)

Preceded by a Shoreditch women's poster parade and other activities, the Holborn Hall rally, 'the first large indoor meeting to be organised, stewarded and addressed entirely by the women', was described as 'a tremendous success'. The 800-seat hall had been 'crowded to capacity with an audience composed almost entirely of women, with only a small sprinkling of men, who had accompanied their wives'. The main speaker, Olive Hawks, accused the government of sending youth to die while failing to improve social conditions. 'Speaking for over an hour she showed real rhetoric ability learned in the hard school of street corner meetings.' Another activist, Marjorie Steele, was reported as launching 'slashing attacks upon the corrupt politicians and their financial masters'. (*Action* 29 February, 7 March 1940.)

In March women's peace meetings were held on successive Sundays in St Pancras, Tooting and Hackney. One such meeting, held in Ridley Road, Hackney, received a particularly glowing account in *Action*.

> Mrs Steele opened the meeting giving a short review of the progress of the Women's campaign and a very brief talk on British Union and the British Peace. Miss Hayes followed and in her brilliant

manner dealt with the many sufferings caused by this war ... The appeal for funds was made by Olive Hawks and a large collection was taken to assist in the Women's fight for Peace.

At the end of the month women members were reported taking part in a poster demonstration and sales drive in the West End, during which several thousand leaflets for women were distributed. Women were also active in Manchester, and the campaign was scheduled to culminate on 13 April in a women's meeting at the Friends House, Euston Road, in support of a negotiated peace, with speakers including Mosley himself. (*Action* 21 March, 11 April 1940.)

The meeting, *Action* claimed, was

> well filled with an enthusiastic audience of women. Mrs Booth, a prominent British Union speaker from Lancashire, opened with a moving appeal to end the horrors of war ... Illustrating her argument with many instances from the life of the cotton towns she soon won the sympathy of her audience for a policy of social reconstruction in place of the destruction which now threatened the youth of Britain. She was followed by Commandant Mary Allen who stressed the great part that women can play in the life of a resurgent nation.

Then Mosley spoke, attacking 'the blunders of the old gang politicians' and urging 'a negotiated peace based upon mutual toleration between the great nations, whose destiny is to lead the world' (*Action* 18 April 1940).

In the event, this was not the last British Union women's peace meeting, and in mid-April Marjorie Steele was arrested during a meeting in Shoreditch, an event which did not stop her from also speaking at Wood Green where 'A good collection was realised for the Women's Peace Campaign Fund, with the assistance of which the meeting was organised.' *Action* called for more reports of 'what the women members of British Union are doing, on their own initiative, to take the message of Peace and Plenty to the women of Britain', but within days the arrests of BUF members began and only three more issues of *Action* would appear. Among the first to be detained were Olive Hawks, Norah Elam and Anne Brock Griggs (the last of whom, Mosley later told his interrogators, had been removed from her position 'on grounds of inefficiency'). (*Action* 25 April, 16 May, 6 June 1940; PRO HO283/13/65.)

The decision to intern selected members of the BUF was motivated not by the fear that British Fascism was strong, but by the belief that it was potentially traitorous. In part, as we have noted, there was concern over secret meetings between the BUF and other extreme right groups. Two of the most prestigious of Mosley's women supporters, Lady Pearson and Viscountess Downe, were among those involved, as were Mary Allen, Norah Elam and another of the movement's prospective parliamentary candidates, Muriel G. Whinfield. (Of these, however, only the last two were interned. Elam, it should be noted, had been found in possession of a letter from Mosley, stating that she had his complete confidence and was authorised to act as she saw fit in the interests of the movement.) While in the case of Lady Pearson, who had initially been arrested, being the sister of the parliamentary undersecretary of war was no doubt an advantage, in general it is extremely hard to tell why some women were detained and others not. In the absence of many of the original documents – only some of the relevant material is available at the Public Record Office – it is not even clear how many of the seventy-one women detained between May and October 1940 were British Union members and why they had attracted the authorities' attention. In some cases, perhaps many, they were probably arrested because as supporters of Mosley they were seen as a threat to national security. But in addition to those who were interned, there were other instances, where women fascists were tried for pro-German activity and sentenced to prison. Two such cases involved sentences of five years' imprisonment. In the first, a woman had distributed material publicising German radio broadcasts, in the other a woman attempted to persuade two soldiers in a public house that Hitler was 'a good ruler, better than Mr. Churchill'. (Simpson 1992: 142–3, 179, 207–8, 169; PRO HO283/48/27; *Daily Mail* 25 June 1941.)

Although British Union internees were progressively released as the danger of German invasion receded, the movement itself remained illegal. During the few years it had existed, the BUF had recruited thousands of women and sought to organise them to bring about a fascist Britain. While class distinction was supposedly transcended in this struggle, the BUF put a great emphasis on its support in the higher echelons of society. In mid-1934 the *Blackshirt* boasted of the recruitment of two cousins of Earl Haig and the assistant commissioner of the Boy Scouts, 'Mrs Hugh Rayner, O.B.E., who was a member of the Council, Metropolitan Area, of the Conservative Party, and Chairman of the Women's Branch of the Conservative Party, Whitechapel'.

Another vaunted recruit, Jean Cossar, 'the first woman Blackshirt to address a meeting in the Tyneside Area', joined the Newcastle branch having previously been women's organiser for the Conservative Association in Wansbeck and in South Hackney, and 'a well-known speaker for the London Municipal Association'. (*Blackshirt* 15, 22 June, 19 October 1934.)

As with Lady Makgill and Lady Mosley in the early days of the BUF Women's Section, some of the movement's prospective parliamentary candidates likewise were from the upper levels of the social scale. Two we have already encountered. The candidate for North Norfolk, Dorothy Viscountess Downe, had been president of the Conservative Women's Association of Scarborough and then chairperson of the Conservative Women's Association of King's Lynn. Lady Pearson, the candidate for Canterbury, was the sister of General Page Croft. Other candidates were not as exalted. Miss L. M. Reeve, the candidate for Norfolk, SW, was described in the BUF press as having 'started life in domestic service' but after succeeding in gaining entry to a business training course had eventually become, first, an assistant to an estate agent and then manager of 'the complete estate of 11,000 acres . . . the only woman in the country managing an agricultural property of this size'. Sylvia Morris, the candidate for Holland-with-Boston, was a doctor's daughter who after 'working in greyhound kennels' had become a free-lance journalist, a destination that resembled that of two other candidates. The candidate for Ilford, Miss L. A. King, was controller of the *Daily Mail*'s Women's Canvass Staff while Olive Hawks, selected for Camberwell (Peckham), had graduated from working in the Amalgamated Press Editorial Department, via being a reader for the Wellington Press, to employment in the Research Department of the British Union. (*Blackshirt* 12 June 1937; 19 December, 21, 28 November 1936; *Action* 16 January, 12 June 1937.)

Yet if the movement publicised its recruits among the upper and middle class, it also wanted to emphasise its popular appeal. Nellie Driver, the woman district leader for Nelson, was a chainbeamer who often wrote for *Action*, sometimes in local dialect. Another woman activist referred in one article to three women members in a Manchester waterproof clothing factory, while an early account of a Speakers' Class at Women's Headquarters noted that among those attending were 'working women of every calibre – nurses, typists, laundry maids, and the sterner side of feminine society'. (Mayall 1990: 33, 29; *Action* 22 October, 19 November 1938; 25 March 1939; *Blackshirt* 22 August 1936; *Fascist Week* 17–23 November 1933.)

For the BUF to attempt to recruit across class lines was not, of course, without problems. The class conflict that the BUF abhorred could be smuggled into the organisation and, as Kushner has pointed out, when in 1934 the *Blackshirt* printed an article criticising the conditions of domestic servants, it drew a quick reply from an anonymous 'Potential Fascist' who suggested that, in her experience, it was impossible to get decent staff. Despite such tensions, the movement none the less continued to work among women of very different backgrounds. Writing in a local paper, the woman leader for Canterbury branch, Bessie Pullen, described the fascist march in London as giving her the opportunity to

> savour the comradeship of all those women, and to see what Fascism means as a comradeship of all classes. There were jolly factory girls from Bethnal Green, cracking Cockney jokes with all and sundry as they waited; professional women; shabby women; women in fur coats. Beside me, as we marched off, was Lady Pearson – great soul in a tiny, dainty body – stepping out bravely.

Some accounts have suggested a particular social profile. One report of the 1934 Hyde Park march, for instance, suggested that the women 'had the appearance of being drawn very largely from the typist or shop-girl class, and were mostly young'. But those who marched in London may well not give us an adequate picture of those who joined the movement nationally. We might, then, turn to portraits of two different localities. According to its Birmingham women's organiser, the BUF's women members were 'diverse', including 'teachers, secretaries, nurses, waitresses, domestic workers, housewives' while Linehan's account of the BUF in the movement's East London heartland includes among its women members a private language teacher, the secretary to the sales manager of a perfume manufacturer, a battery maker, four textile workers, a metal stamper, a dressmaker and a laundry manageress. (Kushner 1990: 51; *Whitstable Times and Tankerton Press* 9 October 1937; *Manchester Guardian* 14 September 1934; Anon. 1986: 47; Linehan 1996: 123, 111, 216, 221, 222, 255, 264.)

This chapter began by warning of the dangers of relying on a BUF press which combined a hagiographic treatment of its leading figures with an unwillingness to linger on those situations where its efforts proved fruitless or where its activists engaged in recrimination rather than co-operation. As with other sources, fascist publications need to be treated sceptically, compared with other evidence and read not only for what they say but for what they leave unsaid. Used in this way, a major omission in the study of the BUF can be repaired, and women who carried out so much of its activity in the 1930s, if not rescued from the condescension of posterity, can at least be recovered for a history that understands fascism better than hitherto.

4 Patriots – and patriarchs?

The Nazi ambition to bring all those it saw as Germans into the Reich had led to the annexation of Austria, the dismembering of Czechoslovakia and ultimately the invasion of Poland and war. The German invasion of Russia in 1941 unleashed genocidal propensities within both National Socialism and its allies in Eastern Europe. For the former, a doctrine that claimed the Aryan as superior now systematically attempted to destroy those it believed inferior. For the latter, old hatreds once more broke surface amid a confusing array of ethnic groups. But, despite massive loss of life, fascism was not to succeed. As the war unfolded, it faced not only the combined strength of the USA, Britain and the USSR but resistance movements within the occupied countries which turned nationalism against the occupiers. Some of those who had previously supported fascism fell away. In Italy, the continued existence of an independent power-base around the king enabled Mussolini to be arrested and the regime to be brought to an end, although the rescue of the fascist leader by the Germans was followed by intransigent supporters fighting to the end in the northern redoubt of the Salo or Italian Social Republic. Mussolini was killed by communist partisans and the Salo Republic destroyed while in Germany Hitler committed suicide as the Red Army fought their way across Berlin. The Thousand Year Reich had lasted less than thirteen years, Mussolini's new Roman Empire little over twenty and many of the movements that had looked to these regimes in the 1920s and 1930s had ceased to exist. But the ideas that they championed were not to pass away.

They would, however, vary in important ways. In a continent divided into a predominantly liberal democratic West and a communist East, extreme rightists were in some cases suppressed, in others drawn into the camp of one or other of the victorious powers. Some became identified with a nationalist anti-communism which suggested that natural allies were to be found among the conservative and Christian Democratic forces that had risen to prominence. Others, more concerned with opposition to the American presence in Europe and the rise of a hated consumer society, were less hostile to communism than to what they saw as Wall Street domination and, strange as it may seem, were sometimes willing to look favourably upon Moscow as a counterweight to New York. Others still believed that radical nationalism involved rejecting both capitalism and communism and forging instead a third way or, as it was sometimes termed, a Third Position. The changing ethnic composition of the West, as large-scale immigration transformed countries in the process of shedding their empires, gave nationalists a new mobilising issue while older concerns over the relationship between men and women and the future of the white race took on an increased intensity amid changes in the family and the decline of the white birth-rate in a world growing in numbers. The role of eugenics, of racism and of anti-Semitism in the horrors of the Third Reich drove thinking in such terms beyond the margins of the acceptable. In time, however, they would enjoy new life, amid heated debate over race and IQ and, in a less influential but more startling way, in the rise of Holocaust revisionism, the claim that the racial extermination policy of the Second World War was a myth promoted by Germany's enemies. Finally, if the extreme right had already emerged across Western Europe soon after the ending of the war and was to be particularly visible from the 1960s onwards, in Eastern Europe the collapse of communism in the late 1980s unleashed again the ghosts of enmities which, if anything, surpassed Western resentments in their ferocity. (For further discussion of the extreme right in post-war Europe, see Hainsworth 1992b; Merkl and Weinberg 1993, 1997; Betz 1994; Kitschelt 1995; Cheles, Ferguson and Vaughan 1995; Lee 1997.)

The re-emerged extreme right has taken a number of different forms of which the most important has focused on immigration, arguing that the nation is in danger of losing its identity to an alien influx. Such a stance has resulted in electoral success in a number of countries – France, Germany, Belgium, the Netherlands – and has encouraged groups in other countries likewise to attempt to use anti-immigration sentiment to escape from a marginal position within national political systems. While this racial populism represents the most important form of the extreme right, others also need to be considered. In Italy, a party tracing itself back to classical fascism has received significant support in the post-war period while in a number of countries small groupings openly avowing National Socialism have been highly active. Finally, minority strands of the pre-war extreme right (particularly the German conservative revolution and the dissident Nazism of Otto and Gregor Strasser) have continued to exert influence after the war, feeding into both the so-called 'new right' in France and Italy and the anti-capitalist radicalism of those who in a number of countries describe themselves as National Revolutionaries or Third Positionists. The extreme right in post-war Europe has important continuities and discontinuities with its predecessors and in this chapter we will explore its development in three countries – Germany, Italy and France. During this discussion, we will be raising some preliminary questions about the stance such movements have taken on the role of women in society and within their ranks. In the light of that discussion, in the chapters that follow, we will turn our attention to our principal case study, the extreme right in Britain, exploring in greater depth how the modern extreme right has sought to articulate a politics not only of race and nation but of gender.

First, however, we need to examine developments on the Continent. In Germany, in the aftermath of the destruction of the Third Reich, many former members of the NSDAP were interned by the Western powers, and the reconstitution of the party was made illegal. In 1949, however, the Socialist Reich Party (SRP), led by former Nazis and calling for a 'leadership democracy', was established. In 1951 it gained 11 per cent of the vote (and sixteen seats) in elections in Lower Saxony, and was banned as a danger to democracy the following year. The German Reich Party (DRP), hitherto a rival, took its place as the dominant grouping on the extreme right. It gained little electoral success during the 1950s, however, and in 1964 it joined with others on the nationalist right to form the National Democratic Party (NPD). Initially this was to lead to a significant breakthrough. Economic recession and frustration with the entry into coalition of the main parties of the right and the left, the Christian Democrats and the Social Democrats, benefited the NPD and between 1966 and 1968 it won sixty-one seats in state parliaments. (It also reached a membership of around 28,000.) By the 1969 federal elections, however, the NPD vote, at 4.3 per cent, fell below the 5 per cent necessary to gain any seats in the national parliament, and the party went into decline. (Tauber 1967: 690–2, 707, 710, 714; Childs 1995: 294–7; Kolinsky 1992: 62–4.)

In the years that followed, two other significant groupings emerged. In 1971 the German People's Union (DVU) was established and was able even in the late 1980s to forge an alliance with the NPD. The most important development, however, was the inception in 1983 of the Republikaner (REP) party, initially in protest at what it saw as too conciliatory a policy towards East Germany on the part of the Christian Democratic right. Led by a former Waffen SS soldier, Franz Schönhuber, the REPs appeared to be the most successful of the three parties, gaining 7.5 per cent of the vote and eleven seats in West Berlin in 1989, and 7.1 per cent and six MEPs (the DVU gaining only 1.6 per cent) in the European elections the same year. In the 1990 federal elections, however, the first to be held in a reunited Germany, the REPs only gained 2.1 per cent (which was significantly more, however, than the NPD's 0.3 per cent). The REPs subsequently enjoyed renewed electoral success, achieving 11 per cent of the vote and fifteen seats in state elections in Baden-Württemberg in 1992 and 9.3 per cent and ten council seats in Frankfurt the following year. (To a lesser degree, the DVU and even the NPD also achieved successes, with the former gaining 6.4 per cent and six seats in the Schleswig-Holstein parliament in 1992 and the latter making gains at local level, notably the election of seven councillors in Frankfurt in 1989.) In the 1994 European elections the REP vote fell to 3.9 per cent, with the loss of all its seats. None the less, in the 1996 state elections in Baden-Württemberg, the party was still capable of taking 9.1 per cent of the vote and fourteen seats. (Zimmermann and Saalfeld 1993: 57; Kolinsky 1992: 63, 65, 69; Childs 1995: 303; Betz 1994: 19; *National Front News* 118, n.d. (1989); *Searchlight* May 1989, May 1992, April 1993, July 1994, May 1996.)

Emphasising opposition to foreign immigration, particularly asylum-seekers, and declaring that Germany should 'remain the land of the Germans', the three electoral parties have continued to fight for hegemony on the German extreme right. Both the DVU and the REPs had over 20,000 members each in the early 1990s, while the NPD had fewer than 10,000. The REPs, however, suffered damaging splits, not least over relations with the DVU, and subsequently lost Schönhuber too, declining to some 12,000. None the less, the REPs remained the strongest electorally in a situation rendered even more complex by the existence of particularly intransigent sections of the extreme right grouped in small organisations that were far more willing than any of the main parties to openly champion the Third Reich. (Kolinsky 1992: 82–3; Eatwell 1996a: 235; *Searchlight* August 1992, May 1996.)

In the early 1980s, two such groups, the Popular Socialist Movement of Germany/Labour Party and the Action Front of National Socialists/ National Activists, were declared illegal. While the former group took a socially radical Strasserite stance, the latter group, led by the central figure in German neo-Nazism, Michael Kühnen, took a more orthodox position towards Hitler and the Third Reich. Following proscription, the Strasserites regrouped as the Nationalist Front, while Kühnen's supporters first formed new organisations, then moved into another far right grouping, the Free German Workers' Party (FAP). The original leadership of the FAP lost control to the new influx, only for the new leadership in turn to fall into bitter dispute and split into rival factions. (Husbands 1991: 90–9; Jensen 1993: 88–9, 94.)

The FAP, increasingly estranged from Kühnen, contested elections (without success), while a new Kühnen grouping, the National Assembly, was banned in 1989. Membership figures were small – in the late 1980s the FAP numbered approximately 500, the Kühnen group fewer than 200 and the Nationalist Front under 100 – but the collapse of the East German state gave such groups a chance to expand eastwards, with the suppression of the National Assembly merely leading to the proliferation of yet more neo-Nazi groupings, sporting such names as the National List, National Offensive and German Alternative. While it is difficult to be completely clear, members of a secret organisation led by Kühnen and others, initially known as the Bewegung (the Movement), then as Neue Front (New Front), were instrumental in much of the neo-Nazi activity during this period, and continued to operate behind the scenes after Kühnen's death in 1991. (Husbands 1991: 95–6, 98, 99; 1995: 328–9, 337; Jensen 1993: 87–90; *Searchlight* November 1990, June 1991.)

Racist activity in Germany increasingly took on a violent form, and in the early 1990s this was to spiral, most notoriously involving an attack on a refugee hostel in Hoyerswerda in late 1991, the burning down of part of an immigrant housing complex in Rostock in August 1992 and the killing of five people in an arson attack on Turkish families in Solingen in May 1993. In late 1992 the Nationalist Front, German Alternative and National Offensive were banned. In 1994 the Viking Youth, a group dating back to the 1950s, suffered the same fate, and in 1995 so too did the FAP and National List. This did not, however, stop successor organisations being set up, or banned groups continuing to meet covertly, and while these too were numerically weak, the number of neo-Nazis had none the less grown. In 1990, the federal government estimated that in addition to such groups as the DVU and the NPD there were 1,400 members of neo-Nazi groups and 2,900 members of other 'aggressively xenophobic' groups. By 1993 the number of organised neo-Nazis stood at 1,500, but now there were nearly another 1,000 unorganised neo-Nazis and 10,000 others, many of them skinheads, in militantly racist groups.

(Husbands 1995: 334–5, 337–8, 329; *Searchlight* October 1995, January 1996.)

Some fifty years after the collapse of the Third Reich, the German extreme right had found a mobilising issue but proved unable to create a stable national electoral party. In Italy, however, a single party has dominated the extreme right since the late 1940s. Following the demise first of the fascist regime nationwide and then of the Italian Social Republic, fascist groups began to re-emerge, and shortly before the end of 1946 many of the activists came together to launch the Italian Social Movement (MSI). Reconstituting the Fascist Party was illegal but the deliberate reference to the Social Republic in the MSI's name, the background of its leading figures and the language of its party programme made it clear to both supporters and opponents that the movement was neo-fascist. The MSI, however, was divided from the beginning in its attitude towards other parties and the new regime. For some, Italian involvement in NATO and an alliance with monarchists and Christian Democrats against the Communist Party was a key objective, for others the movement should be both anti-American and anti-establishment. While in the 1950s and 1960s, the more conservative elements dominated the MSI leadership, more radical elements (one of whose slogans was 'Less double-breasted suits – more brass-knuckles') were highly visible in the movement's ranks and periodically groups broke away, accusing the MSI hierarchy of betrayal. In part, the MSI's critics harked back to the Italian Social Republic, but they were also inspired by a dissident fascist, Julius Evola, who during the 1930s had espoused a 'spiritual' racism, and after the war called for the creation of an elite who would champion a warrior ethic. While such organisations as Pino Rauti's Ordine Nuovo sought to challenge the MSI's claim to be the inheritor of fascism, other radicals, notably the movement's future leader, Georgio Almirante, remained in the MSI, seeking to alter its course. (Weinberg 1979: 14–17, 23–4, 32–3; Chiarini 1995: 27–8; Drake 1989: 122–4.)

During the 1960s and early 1970s, neo-fascists both outside and inside the MSI were involved with sections of the military and the intelligence services in efforts to create an authoritarian right-wing regime. Their activities ranged from preparations for a coup to infiltration into the left to carry out terrorist bombings for which their enemies could be blamed. In the late 1960s, of course, their enemies were often to the left of the Communist Party in the radical student and workplace movements of the period. While the radical left was extremely visible in 1968 and 1969, the MSI was in electoral decline (gaining 4.5 per cent in 1968 as against 5.1 per cent in 1963, 4.8 per cent in 1958 and 5.8

per cent in 1953). Following the death of the MSI's national secretary in mid-1969, Almirante succeeded to the position and broadened the party in both radical and conservative directions, with the return of Rauti and a section of Ordine Nuovo on the one hand and a common electoral list, and eventually fusion, with the monarchists (Italy had become a republic after the war) on the other. The rise of left-wing terrorism, particularly on the part of the Red Brigades, enabled the MSI to claim that Marxists had launched an attack on the nation. The MSI grew in the early 1970s, claiming a membership of 420,000 in 1973, and its joint list with the monarchists gained 8.7 per cent in 1972, parliamentary representation leaping from twenty-four deputies to fifty-six. In 1976, in the next general election, however, the MSI vote fell back to 6.1 per cent and a large section of the more conservative elements broke away. (Ferraresi 1988: 87–93; Weinberg 1979: 42–3, 48–50, 55: Chiarini 1995: 21, 33; Ignazi 1989: 165.)

By 1976 the MSI had declined to a still substantial 279,000 and in the late 1970s and early 1980s a second wave of right-wing terrorism saw the rise and fall of such organisations as Construiamo l'Azione (Let's Build Action), the NAR (Armed Revolutionary Nuclei) and Terza Posizione (Third Position). The MSI itself aimed much of its propaganda at radical youth and was profoundly affected by the rise of the Nuova Destra (New Right), an ideological grouping which emerged in opposition to what it saw as the Americanisation of Europe, and which both radicalised some who stayed in the MSI and led to others leaving to form yet more groupings. While the MSI boasted a membership of 382,000 in 1984, electoral results for the MSI remained disappointing (6.8 per cent in 1983, 5.9 per cent in 1987), and in 1987, when Gianfranco Fini became the new party leader, the organisation was divided into a large number of factions. For the leading radical, Rauti, the future for the movement lay in a particularly militant policy, involving anti-capitalism, alliance with anti-imperialist regimes in the Third World, support for ecology and opposition to the consumerist 'pseudo-values imported by Americanism' at home. Briefly, in 1990, he even gained the movement's leadership. Instead, however, of his radical fascism, Fini's return to leadership was to take the MSI increasingly away from the open enthusiasm for Mussolini so common among its activists. Following the collapse of the Christian Democrats at the beginning of the 1990s, the MSI became the leading element of the new Alleanza Nazionale (AN), and in 1994 it entered government alongside Forza Italia, a new movement led by the conservative television magnate Silvio Berlusconi. The following year the

MSI ceased to exist, finally dissolving into the AN. Membership, which had fallen to 150,000 at the beginning of the 1990s, increased to 202,000 in 1993. Its seats in the European Parliament rose from four in 1989 to eleven in 1994, with its vote increasing from 5.5 per cent to 12.5 per cent. At national level, in 1992 the MSI received 5.4 per cent of the vote. In 1994, running as the AN, it gained 13.5 per cent, its seats rising from thirty-four to 109. After a short period in office, the right-wing coalition fell from power and in fresh elections in 1996, despite the Alleanza increasing its vote to 15.7 per cent (which resulted in ninety-three seats), an alliance of the centre and the left came to power. A breakaway organisation led by Rauti, Fiamma Tricolore (the Tricoloured Flame) gained 0.9 per cent. (Ferraresi 1988: 99–100; Sidoti 1992: 164–5, 158–9; Chiarini 1995: 21, 37; Ignazi 1989: 293; 1994: 9; Carioti 1996: 67, 73–4; Newell and Bull 1996: 634.)

If the German situation, where no single party emerged as hegemonic on the extreme right, is to be contrasted with the persistent dominance of the Italian Social Movement, our third example gives us a further variant – dominance by a single organisation but not until after an extended period of fragmentation. Defeat by Nazi Germany shortly after the outbreak of war had led to the division of France into two, with the unoccupied zone ruled from Vichy by the ultra-conservative Marshal Pétain. The brutal war against the Resistance and the subsequent 'popular justice' against collaborators following the Liberation all but silenced the extreme right until the mid-1950s, when the sudden emergence of the small business and small farmer populism of Pierre Poujade brought over fifty deputies into the French National Assembly, including Poujade's lieutenant, Jean-Marie Le Pen. The movement subsided almost as quickly as it had risen but for the French extreme right a new and more important issue had emerged in the shape of Algerie Française. The ultimately unsuccessful struggle to keep Algeria part of France led to a bitter terrorist war by the extreme right Secret Army Organisation (OAS) and militants shaped by that conflict continued to be active in French politics, not least in attempts to secure electoral support against what they saw as the traitorous policies of President de Gaulle. The strength of the Communist Party in France, although eventually eclipsed by the revival of the country's Socialist Party, engendered considerable anxiety, and the events of May–June 1968, in which student rebellion meshed with working-class unrest, gave increased impetus to the extreme right. This took two particular forms. First, a number of intellectuals, some with backgrounds in extreme right organisations, had established a discussion group that would become known as the Nouvelle Droite (New

Right). Led by Alain de Benoist, the Nouvelle Droite denounced egalitarianism but sought to avoid association with the extreme right. (Where initially it expressed strong interest in eugenics and the 'superiority' of Western civilisation, in later years it would emphasise opposition to American domination and the threat this was seen as posing to other cultures.) A second grouping, Occident, emerged in the mid-1960s, only to be banned in 1968. Re-established as Ordre Nouveau the following year, it believed that the only way to gain significant support was by uniting the scattered forces of the French extreme right. In 1972 most of these forces were brought together in the Front National (FN). (Where the French Nouvelle Droite had influenced the Italian Nuova Destra, in turn the example of the MSI influenced the creation of the Front National.) Led by Le Pen, the FN's early years were ones of electoral failure and bitter internal fighting in which some of Ordre Nouveau's former leaders turned instead to another formation, the Parti des Forces Nouvelles. But it was to be the FN which survived the 1970s in good shape ready for the opportunities which suddenly emerged following the election of a socialist–communist government in 1981. Benefiting from the disarray among the mainsteam right and falling support for the left, the FN entered the 1983 municipal elections in the Paris dormitory town of Dreux, proclaiming that immigration into the area was at the root of unemployment and crime. The French system of a second ballot in the event of no party gaining an absolute majority proved crucial here, with the FN achieving enough votes in the first round to bring about a joint slate with the orthodox right on the second ballot and the election of four FN councillors. Benefiting from national publicity, the FN threw itself into the 1984 European elections which both offered a less demanding electoral system than national elections and allowed Le Pen to attack the orthodox right for putting forward Simone Veil, the minister in the previous conservative government responsible for the liberalisation of abortion. The FN gained over 2 million votes (11 per cent) and ten European seats. President Mitterrand's subsequent decision to change the electoral system for the national legislature to a PR basis turned the 1986 elections into a significant opportunity for the FN, and its 9.8 per cent of the vote gave it thirty-five seats. The Front grew in numbers, winning over recruits from the mainstream right. In 1988 Le Pen himself stood as presidential candidate, challenging the two rival conservative candidates as well as the communists and the incumbent Mitterrand. He gained 14.4 per cent of the vote (nearly 4.4 million votes), although in the legislative elections that followed FN support fell to a still significant 9.8 per cent. Importantly, however, the electoral system had been changed back again to the two-ballot system, and only one FN candidate, Yann Piat, was ultimately elected (and she would break with the Front later in the year). (Warner 1981: 319–27; Vaughan 1995: 217–19, 228; Johnson 1995: 235; Taguieff 1993–4: 99–125; Marcus 1995: 16–21, 38–9, 52–64; Mayer and Perrineau 1992: 124; Hainsworth 1992: 42–3.)

However, the organisation soon experienced a revival in its fortunes, first in the 1989 European elections, in which an 11.7 per cent result again gained ten seats and then, once again, in Dreux with the parliamentary by-election victory of its candidate, Marie-France Stirbois. Regional and municipal elections also brought successes (in 1991 the FN had over 1,600 councillors) but, despite gaining 12.4 per cent, the legislative elections in 1993 saw even Dreux (narrowly) lost. Local elections in 1994 were equally disappointing but the 10.5 per cent (and 11 seats) in the European elections that year and the 15 per cent Le Pen gained in the 1995 presidential election demonstrated that the FN remained a significant force in French politics. In municipal elections shortly after, it elected over 1,000 councillors and took control of three city councils in the south of the country. In 1997 it gained a fourth council and in the legislative elections won 15 per cent of the vote (and one seat). Claiming in 1993 over 70,000 members (other estimates have been significantly lower), the organisation has suffered from internal rivalries and tensions. (Most importantly, these revolve around who will succeed Le Pen and whether the FN, or perhaps a significant section of it, will move closer to the mainstream right.) Some on the extreme right have even tried to build independent organisations, such as the radical Parti Nationaliste Français (PNF) or the pro-Nazi Parti Nationaliste Français et Européenne (PNFE). To date, however, Le Pen's leadership and the organisation he had built has remained dominant not only on France's extreme right but, in many ways, on Western Europe's. (Vaughan 1995: 230, 233; Hainsworth 1992: 43–4; Marcus 1995: 127, 68–70, 159, 41–2; Simmons 1996: 111; *Searchlight* January, July 1994, November, December 1995, August 1997; *Nationalism Today* 42, n.d. (1988); *Independent on Sunday* 23 March 1997.)

Ideologically, neither the Italian nor the French parties are easily definable as one particular strand of the post-war extreme right. The FN in the 1980s saw itself as defending free market values and claimed an affinity with Reaganism in the United States. More recently, however, fears over globalisation have caused it to emphasise the defence of the French economy and culture against foreign competition and foreign influence. The MSI's factional warfare has become complicated by its mutation into the AN and claims by Fini that the movement should now be seen as 'post-fascist', claims which have contributed to the breakaway of Rauti's group but which others in the organisation (and among its opponents) see as a ploy rather than a genuine renunciation of the past. Certainly, its prominent role in the short-lived Berlusconi government has marked its new strength within the Italian party system. At the same time, however, it has posed new problems for the AN, not least in the tensions between a historic commitment to corporatism and the free market policies popular among many on the right. As for the far weaker German groupings, the Republikaner has forged links with the Front National in the European Parliament while the NPD has denounced the newer party as 'an Establishment safety valve' and, particularly in its youth and student groups, displayed sympathy for the most radical strands of the international extreme right. As elsewhere in Europe, the wartime experience continues to haunt the extreme right in all three countries. In Italy, the MSI originated as a movement which, save for legislation forbidding the reconstitution of the Fascist Party, would have been even more open in its veneration of Mussolini. The electoral parties of the German extreme right, similarly endangered by legislation forbidding the recreation of the NSDAP, largely deny any continuity with the Third Reich, and, unlike many of the smaller neo-Nazi groups, have retained their legality and their ability to gain seats on local councils and in state parliaments. France, as a country whose right was divided by the Second World War, provides a particularly difficult picture. For some of the FN's militants, Vichy represented, as it claimed, the National Revolution; for others, it betrayed the nation. While figures such as Marie-France Stirbois claim the FN to be the new Resistance movement, this time against occupation by immigrants, some of its own activists fought on opposite sides when France was occupied by Nazi Germany. (Flood 1997; Griffin 1996; Marcus 1995: 160–5, 14, 49–50; Griffin 1995: 383–4; *Nationalism Today* 43, n.d. (1988); *National Front News* 118, n.d. (1989); *Guardian* 5 December 1989; Vaughan 1995: 229.)

This reference to immigration, of course, takes us back to the most important feature of the extreme right since the Second World War. In all three countries, nationalism and anti-communism have been of central importance in recruiting activists and defining where the movements stand on the political spectrum. In France, Germany and Italy, the extreme right have benefited from economic insecurity and concern over law and order. But in France and Germany (and in other countries too), it is immigration which has taken the extreme right from small coteries to mass politics. North African immigration into France, the presence first of Turkish guest workers, then of refugees and asylum-seekers in Germany, have enabled parties such as the FN and the REPs to link together unemployment, fear of crime and hostility to 'the Other' into a potent appeal that the mainstream right has then emulated in an effort to recover its voters. Nor has support for the extreme right come solely from erstwhile voters for the orthodox right. Former supporters of the mainstream left and of minor parties, along with new voters and those who previously abstained, can also be found in the electoral bloc that has sustained the advance of the extreme right. The Italian situation is significantly different, with immigration only recently becoming an issue. For the FN and the German extreme right, however, it is central. (Cheles 1995b: 170, 163.)

In each of the three countries, the extreme right has secured significant support from both men and women, but in a significantly disproportionate way. In the 1989 Berlin election, for instance, 10.8 per cent of men voted REP as against 5.9 per cent of women. A more detailed breakdown can be found in a German-language article on the gender gap in such parties' electoral support. Here, looking at the 1989 European elections, where the REPs gained 7.1 per cent, we find that 9.6 per cent of males supported the party as against 4.9 per cent of females. If we look in particular at the results for Bremen, where both the REPs and the DVU ran candidates, we find a gender disparity once again, with the REPs on 4.6 per cent (6.2 per cent of males, 3.3 per cent females) and the DVU on 3.2 per cent (4.3 per cent of men, 2.3 per cent women). (Betz 1990: 16–17; Hofmann-Göttig 1989: 26, 29.)

In Italy too we find a gender gap. In 1980 a survey suggested that a little over a third (35.7 per cent) of MSI voters were women, while in 1991 the figure stood at 34.2 per cent. In the 1996 election, one account notes, voting for the conservative Forza Italia was around one-third higher among women than men, while support for the AN was 25 per cent lower among women. (Cheles 1991: 84; Newell and Bull 1996: 639–40; Chiarini 1995: 36.)

In France in the 1986 legislative elections 12 per cent of males supported the FN, and 7 per cent of females. In the 1988 presidential election, Le Pen received the votes of 17 per cent of the male voters and 10 per cent of females. (In legislative elections the same year, the divide was 13 per cent and 6 per cent respectively.) To take two final examples, in the 1992 regional elections, the FN received 14 per cent, 15 from men, 12 from women. The following year, at 12.4 per cent, FN support at legislative elections stood at 15 per cent among men,

10 per cent among women. (Safran 1993: 25; Betz 1994: 143; *International Viewpoint* 8 June 1992.)

For the main groupings on the extreme right, a third or even more of their electoral support comes from women. But what policy does the modern extreme right adopt towards women, and what place do women occupy within its ranks?

Within the German extreme right, the early groups, shaped by the Nazi experience, emphasised a traditionalist stance, with the DRP in its 1958 programme declaring that only in an emergency should women abandon their maternal tasks and become 'a second breadwinner'. The theme of anti-permissiveness, combined with an anti-Americanism, was particularly evident, with the party paper in 1955 calling upon boys to be 'brave' and girls 'pure', and urging men to see 'the mother of your children' as their 'queen' rather than 'the beauty queen or the "sex bomb"'. Soon after the NPD's creation, its chairman likewise denounced the portrayal of women in magazines for undermining 'moral and traditional values', while the party's 1965 manifesto called for 'the elimination of public immorality which does daily injury to . . . the dignity of woman'. If the increased visibility of sexualised images of women was of particular importance to German nationalists, they have increasingly become concerned with the legalisation of abortion, with the FAP describing it as a 'crime against the laws of a healthy nature and against God' while the REPs' 1990 programme opposed it except when the mother's life was in danger. Such views, however, are not universal among extreme right activists. According to the REPs' 1987 party programme, women should be seen as mothers and the focal point of the family. However, Mushaben notes, women activists tend to reject such a traditionalist stance and the party's 1990 programme argued instead: 'Women and men have equal rights. The right to self-actualization applies equally to women and men; this is especially true in occupational life.' REP women, she notes, were also unhappy with the party's opposition to abortion, with one declaring that it was 'a thorn in the eye for me, the way it stands in the party platform'. (Tauber 1967: 823, 851–2, 1321, 1333; Montagu 1967: 47, 130; Nagle 1970: 91; Betz 1991: 119; Biehl and Staudenmaier 1995: 39; Mushaben 1995: 29, 36.)

If there have been differences as to what policy to espouse on women, there have also been differences as to how they might be organised. While in the majority of cases, women simply belonged to extreme right parties, there have been attempts to create structures specifically for women. In the early 1950s the Socialist Reich Party included a short-lived Frauenbund led by a former activist in the Nazi women's movement. The REP and the other main electoral parties of the extreme right have not sought to organise women separately from men, and it is only in the smaller neo-Nazi formations that this has occurred. In the early 1980s the Action Front of National Socialists created a Girls' League which, following the banning of the parent organisation, was relaunched as the Deutsche Frauenfront (DFF, German Women's Front). The Women's Front, despite suffering splits, has an estimated 100 to 150 members. Another organisation, the Deutsche Frauenschaft, the women's section of the FAP, was dissolved in 1990. In recent years, however, there have been new developments, including the creation of the Skingirl Front Deutschland (SFD), which recruits among skinhead women. The SFD was set up in 1991 and is linked in turn with a North American-based organisation, Women for Aryan Unity. As a number of accounts have emphasised, women play different roles on the German extreme right. Thus, one article in *Der Spiegel* points out, while some go hiking with the Viking Youth and some even take part in racial attacks, yet others form mothers' circles to ensure their children do not go to kindergarten alongside Turkish children. The DFF, it is also worth noting, did not split only over Kühnen's leadership but over whether women should take part in street violence. (Tauber 1967: 693–4; Mushaben 1995: 24–5; Stöss 1991: 186; *Der Spiegel* 7 December 1992; *Antifa-Info* May–June 1993.)

If the central feature of women's organisation on the German extreme right is its fragmentation, then the Italian case reflects two characteristics of the single organisation that dominates it – factional differences and an often surprising combination of radicalism and traditionalism. In 1974, the latter was to the fore when the MSI was the only party other than the governing Christian Democrats to oppose divorce in the country's referendum on the issue. Defeated by a six to four pro-divorce majority, the movement had used such slogans as 'Now they want to destroy even the family', but, significantly, had been criticised by some within its own ranks for so closely identifying with the Catholic Church's stance. (Clark, Hine and Irving 1974: 345, 349, 352; for an anti-divorce poster produced by the MSI, see Cheles 1995a: 64.)

Defeated on divorce, the MSI has turned to the abortion issue and in the late 1980s, for instance, held meetings with Christian Democrat European deputies active in the anti-abortion movement. But if divorce and abortion were central to the MSI's attempt to appeal to women, they were not its only concerns. A particularly interesting guide here is Cheles' discussion of MSI posters aimed at women. In 1975, he notes, the movement produced posters for International Women's Year and then began to produce them for Women's Day, with one in 1983, for instance, declaring 'Women's Day? No chance, not as long as there's hatred, violence and injustice. Let's fight united for the New Republic.' Another the same year declared that it was women's right to choose whether to stay at home or go out to work: 'You too must sign our petition for a bill that would give housewives a monthly allowance.' Most interestingly of all, the MSI in 1985 produced a poster declaring that 'women of the right' opposed not only Marxist feminism ('which is based on an equality which goes against nature') but also 'the exploitation of traditions, which relegate women to restricted and historically obsolete roles'. In place of both, it went on, women of the right sought equal rights, the complementarity of the sexes and 'the unrelinquishable freedom to choose which roles to pursue in society'. (Tassani 1990: 140–1; Cheles 1991: 69–71, 84, 76–7.)

As our earlier account has suggested, the MSI has been bedevilled by internal conflict, and its organisation of women was in no way immune. In the late 1970s the veteran organiser of its women's section, Amalia Bacelli Rinaldi, resigned in protest against the MSI's expulsion of a deputy involved in a shooting. The section was dissolved, but the party paper continued to give regular coverage of its women's policies and the emergence at the beginning of the 1980s of Adriana Poli Bortone as the head of its National Secretariat for Women marked a renewal of its work in the area. In 1988, for instance, the Women's Secretariat held a National Festival for Women on the Right which involved both a display of handicrafts and a photographic exhibition of right-wing women since the 1920s, and a convention discussing subjects including ecology, the family, equal opportunities and the need to revise the abortion law. Crucial to the convention's deliberations was the issue noted earlier, the proposal of a salary for housewives, a concern that has remained central to the movement. Six years later, as the MSI was about to become the Alleanza Nazionale, Bortone was appointed as minister of agriculture in the Berlusconi government. Insisting that the movement did not propose 'chasing women back into the kitchen', she declared that instead it wanted to shift the emphasis of Italian debate from 'a mother's right to work' to 'a mother's right to stay at home'. (*Il Messagero* 12 May 1980; *Panorama* 28 August 1988; *La Repubblica* 24 September 1988; Cheles 1991: 83; *Searchlight* June 1994; *European* 6–12 May 1994.)

If the MSI leadership saw itself as representing women on the right, this did not go unchallenged. In the mid-1970s, dissidents associated with Rauti and the incipient Nuova Destra launched a magazine aimed at establishing 'a new way of how to be a woman of the right'. Named after the warrior queen in *The Lord of the Rings* (somewhat surprisingly, Tolkien was a powerful source of imagery for the Italian extreme right), *Eowyn* was selling 2,500 copies per issue by the time of its first convention in 1980. Calling for men and women to unite 'against the system', *Eowyn* believed that strong families were sites of 'cultural and political resistance' and attacked feminism as 'A phenomenon which derives directly from liberal ideology; essentially it is a symptom of the decadence of the modern world, a world of confusion and of destructive ideologies.' Opposed to abortion (but not to contraception), *Eowyn* wanted substantial increases in family allowances rather than either 'the degrading idea of a salary for housewives' or women going out to work. ('Working women, an idea introduced by the French Revolution, are the biggest attack on the family', claimed one speaker at its convention.) Nurseries too were opposed as helping 'the state to destroy the family and to appropriate the children' and the emphasis was on woman as militant educator of her children and companion to her husband. *Eowyn* was at the same time conservative and radical in its views of women, with the convention discussion including disputes about whether men should be dominant in the family and the advisability or otherwise of interfering with natural processes in childbirth. ('We need to be more scientific when we talk about things like this', declared one militant in defence of anaesthetics in childbirth.) Women were seen as both home-makers and political activists (thus one *Eowyn* writer complained that some women were too concerned about appearance to engage in 'propaganda activities which require them to wear practical and unpretentious clothes') and the letters section of the magazine showed even clearer evidence of ferment among rightist women, with one writer criticising defenders of Evola ('the kind uncle ... who shows women as second class citizens') and another noting that many young women joined the movement only to leave it 'because they are either seen as women to get into bed or as inferior individuals who are not to be put in charge of any task'. (*Il Messagero* 12 May 1980; Ferraresi 1987: 140–2; for the magazine's response to an unsuccessful attempt to amend the abortion law, see *Eowyn* March–April 1980, June–July 1981.)

Eowyn sought to forge links with groups elsewhere and was in touch with the women's section of a Spanish neo-Nazi grouping, CEDADE (Spanish Circle of Friends of Europe) which in the late 1970s produced two issues of an international women's magazine bringing together contributions from 'young comrades' from Italy, France, Germany, Spain and a number of other countries. But just as this initiative failed to be sustained, so too *Eowyn* did not survive, and the MSI was to continue to organise the largest group of women on the European extreme right. (In 1986, 21 per cent of its membership of 380,000 were women.) But dissent with its policies towards women has continued, as events in the 1990s have demonstrated. Shortly after the announcement of new elections in 1992, the MSI revealed that one of its candidates would be the Duce's granddaughter, Alessandra Mussolini. Selected for one of the movement's southern strongholds, she was elected and in the years that followed was to be the subject of considerable media attention, much of which centred either on her unabashedly enthusiastic support for her grandfather or her past as an actress and soft-porn model. Yet closer examination shows that she also voiced disagreement with the party's stance towards women. While she declared that she supported encouraging 'more women to stay at home', she expressed doubts about the MSI's policies on both abortion and divorce and in 1994 was to call for measures to curb male domination within the movement. 'It annoys me', she declared, 'that of 109 National Alliance deputies, only six are women. We are going to have to work to change this from the grass roots, to persuade more women to get involved on every level.' These were not her only disagreements, and in 1997, following a number of clashes, she left the Alliance's parliamentary contingent and subsequently addressed the congress of Rauti's organisation, declaring that Fini had 'betrayed our movement' and that she wanted to 'come home as a prodigal daughter'. Soon afterwards, however, she returned to the National Alliance. (Ó Maoláin 1987: 252; *Searchlight* February 1981; *League Review* May 1977; *Pensamiento Femenino Europeo. Colección Erika* 2, February 1978; Cheles 1991: 84; *Daily Mail* 9 October 1992; *Guardian* 22–23 February 1992; *European* 6–12 May 1994; *Corriere della Sera* 15 November, 7 December 1996; *Times Magazine* 17 May 1997.)

If the MSI and the German organisations are opposed to abortion, so too is the Front National. The abortion law, Le Pen declared in 1984, was 'official anti-French genocide'. During a demonstration in 1991, he likewise called for a minute's silence 'in memory of the millions of French children' murdered as a result of legalised abortion. In part, these pronouncements reflect the strength of the grouping around an extreme right daily, *Présent*, which supports the FN not simply because of ultra-nationalism or opposition to immigration but because of a commitment to Catholicism and the defence of what it sees as traditional family values. FN activists have become involved in anti-abortion activity in France, and much of the attention given in recent years to the small movement that, along American lines, engages in direct action at clinics and hospitals is around the degree of involvement of the FN or other right-wing groups in such activities. Indeed, there has been some tension within the FN because of what is seen as Le Pen's lack of support for anti-abortion militancy. (Marcus 1995: 112, 193; *International Viewpoint* 9 December 1991; Lesselier 1992/3: 16–17; Camus 1992: 7–8; *Le Nouvel Observateur* 13–19 July 1995, 31 October–6 November 1996; Roux 1995: 9.)

This opposition to abortion, while often motivated in terms of defending unborn life, is linked in turn to the pressing concern of the FN with the birth-rate. Writing in 1985, Le Pen argued that the state needed to pursue a pro-natalist policy to ensure its survival and, as he cheerfully told an interviewer for the *Daily Mail* the following year, 'We want to have many more French mothers having French babies to keep the country full of Frenchmen and will pay them to stay home and breed a proud healthy people.' A brochure produced for Le Pen's 1988 presidential campaign (and appearing in translation in the main extreme right paper in America, the *Spotlight*), argued that one of 'ten good reasons' for supporting his candidacy was to defend the family through a maternal income for the mothers of large French families and priority for French families in housing. This emphasis on French mothers and French families, of course, links to the emphasis in the brochure (as elsewhere) on opposition to immigration. The nation was threatened, the FN claimed in 1984, by 'demographic submersion'. Most vitriolically illustrated by Le Pen's infamous quotation of the 1980s, 'Tomorrow, the immigrants will move in with you, eat your soup and sleep with your wife, your daughter or your son', the FN sees immigration as the primary danger to French identity, and the 'frequent articles' in its weekly paper, recounting 'rapes and other crimes committed by immigrants' are a particularly graphic indication of its attempts to appeal to both women and men against a multiracial France. Thus, during a 1989 demonstration protesting against an attack on a woman, Le Pen declared that the crime was 'a veritable taking symbolic possession of our earth and our people'. (Betz 1994: 132; *Daily Mail* 22 March 1986; *Spotlight* 23 May 1988; Taguieff 1989: 45, 62; Kofman 1993: 106; Levy 1989: 103; Simmons 1996: 240; for a discussion of an FN article linking immigration to attacks on women, see Dupont 1988: 18.)

Interviewed for a programme on women and the extreme right, these themes appeared again. Its former deputy for Dreux, Marie-France Stirbois, argued that if more women stayed at home it would both lower unemployment and lead to an increase in the birth-rate. But while she declared 'We don't want to oblige women to stay at home', she also argued that they were not safe when they ventured outside. In her constituency, she claimed, women could not go out for fear of young blacks pestering or attacking them. Women, she argued, often wanted to stay at home but should not be compelled to do so. In an earlier interview, she had described her supporters as including 'cops who are told not to mention that this rapist or that burglar is a foreigner'. (Stirbois interview 1994; Cleary 1994; *Newsweek* 11 December 1989.)

In 1985 the Front National launched the National Circle of Women of Europe (CNFE). Led by Martine Lehideux (an FN MEP and central committee member), it was established under the slogan 'the women of France are back!' as 'a discussion group enabling women to become more aware of the family, educational, cultural and political problems with which they are confronted daily'. Claiming 3,000 members at its first Congress in 1987, it gave pride of place to the declining birthrate in France and Europe, warning that Third World births were increasing and that foreigners would flood into France. What was needed, it declared, was to end the situation where marriages and births were declining, divorce rising and mothers who stayed at home were devalued. French families should receive an increased dependent's allowance, assistance for mothers-to-be and an income for mothers of three or more children, equivalent to the guaranteed minimum wage. The abortion law should be repealed, a media campaign should be launched to defend the family and opportunities extended for mothers to take up part-time work or work at or close to home. (Foucault 1990: 9–11; Lesselier 1991: 103; CNFE 1989.)

In a subsequent interview, Lehideux argued that the key issue was a maternal income:

> What I want is for women to have the possibility throughout their lives, either to stay at home for a while, to go to work, or to do both (with flexible hours or part time job) and that at the end of their lives, they have a pension that would be theirs and would not depend on their husband's pension.

This policy of a maternal income is here argued as giving women a choice of how to live. In speeches before the European Parliament, for instance, she has argued that women who wish to stay at home with their children are also workers, and should be rewarded accordingly. Millions of women, she claimed, would rather not 'leave their children in crèches every day or pay expensive child-minders' solely in order to spend hours commuting to and from repetitive and ill-paid jobs. 'If they had the material choice', she declared, 'many of them would opt for staying at home to raise their children.' But if a maternal income can be argued for as extending women's choice, it can, of course, be argued differently. Thus Bruno Mégret, a central figure in the organisation, argued that mothers deserved official recognition because they were 'in charge of one of the noblest of tasks. Those who work towards the survival of our people merit at least the same treatment as women who work only towards its prosperity.' (Lehideux interview 1994; Cleary 1994; *Official Journal of the European Communities. Debates of the European Parliament* 2–318: 84 (1984), 3–431: 36 (1993); Simmons 1996: 245–6, 250.)

In discussing the post-war extreme right, a number of themes have emerged. Electorally, women make up a minority, but a significant minority, of its support. They are a minority too within extreme right organisations. (In Germany, for instance, of the approximately 28,000 members of the NPD in 1968, 9 per cent were women, a percentage that is replicated in Mushaben's estimate that women made up some 10 per cent of REP and DVU members in the mid-1990s.) Within its ranks, women sometimes participate in the organisation as a whole but on occasion are to be found in special women's structures. The parties have a particular concern with abortion (and, to a lesser degree, with the birth-rate) and in France and Italy, in particular, argue for economic and social policy to make full-time motherhood a more attractive option than it has proved to be in recent years. The use of the word, option, is of particular importance. The modern extreme right frequently declares itself opposed to feminism. (In one issue of its bulletin, a woman teacher was to argue that where the feminist movement believed in a battle between the sexes, the CNFE believed in their complementarity and natural harmony.) But this does not mean that feminism is attacked because it believes women have the right to work outside the home. Instead, such figures as Martine Lehideux or Adriana Poli Bortone argue that it is a matter of choice whether or not women enter the labour market. (Childs 1995: 295; Mushaben 1995: 27–8; Lesselier 1991: 103.)

Other aspects too have been raised. Some extreme right material, we have noted, has deplored sexualised images of women. For the Front National, the vehement opposition to immigration has a gender dimension in the notion of white women as under threat from the interloper. Finally, in both Germany and Italy, we have seen evidence of disputes among extreme rightists as to what role women should play in the movement and what policy parties should adopt towards such issues as abortion or women's role in the family. In the following chapters, we will examine how one particular movement has dealt with all these questions. Earlier, we discussed fascism in Italy and National Socialism in Germany before examining how the British Union of Fascists organised women and forged a policy towards them. The pre-war British case, it was suggested, was particularly disruptive of our assumptions about how fascism sees women. What continuities and discontinuities have there been between the BUF of the 1930s and its successor organisations? How has the extreme right reacted to a changing family, a shifting relationship between men and women and a different demography? As with the British Union of Fascists, while the modern British extreme right has been the subject of considerable study in recent years, the questions with which we are concerned have remained neglected. Furthermore, only one strand, the National Front of the 1960s and 1970s, has received much attention. The extreme right of later years, particularly the rival groups claiming the name National Front and a third (and ultimately more important) grouping, the British National Party, have been far less discussed. While electorally weak, the modern British extreme right has proved able to gain significant support in particular localities and has put considerable effort into both recruiting women and formulating policies towards them. We will turn our attention to those developments.

5 For race and nation

While the banning of the BUF and the internment of many of its activists had put an end to the most important pre-war fascist organisation, the British extreme right was not to disappear. Some activity by those who had not been detained continued, albeit on a small scale, and, with the increasing release of the internees themselves, by the end of the war a number of groupings had become active. In 1948 Mosley was able to bring together many of those who still supported him into an organisation which, while no longer calling itself fascist, deliberately harked back to the pre-war British Union in calling itself the Union Movement. Many had fallen away, and both personal rivalries and Mosley's decision to abandon a British nationalism for a policy of European nationalism deterred others. Some continued to look to Arnold Leese and his uncompromisingly racial fascism, while a few were attracted to the controversial figure of Francis Parker Yockey, whose shortlived European Liberation Front argued that opposition to America was more important than opposition to communism. Most importantly, the former editor of *Action*, A. K. Chesterton, believed that Britain's future lay in empire not Europe and in the early 1950s launched first a journal, *Candour*, and then an organisation, the League of Empire Loyalists. The League occasionally took part in elections but devoted much of its energies to the disruption of public events organised by those it saw as the enemies of the nation. Never a large organisation, the League none the less suffered periodic internal dissent which resulted in the creation of rival groups, most notably organisations that prioritised an issue that Mosley's organisation also had taken up – opposition to black immigration. In 1960 two such splinter groups, the White Defence League and the National Labour Party, joined together to form the British National Party (BNP). In 1962, however, the BNP's leader Colin Jordan and others broke away to create the National Socialist Movement (NSM) which in 1964 underwent yet another split into the NSM and the Greater Britain Movement (GBM). Amid this fragmentation, caused by both personality and disputes over the appropriateness or otherwise of an openly Nazi identity in a country that had only recently fought against Nazism, race continued to offer opportunities as an issue and anti-immigration groups sprang up in different localities. In the mid-1960s, it began to become possible to bring together the scattered forces of the British extreme right into one organisation. The League of Empire Loyalists and the British National Party were the central movers in this and in 1967 the formation of a new organisation, the National Front (NF), was announced.

The NF's founders had long campaigned against both immigration and what they believed to be an international conspiracy to destroy the British Empire. But for the new organisation to succeed, they believed, it was vital that it be seen as a British nationalist organisation with no links to the fascism of the past and the Greater Britain Movement, viewed as too obviously linked with National Socialism, was initially excluded. Subsequently, however, it was to dissolve and members, including its leading figures, John Tyndall and Martin Webster, joined the NF as individuals. By the early 1970s, they would be the most important figures in the organisation. (Tyndall became its chairman in 1972.) The continued exclusion, however, of the National Socialist Movement (from 1968 the British Movement), ensured that for some on the extreme right, rather than being seen as covertly promoting National Socialism, the NF would be accused of betraying it.

The NF called for a predominantly private economy which would be controlled by the state in the national interest. As the empire increasingly disappeared, the organisation opposed membership of the Common Market, arguing instead that the economic, and political, future lay in reviving links between the mother-country and the white Commonwealth. But it was not economics but the NF's opposition to immigration that was to be crucial to its development. Not only should black immigration be stopped altogether, it declared, but all those who had entered already, along with their descendants, should be removed from what ought to be a wholly white Britain. The widespread popular support for the anti-immigration speeches of Wolverhampton Conservative MP Enoch Powell in the late 1960s presented new opportunities to the NF. Under both its first chairman, A. K. Chesterton, and his successor, John O'Brien (himself a former Powellite), the new organisation experienced some growth, but it was not until the furore over the admission of Ugandan Asians in 1972 that membership numbers really took off. Strenuous efforts were made to win over recruits from the Conservative right, particularly within the anti-immigration Monday Club, but the organisation also tried to establish a base among white trade unionists and even launched a short-lived student organisation. Growing to some 17,500 members, the NF also enjoyed rising electoral support, achieving a sixth of the vote in the West Bromwich by-election in May 1973, and a little over 3 per cent where it stood in the two general elections of the following year. Strongest in parts of north and east London, the NF also gained 119,000 votes in elections to the Greater London Council in 1977, having survived a split which had taken many of its leading activists into the breakaway National Party. (It was to be the National Party, and not the NF itself, which, in Blackburn, gained, albeit briefly, the only two council seats won by the extreme right in this period.) The rival group was to prove to be highly unstable, containing some who held that the NF had failed to make an electoral breakthrough because of Tyndall and Webster's past affiliations and others who believed that the movement could only succeed if it adopted radical economic policies and concentrated on trying to win support among the white working class. As the National Party disintegrated, some of its members would return to their earlier allegiance. But if for much of the 1970s the NF was able to gain credible election results and avoid succumbing to internal discontent, this was no longer true by the end of the decade.

As with the British Union of Fascists before the war and the Union Movement after, in part the NF's failure can be attributed to a combination of the failings of its leadership and the activities of its opponents. Furthermore, there were already signs before the 1979 general election that the party was experiencing problems in gaining electoral support. But one factor deserves particular emphasis. The NF's support derived not simply from opposition to immigration, but from disappointment with both the main political parties. The emergence of Margaret Thatcher as leader of the Conservative Party and her championing of strongly right-wing policies, not least her promise to do something about popular concerns about immigration, was to draw many of those who had previously voted for the NF towards the Conservatives. The NF vote in the 1979 general election fell to an average 1.3 per cent and inner-party disputes tore the organisation apart. Two groupings, the Midlands-based British Democratic Party and the London-centred National Front Constitutional Movement, objecting to both John Tyndall's continuation as chairman and Martin Webster's homosexuality, broke away. Tyndall's belief that he needed more power as leader, not less, in turn separated him from many who remained in the NF, and in 1980 he and his supporters also left to form, first, the New National Front (NNF); two years later, adopting the name of one of the original components of the NF, the NNF became the British National Party (BNP). This change of name denoted not only Tyndall's wish to disassociate his organisation from the movement he had formerly led but also the successful winning over of some not initially willing to join with him. Some came from the disintegrating British Democratic Party but, in particular, the BNP won over a section of the British Movement which, having enjoyed its own period of growth, was now itself in severe decline.

For a moment, it appeared that the British extreme right was being gathered predominantly around two poles, the National Front and the British National Party, with only a small number in other groupings. (Chesterton and his supporters had broken with the NF shortly after its foundation and, following his death, they continued to produce *Candour* as an independent magazine. Other former National Front activists were to be found, for instance, around a stridently anti-immigration publication, *Choice*, produced by a veteran right-wing activist, Lady Jane Birdwood.) In the mid-1980s, however, the lines were drawn again with the breaking of the NF into two rival groups. Following Tyndall's departure from the NF, a younger generation had come to prominence committed not only to racial but to radical nationalism. Influenced by the ideas of the Italian group Terza Posizione, and putting forward their ideas in an initially unofficial publication, *Nationalism Today*, the radicals were drawn to a heady mixture of foreign and indigenous heroes. Among the former were to be found the Romanian Iron Guard leader Corneliu Codreanu and the dissident National Socialist, Otto Strasser. As for the latter, militants were particularly drawn to the early-twentieth-century writers G. K. Chesterton and Hilaire Belloc and their argument that the only alternative to both capitalism and communism was Distributism, the widespread distribution of ownership and the encouragement of a rural and rooted way of life. Claiming affinity not only with earlier traditions on the right but with the green movement and even some aspects of (non-Marxist) socialism, radicals called on the NF to oppose both the multiracial society and big business. Such a stance, overtly critical of the NF of the past, inevitably worsened the tensions on the extreme right. Where the supporters of *Nationalism Today* denounced Tyndall for what they saw as his reactionary objections to their anti-capitalism, the former NF chairman in turn used his magazine, *Spearhead*, to accuse his critics of sounding like the very leftists they claimed to oppose. By the end of 1983, the radicals were strong enough to displace Webster from the NF leadership and in early 1984, from the organisation itself. Soon, however, they were to come to a parting of the ways. For the more radical section, the so-called political soldiers, membership of the NF was only for a dedicated racial elite and the movement's opposition to both Israel and the United States suggested the need for co-operation with the Iranian and Libyan regimes, just as opposition to multiracialism made America's black separatist Nation of Islam and its leader Louis Farrakhan attractive as potential allies. Some members proved unwilling to accept the direction the NF was taking and in 1986 it divided into two groups, with the political soldiers continuing to control the party paper, *National Front News*, and their opponents launching a rival publication, the *Flag*. While the latter group took the name National Front Support Group, they quickly decided to drop the last two words and until 1990 both groups claimed to be the real National Front.

In 1989, one estimate suggested that the *Flag* group had a little under 3,000 members, the BNP almost 1,000 and the political soldiers between 600 and 800. The smallest of the three, whose radicalism now involved support for the militant wing of Welsh nationalism and schemes for building small agrarian communities, grew weaker still and in 1990 was to declare that the NF was no more. The *Flag* group, rather than prosper, found the 1990s an unpropitious period that left it with a few hundred members, and, in an attempt to reverse its fortunes, in 1995 it too declared that the National Front had ceased to exist, changing its name to the National Democrats. (A breakaway grouping, however, retained the old name.) But if the 1970s had been the decade of the NF, in the 1990s it was the BNP that emerged to centre stage. Growing to some 3,000, it concentrated much of its activities in East London and received considerable publicity in late 1993 after it gained a council seat in Tower Hamlets. For a time, it appeared that it might gain further seats. This, however, proved not to be the case and the loss of its one electoral gain the following year encouraged critics of Tyndall's leadership. Hardline National Socialists, who had organised a paramilitary organisation, Combat 18 (18 standing for AH, Adolf Hitler), came into conflict with the BNP leadership and created their own political grouping, the National Socialist Alliance. Much of their support came from the rise of a racist skinhead movement which in particular coalesced around a magazine, *Blood and Honour* (the name coming from the slogan of the SS). By the mid-1990s, the National Socialist Alliance had brought together supporters of *Blood and Honour*, a section of the British Movement and others in a fundamental challenge to the electoral strategy of the BNP. In rapid succession, tensions became evident within both the BNP and Combat 18 and while the latter rapidly went into decline, the future of the BNP, now reportedly less than 1,000 strong, was also unclear, not least because of the political resurrection of a former leader of the political soldier wing of the NF, Nick Griffin, who having been a bitter critic of Tyndall's organisation had subsequently not only joined it but come to play a prominent role in internal arguments about its future. (For the extreme right in Britain after the dissolution of the BUF, see Walker 1977; Billig 1978; Billig and Bell 1980; Fielding 1981; Taylor 1982; Husbands 1983, 1988; Hill and Bell 1988; Kushner 1989; *Searchlight*, n.d. (1989); Gable 1991, 1995; Eatwell 1992, 1996b; Toczek 1992; O'Hara 1993a, 1993b; Copsey 1994; Durham 1996. For estimates of membership numbers, see *Searchlight* January 1989, January 1990, January 1993, July 1995.)

As the account above suggests, the British extreme right since the war has seen a considerable amount of organisational conflict and turnover. Two groupings, however, have been of particular significance – the National Front and the British National Party. It is these organisations that have achieved the largest memberships, the greatest amount of publicity and, despite the short-lived success of the National Party in the late 1970s, have been the most important electorally. Any consideration of their development has been complicated, as we have seen, by the existence of two National Fronts in the late 1980s and by the fluid situation on the extreme right since the emergence of Combat 18. In a situation where no grouping has made a sustained electoral breakthrough, disagreements over strategy and leadership have again and again caused members, sometimes prominent ones, to defect to rival groupings. But it is the NF and the BNP which have dominated the British extreme right over recent decades and it is on these parties that we will focus our attention. In subsequent chapters, we will discuss the British extreme right's conception of women. In this chapter, however, we will be concerned with women's role in the movement. As we will see, both the organisation of this account and how it has been constructed have important differences from our discussion of the BUF. In both cases, a close examination of the party press has been supplemented with other sources – in particular, where in the case of the BUF the Public Record Office holds some extremely useful documents, notably on Special Branch and MI5 surveillance of its activities, in the case of the NF it has been possible to draw on a number of internal documents, ranging from National Directorate minutes to bulletins for both members and local organisers. Other material, for instance from local newspapers, has been used in both cases but one area of difference will soon become evident. Unlike the BUF, neither the NF nor the BNP has organised women separately. They have given considerably less attention to the role of women in their ranks and, furthermore, while there has been no shortage of extreme right publications in recent decades, no group has ever been able to emulate the BUF in producing weekly publications within which substantial coverage can be given to local activities. Our account of Britain in the 1930s was of a movement in which women were a highly organised and important part. Within the organisations in this chapter, however, women are far from invisible, but we glimpse them in much more fragmented ways, active in a movement which is not only led by men but finds the recruitment of women to be both desirable and problematic.

Of the groups which came together to form the National Front, women had been particularly visible in only one – the League of Empire Loyalists. This was true both in organising the League and in carrying out its most typical activity, the public denunciation of 'traitor' politicians. In late 1956, for instance, its organising secretary, Leslie Greene, disrupted a speech by the prime minister, Sir Anthony Eden. Weeks later Eden was interrupted again, this time by another of its women activists, Rosine de Bounevialle, joined by Greene and others. (Nor were such activities confined to Conservative events. Ten years later, de Bounevialle would be disrupting a speech by another prime minister, this time Harold Wilson.) While, unlike the National Front, the League rarely entered election contests, Greene stood in 1957 as an Independent Loyalist candidate in the first by-election after the Suez farrago, while in 1964 both she and de Bounevialle ran as Loyalists in the general election. In the early years of the NF, women's prominence in one of its main components was reflected by their involvement in the higher levels of the new party. Greene (subsequently Leslie Von Goetz) and Lady Elizabeth Freeman, a central figure in the founding of *Candour*, were among the members of the NF's National Council (effectively an honorary body) in the organisation's early years, while de Bounevialle and another prominent former Empire Loyalist, Avril Walters (subsequently Avril Munson) were members of the NF's leading body, the National Directorate. The decision by A. K. Chesterton and his supporters to leave the NF at the beginning of the 1970s was to end this period in the organisation's history but did not mean that women were henceforth absent from key positions. On the contrary, women could be found on local branch committees, as electoral candidates or even on the national leadership itself. (*Candour* 7 September 1956, 23 November 1956, November

1966, 11 January 1957, September 1970, June 1973; *Spearhead* 25, September 1969; Empire Loyalist (leaflets) 1964; Scott 1972: 552–3; Walker 1977: 89.)

In the early 1970s, the Huddersfield branch was chaired by a woman, while examples of women as branch organisers can be found in Havering and Brentwood in the late 1960s or in Cardiff or Newham during the 1970s. For women to take such prominent roles, however, was untypical, and they were more likely to be found in other branch positions. Exactly which positions they occupied could vary. In 1974, for instance, the Bristol branch committee included two women, one the treasurer, the other its librarian, while in 1976 the Leicester committee included a woman activities organiser. In 1970 it was one such officer, the secretary of the Wolverhampton branch, who was to be the first woman to run as an NF parliamentary candidate. Described as 'a Wolverhampton housewife with two sons', Sheila Wright joined nine men as a party candidate in its first general election. Such was the level of support in the Wolverhampton area, the NF claimed, that the Conservative candidate had tried to get it to stand down in order not to split the anti-immigration vote. Wright gained 1,592 votes, 4.7 per cent, and at the National Front's Annual General Meeting shortly after was to be among the activists singled out to receive 'special badges of merit' in recognition of their 'outstanding services' to the party. (*Bristol Evening Post* 7 June 1974; *National Front News* 2, May 1976; *Spearhead* 56, September 1972; 27, November 1969; 113, January 1978; 134, December 1979; 34, June; 35, August; 36, September 1970.)

In February 1974, the next general election saw the NF run fifty-four candidates. Wright was not among them (she had defected to the British Movement, becoming its Wolverhampton branch chairman) but three women were. One, Sheri Bothwell, gained 4.3 per cent in Leyton while Jo Reid gained 4.4 per cent in Feltham and Helston. The other woman candidate, Gillian Goold, a former Monday Club activist who would later return to the Conservatives, gained a less impressive 1.3 per cent in Norwich North. In the second general election that year, in October, the NF ran more candidates (ninety), and more women (five), with Reid and Bothwell standing in their old seats achieving a better result (3.7 per cent and 5.4 per cent respectively) than the other three, who averaged 2.5 per cent. (*British Tidings* September 1973; *Guardian* 21 June 1988; *Spearhead* 74, April 1974; Craig 1984.)

In the years that followed, women were highly visible in council elections and, to a lesser degree, in parliamentary by-elections. In the 1976 municipal elections, over 20,000 voted for NF candidates in Leicester. Three candidates ran in each of the sixteen wards and nine of these were women. In 1977, twenty of the Front's ninety-one candidates in the Greater London Council election were women, with particularly strong support in Newham South (over 15 per cent) and creditable results in Chingford (nearly 8 per cent), Hackney North and Stoke Newington (nearly 7 per cent) and Romford (5.7 per cent). (*Spearhead* 94, May 1976; 105, May 1977.)

Women council candidates ran in a number of areas in the following two years. In 1979, for instance, eight of the twenty candidates in the elections for Wolverhampton council, and four of the ten for Coventry, were women. But they were also evident in contests for parliament. In 1978 *Spearhead* proudly announced that 'Housewives and mothers' Helena Steven and Sylvia Jones were 'fighting both the forthcoming Parliamentary by-elections for the National Front'. In the general election the following year, both were among the thirty-six NF women out of the overall total of 303 NF candidates standing. While this was to be the highest number of candidates the NF would field in a general election, their generally low percentage of the vote, as we have seen, was to have catastrophic results for the party. While women candidates gained 2.6 per cent in Greenwich, 3 per cent in Hackney North and 4.4 per cent in Peckham, among the better of the results, they also received 0.8 per cent in Brighton, Kemptown, 0.6 per cent in Lichfield and Tamworth and 0.2 per cent in Glasgow Pollock, among the worst. (*Searchlight* June 1978; *Birmingham Evening Mail* 30 April 1979; *Spearhead* 117, May; 116, April 1978; Craig 1984.)

In the four general elections of the 1970s, approximately 10 per cent of the NF's parliamentary candidates were women. In internal elections, too, women stood some chance, if not in great numbers, of achieving significant positions. Before Chesterton's departure, members of the National Directorate had been appointed rather than elected and in the first election to be held to it, those members who attended the NF's 1971 AGM gave the third highest number of votes to Clare Macdonald, the organisation's treasurer. Not for the last time, however, election to the Directorate would be followed by a break with the organisation. Along with another woman activist, Macdonald attempted to get the NF to change its name, arguing that the term Front was 'not understood by ordinary electors' and gave an unfortunate impression of extremism. Unsuccessful, Macdonald defected to a short-lived rival grouping. In 1972 Huddersfield branch chairman Rita Buckley was elected to the Directorate, and in 1973 she was joined by a woman activist from Leicester, Beryl Brakes.

Buckley died shortly after but at the 1974 AGM another woman, Joan Sandland, was elected to the Directorate. The organisation, however, was by now riven by disputes and Sandland was to be among those who defected to create the National Party. (Walker 1977: 101; *Spearhead* 47, October 1971; 60, January 1973; 55, August; 56, September 1972; 69, October; 70, November 1973; 80, January; 86, August 1975; *Britain First* 35, January–February 1976.)

While a more substantial breakaway than that involving either Macdonald or Chesterton's supporters, the National Party did not significantly deprive the NF of women activists. In 1977 one NF loyalist, Beryl Mitchell, was elected to the Directorate. The Head Office secretary since 1976 and a founder member of the NF, she, like Sandland, Buckley and Wright before her, had received an award for her services to the party. In 1979 Mitchell was joined on the National Directorate by another woman, Helena Steven. This, however, was to be the last NF AGM for many of those involved in the organisation. These included a number of women, four of whom ran unsuccessfully as candidates for the National Directorate. One of them, Marilyn James, secretary of the Northampton branch and a parliamentary candidate in 1979, had once been quoted in *National Front News* denouncing claims that the NF was really a Nazi party. 'I used to be a dedicated Tory follower,' she had declared, 'but then I met NF members and saw how genuine they are.' In 1980, however, she resigned, accusing the NF of attracting 'thugs and bully boys'. The other three, Jean White, Susan McKenzie and Beverley Matthews, stood together as part of an opposition slate. The opposition's leaflet for the Directorate elections, which criticised the quality of party propaganda, the efficiency of its administration and the leadership's treatment of inner-party critics, included profiles of each candidate, emphasising their contribution to the building of the NF. White was described as having been a member since 1975, a branch treasurer, parliamentary candidate and recipient of an award for services to the movement; Matthews as a founder member of the Tower Hamlets branch in 1973 and having twice been a council candidate. McKenzie, it noted, was not only a former branch treasurer and a member since 1976, but had been an active supporter since 1970, when she was only ten years old. They were subsequently among the founding members of the breakaway National Front Constitutional Movement. (*Spearhead* 110, October; 108, August 1977; 70, November 1973; 58, November 1972; 132, October 1979; *National Front News* 15, September 1978; *Chronicle and Echo* 12 January 1980; *Searchlight* January 1980; NF opposition leaflet 1979.)

Following the 1980 split, as we have seen, only the NF and the NNF (subsequently the BNP) were to long survive, with the NF itself breaking in two in the mid-1980s. In the 1983 general election, of the six NF woman candidates (of a total of sixty), one gained 2.5 per cent in Peckham, another 1.9 per cent in Bow and Poplar. The remaining four gained an average of 0.9 per cent of the vote. Women continued to hold branch positions within the organisation. Thus in 1984 the NF's Tower Hamlets branch had a woman treasurer (as did Wandsworth in 1981 and Croydon in 1986), while in 1985 *National Front News* published a profile of its Hounslow branch. Illustrated with two photos, one of five paper-sellers (two of them female) and the other of the male branch organiser with 'one of Hounslow's numerous lady members', the report described a branch meeting where the woman branch treasurer gave the branch accounts and the woman branch secretary read out the minutes of the previous meeting. (*National Front News* 48, July 1983; 57, June 1984; 63, February 1985; 76, n.d. (1986); *Searchlight* July 1984.)

Women also continued to be elected to the National Directorate. In 1980 two women were first co-opted, then elected, onto the Directorate. Peggy Caine ('Secretary of the successful Havering Branch') had been active for ten years while Carole Neil, a member for five, held a key position in the NF's electoral work as its East Midlands Regional Agent. The Directorate now stood at its peak of four women members, the others being Steven and Mitchell, but by the next round of elections a year later only Caine and Mitchell remained. In 1983 Mitchell, who had been ill for some time, died. Caine was re-elected, now the only woman on the Directorate. Subsequently, however, she left and was involved with Martin Webster and others in an abortive attempt to set up a 'non-party association' following Webster's expulsion from the NF. (*National Front News* 24, July; 28, November–December 1980; 51, November 1983; *Members' Bulletin* Spring 1984; *Our Nation* n.d. (c. 1985).)

As we have seen, women were to be found on both sides of each of the frequent arguments that have divided the British extreme right, and the emergence of two rival NFs in 1986 was to be no exception. The most prominent women, however, were to be found in the *Flag* group. Caralyn Giles (subsequently Caralyn Taylor), a multilingual secretary who had joined the organisation in the late 1970s, was a particularly prominent activist, her involvement ranging from attending numerous national events and representing the NF in a televised debate to standing as a candidate in local elections and holding the position of branch organiser in Brighton and branch secretary in

Worthing. (She had been one of five activists to receive 'Gold Badge awards' at the NF's 1983 Annual General Meeting.) Another southern activist, Tina Denny (previously Tina Dalton) was similarly highly visible at NF activities and in the late 1980s was both Worthing branch chairman and the national administration officer. Shortly after her marriage to the party deputy chairman, Martin Wingfield, in 1989, both she and Caralyn Taylor were elected to the National Directorate, coming fourth and sixth respectively. Taylor subsequently seems to have left the organisation. Wingfield, however, while also reportedly leaving for a while, has remained a prominent member of the National Front and subsequently the National Democrats. (*National Front News* 76, n.d. (1986); 51, November 1983; *Flag* 18, April; 22, August 1988; 8, May 1987; 35, October 1989; 24, October 1988; 36, November 1989; 85, April 1995; 93, n.d. (1996); *Searchlight* September 1994; *Members' Bulletin* Spring 1991; n.d. (late 1994).)

We have so far concentrated on women as branch officials, election candidates and National Directorate members. But how else have women been active in the NF? As has been suggested already one important activity was paper-selling. In the mid-1970s women were among the organisation's leading sellers in the Manchester and Salford area while in late 1986 a woman member of Wandsworth branch was among four activists arrested for paper-selling outside Chelsea Football Ground. (Papers were not only sold in city centres or outside football matches. One woman member was to write in the party paper how door-to-door selling was a particularly effective way of telling 'people what we really stood for, not just about immigration'.) (*Britain First* 34, November–December 1975; *Flag* 6, February; 7, April 1987.)

For the NF, as for the BUF before the war, considerable attention was given to the organisation of marches. On occasion, women's involvement in such activities was deliberately pushed to the fore. Thus, in 1973, a photo of a march during Martin Webster's by-election candidacy in West Bromwich shows a young woman either side of him carrying 'Stop Immigration Vote Webster' placards while in 1980 it was the turn of two leading figures, Richard Verrall and Andrew Brons, to march against the import of foreign steel accompanied by what *National Front News* called 'two pretty bodyguards'. The same technique was used yet again both when Verrall, Brons and NF president Blaise Wyndham led off an anti-IRA march the following year and when another key activist, Joe Pearce, stood as a candidate in Mitcham and Morden in 1982. But women marchers were not restricted to what the NF leadership appears to have seen as a decorative role. Particularly important for the organisation, and not only for its male members, was its annual Remembrance Day march in commemoration of British losses in the two world wars. (The march, of course, was significant both for its patriotic symbolism and for the NF's unending efforts to refute allegations of sympathy for National Socialism.) In 1972, for instance, *Spearhead* noted that among the ex-Servicemen and women's section of the march were 'many war widows wearing their husbands' campaign medals'. (Similarly in 1978 *National Front News* noted the 'hundreds of male and female veterans and war widows, many with impressive rows of glinting medals'.) In the 1980s women's attendance became visible in a different way. The 1984 Remembrance Day march was the subject of a report in a National Front *Organisers Bulletin* which commented that the participation of two Drum Corps and a 'girls' flag party' had 'all helped' to make the event 'one of the best turned out' marches for a long time. A Women's Flag Party likewise appeared the following year, the *Organisers Bulletin* declaring that 'lady members' should be encouraged to attend not only the parade but a practice session immediately before so as to add 'to the appearance and image' of the march. (*Spearhead* 65, June 1973; 59, December 1972; *National Front News* 23, June 1980; 30, March 1981; 41, July 1982; 75, n.d. (1986); 16, December 1978; *Organisers Bulletin* 15 November 1984; 1 October 1985.)

Women would continue to be evident in later marches. In 1985 *National Front News* reported that a march in Leicestershire had been led off by 'two drum corps' and a 'flag party', emphasising the presence of 'ladies' among the latter. In both 1987 and 1989 the Remembrance Day parade included women in its Drum Corps. But the NF leadership's concern for 'appearance and image' had not disappeared. In 1986 a march through London was led off by the London Drum Corps and 'twenty young ladies holding burning torches', an innovation which followed an internal bulletin urging units to 'encourage attractive female members' to thus lead off the march. (*National Front News* 67, June 1985; *Flag* 15, January 1988; 37, December 1989; 1, August 1986; *Organisers Bulletin* 25 April 1986.)

Women were involved in other kinds of activity too. Thus in 1975, they were among those carrying placards when the Hillingdon branch picketed the local council in protest at the provision of council housing to immigrants. The same year six women attended a meeting addressed by Labour home secretary Roy Jenkins to protest against government race relations proposals. Hurling bags containing flour, soot and manure, the women gained publicity in the national press, the NF declaring that while most were members, the action had not been an official one. In 1988, women were also involved in an NF picket of a local paper, protesting against its withdrawal of an advertisement for the organisation, while the following year they were among those carrying placards outside a meeting addressed by Sinn Féin spokesman Gerry Adams. (A woman member also threw a glass of water over Adams inside the meeting.) (*Britain First* 32, September 1975; *Spearhead* 88, October 1975; *Flag* 22, August 1988; 35, October 1989.)

Despite their visibility on branch committees or as candidates, women speakers appear to have been comparatively rare in the NF. In 1971, reporting on a Tunbridge Wells anti-Common Market meeting where the branch secretary had argued 'from the position of a British housewife', *Spearhead* commented that this had 'revealed an example of the hidden talent waiting to be tapped in the way of female speakers, which in the movement have up to now not been numerous'. Such talent, however, seems to have remained largely untapped. Sometimes, women council candidates addressed public meetings and in 1980 the speakers at the end of a march in south east London against mugging included '72 year-old Mrs Nellie Cecil, a longstanding member of the NF's Wandsworth Branch who told the rally how in recent years she had been mugged no less than four times!' In general, however, reports of women representing the NF as speakers are few and far between, but there is one interesting exception. Whatever their failings in developing women speakers, the NF leadership certainly realised that they would be of advantage in election broadcasts. In one, 'a young housewife and mother' declared that paying more for food for her family brought home the need to withdraw from the Common Market, while in another a familiar theme surfaced as a woman declared how she worried about 'what sort of future my children face especially since employers are being pressured to give preferential treatment to immigrants'. (Hanna 1974: 51; *Spearhead* 46, September 1971; 86, August; 84, May 1975; *National Front News* 21, April 1980; NF election broadcasts February 1974, 1983.)

If few women members addressed public meetings, the NF certainly saw them as useful in raising money for the organisation. Writing on the subject in 1974, Webster advised that every branch should set up a fund-raising committee and that 'Ladies in particular' often showed talent and ability in this area. In the same period, once again invoking the leadership's fascination with the appearance of its women members, Tyndall advised branches when conducting collections that 'attractive lady members should when available be used' for passing boxes or buckets around the meeting. Both he and Webster addressed a youth rally later in the decade where a 'team of girls, buckets at the ready' collected nearly £100. This emphasis on women as useful in the generation of funds continued in the years that followed. In the mid-1980s Tina Denny was appointed organiser of the NF's Social Club while another young woman activist, Newham branch committee member Jackie Cosgree, was praised in *National Front News* for organising a particularly successful jumble sale. Cosgree, later a council candidate in Essex, was also one of the members of an NF Women's Support Group described in another NF publication as providing food and drink at an NF event in 1986. While the Women's Support Group appears to have had a short existence, in the same year it also raised money for racist 'political prisoners'. An initiative of the political soldiers, it had been partly anticipated by an earlier proposal by Beryl Mitchell at the beginning of the 1980s to launch a Women's Committee to organise social functions for the party. (*Spearhead* 75, May 1974; Tyndall n.d. (1977): 14–15; *Bulldog* 14, n.d.; *National Front News* 70, September; 72, November 1985; *Searchlight* May 1989; *Flag* 1, August 1986; letter to NF Organisers, 25 April 1986; NF National Directorate minutes, 5 January, 2–3 February, 29 March 1980; *Organisers Bulletin* 11 April 1980.)

It was not until the late 1970s that the NF launched a youth wing, the Young National Front (YNF). In some ways YNF membership replicated the experience of older members. Thus *Bulldog*, the YNF publication, in 1982 profiled two young Brighton women who had joined the YNF after taking part in one of its marches and had since been involved in selling the paper outside the local football ground. A local NF publication, in an issue earlier in the year, described them as deciding to join after attending both the march and a branch meeting. Both factory workers, they had 'immediately got involved with activities, helping with food for the Christmas Social' as well as paper-sales. (*Bulldog* 28, July 1982; *Sussex Front* 15, March 1982.)

There were, however, important generational differences. Emphasising sport, discos and holidays, *Bulldog* in 1978 urged 'white racialists' to join 'The best social club in the country'. The discos, it noted, not only gave members a chance to drink but 'more important, our female members are all the right colour'. The call for members was accompanied by a report of a YNF disco in which there had been 'as many girls . . . as boys, this obviously made things more interesting!' In one of the earliest issues, indeed, a 19-year-old member, Sue McKenzie, had urged girls to join, promising that politics was not just 'stuffy meetings and speeches' but had a lively social side: 'there's always lots of guys to chat you up in the bar afterwards . . . You never know, if you come to our socials, you might meet your future hubby.' (*Bulldog* 9, August 1978; 4, December 1977.)

No doubt appealing to such future spouses, in early 1978 *Spearhead* accompanied a report of the launch of the youth wing of the party with a photo of a young woman wearing a YNF T-shirt captioned 'One good reason for joining the YNF!' The following year a photo of another such young woman was captioned 'One of These Could Be Yours For Only £2.00!' 'No, the T-Shirt, you fool!', it added. This sexualisation was even more evident in *Bulldog*, which took to publishing regular music reports, accompanied by photos of young women, usually on NF marches. They were sometimes unidentified, sometimes named as members. Thus on one occasion a London member ('The Blonde Bombshell of Southwark') was shown wearing a White Power T-shirt standing in front of a Union Jack. One of the final issues of the publication called for girls who fancied 'being a *Bulldog* . . . Bird' to 'send a photo of yourself with personal details. The sexier the better. . . .' Yet, while pictured as sex-objects, this did not mean that women could not play a politically active role in the YNF. One young woman appeared on the cover of *Bulldog* modelling a YNF T-shirt under the caption 'Jane is Out in Front!' As the accompanying article noted, she was one of its branch organisers. (*Spearhead* 115, March 1978; 127, March 1979; *Bulldog* 22, n.d.; 40, n.d.; 12, April 1979.)

Women in the NF occupied many different roles. If they were mothers (and concerned at Vietnamese refugees entering the country), then their support was wanted for the NF's British Mothers' Campaign to Keep Out the Boat People. If employed, they could be encouraged to join the NF Trade Unionists Group (although a membership list published by anti-fascists suggests that very few did). If housewives or pensioners, they could be urged to call into radio phone-ins, putting forward the NF's view. This diversity of activity was reflected in the party's own propaganda literature. Thus *We Are NF*, a book of photographs published in 1981, brings together pictures of a 'Blonde seller at Brick Lane', a woman electoral candidate, a 'Lovely YNF girl', a 'drum corps girl' and women placard carriers flanking Brons and Verrall during a march. Another NF photo book, *Marching On With The National Front*, included a page 'Women in the Front' showing two young women in YNF T-shirts, two other young women at a 'Rights for Whites' rally and a group of women, one with a child in a buggy, with Union Jacks behind them and the caption 'Mothers concerned for their children's future'. (*Spearhead* 129, July 1979; *National Front News* 18, August 1979; *Searchlight* June 1984; *Members Bulletin* May

1974; National Front 1981: 16, 36, 39, 51, 60; Nationalist Welfare Association n.d. (1984): 11.)

But if women were active in the National Front, some women within it were concerned that they were not prominent enough. Writing on the role of women in the NF in the mid-1980s, Jackie Griffin noted that frequently women were to be 'found behind the scenes, making cups of tea, addressing envelopes and folding circulars' and that apart from 'a few women on local committees' and the Women's flag party on Remembrance Day little was heard or seen of NF women. Women, she declared, needed to 'find their role in our revolution' and 'raise their fist in defiance', not only by 'organising food, raffles and functions', necessary as this was, but by writing to imprisoned members, organising against nuclear war and emulating the women of the miners' strike in supporting their community's struggle. This, we should recall, was the radical wing of the movement, which believed that both ecology and working-class militancy were far from incompatible with a racially based politics. Writing shortly after the appearance of Griffin's article, the NF's Liverpool branch organiser likewise argued that women should become more active. They should, she wrote, no longer leave leafleting and postering to the men but should 'equal and perhaps better the efforts of our menfolk. Women must become more willing to take part on committees, make decisions and ultimately carry out those decisions on the streets of our battered homeland.' Nor were these the only such observations. In 1984, another activist, Michelle Wiltshire, had used the letters column of *Nationalism Today* to comment on an article it had published on women and the miners' strike. Miners' wives, she declared, were 'rightly fighting for the future of their local community' and NF women likewise not only ran a home but sold papers, leafleted and demonstrated for the national community. (*Nationalism Today* 33, September 1985; 36, February 1986; 23, July–August 1984.)

One way in which the political soldiers tried to involve women members was in their attempts in the late 1980s to 'sink local roots' through community self-help projects. Women, it argued, could 'play a particularly valuable role' in this by organising baby-sitting circles, running play groups or 'pressing for a safe playground'. But concerns about women's participation in the NF had persisted after the 1986 split and surfaced in the rival grouping. Interviewed in the *Flag* group's magazine, *Vanguard*, following their election to the Directorate, Tina Wingfield and Caralyn Taylor were asked why there were 'so few women at the top, in the National Front'. For Wingfield, the problem was that while there had been many inactive women members, women who wanted to be politically active had looked elsewhere. Women had joined through husbands and boyfriends and perhaps had not yet gained the experience or confidence to stand for election. Taylor took a stronger line, arguing that women had 'been brainwashed by male members into thinking that running the National Front is a "job for the boys"'. Neither, however, supported the idea that the NF needed a women's section. According to Wingfield, while there might be 'some injustice with regard to opportunity because of their different roles', the sexes were 'complementary parts of one whole, the Race'. If any women believed there was discrimination in the party, she suggested, it could raise it at the NF's Annual Conference or in the pages of *Vanguard*. (*National Front News* 88, April 1987; *Vanguard* 28, November–December 1989.)

In raising the subject of a women's section, the *Vanguard* interviewer had referred to the example of the Labour Party, rather than the MSI or the Front National. There had been attempts in the past to bring together British fascist women in their own organisation. Not only had the pre-war BUF and the post-war Union Movement done so, but so had the British Movement in the late 1970s and a short-lived BNP splinter group, the National Action Party, in the early 1980s. (For post-war Mosleyism, see e.g. *Union* 26 November 1949, 17 June 1950; for the British Movement Women's Division, see Ware n.d. (1978): 16, 18; for the National Action Party, see *Searchlight* January, March 1983.) But if a women's section was not seen as appropriate for the NF, not only the difficulty of involving women members but their low number in the first place attracted comment within the movement, and (recurring) claims were made of success in increasing female involvement. The first issue of *Nationalism Today* claimed that as the YNF 'moved into 1979 it was noticed that more and more girls were becoming active on NF demonstrations'. This, it said, 'was a welcome development because, up until then, the vast majority of YNF activists were male'. One area, West Bromwich, had its own YNF girls' unit, and already in 1978 *Bulldog* had claimed that there had been a recent 'large increase in the number of girls joining the National Front'. (*Nationalism Today* 1, March 1980; *Bulldog* 15, n.d.; 9, August 1978.)

The issue arose again in the late 1980s. In a pamphlet in 1987, the future leader of the NF (and subsequently the National Democrats), Ian Anderson, had noted that while the movement was predominantly male, 'over the last few years this imbalance has been slowly decreasing and we hope that this will continue to be the case'. The subject returned yet again in the next decade too. In 1992, looking back at an article on building the organisation which had appeared in the first issue of

Vanguard, he noted that 'no mention' had been 'made of the recruitment of women'. In the past twelve to fifteen months, however, this had been addressed and, 'although we have a long way to go', progress was being made. A third of those taking part in the 1991 Remembrance Day march, Anderson pointed out, were women. The *Flag*, shortly after the 1992 general election, likewise claimed that it was delighted that 'ladies . . . are now making up an increasing proportion of National Front membership' and that figures of 'ladies sitting on NF Committees' were likewise 'rapidly increasing' while a little later, discussing an increase in support in South London and Kent, it reported that 'we are delighted to see an increasing number of ladies attending our meetings – always a sure sign of our growth'. (Anderson n.d. (1987): 29; *Vanguard* 37, n.d. (1992); *Flag* 64, n.d. (1992); 71, n.d. (1993); 80, August 1994.)

Estimates of the proportion of women in the NF have varied. In the late 1970s, one account suggested an improbably high 25 per cent while more recently the NF itself has been quoted as claiming that 10 per cent of its membership is female. But if the NF leadership has given some attention to the low level of women's involvement, so too has the British National Party. This, however, has been even less sustained. While in 1983 paper sales in East London's Brick Lane were described as including 'the intrepid *Christine Yianni*', it was more typical to describe BNP activity as including 'two attractive young lady flag-bearers'. Every branch meeting, *Spearhead* readers were told in 1982, should include a literature display, and a member should be assigned to collect the money for sales ('one of the most attractive lady members of the branch is ideal for this purpose!'). This did not mean that women could not play leading roles. They could be branch organisers, *Spearhead* noted in 1982, and the previous year it had reported that the most active of its Young Nationalists groups was in Grimsby, where the organiser, the daughter of the city's NNF organiser, sold the paper in the town, and leafleted dole queues, 'the local football ground, shopping centre and housing estates'. Another woman was organiser of the Greenwich Branch while a third was praised by the magazine for building the initial NNF organisation in Manchester, having been 'repeatedly let down and left to do almost everything herself'. Electorally, however, they were far from prominent. In 1983 only two women, one John Tyndall's wife, the other her mother, were among its fifty-four general election candidates. Valerie Tyndall gained 0.98 per cent in Hackney South and Shoreditch while Violet Parker, who was also the BNP's head of administration, gained 0.62 per cent in Wakefield. The minimal involvement of women as candidates was to be repeated subsequently. Having, like both wings of the NF, decided not to take part in the 1987 election, in 1992 of the thirteen BNP candidates, one was a woman (and non-member), Lady Jane Birdwood, who gained almost an exact average of the results with 660 votes (1.1 per cent). The NF also ran one woman in 1992, in this case alongside thirteen men. She gained 192 votes (0.4 per cent), one of the weakest results, the average being a little under 0.7 per cent. In 1997, due to illness and legal problems, Lady Birdwood was unable to stand again as a BNP candidate but it increased both its number of candidates (to fifty-six) and its number of women (to six), with results ranging from one of the best of 2, 232 votes (5.2 per cent) to one of the worst of 238 votes (0.5 per cent). As for the National Democrats, they ran twenty-one candidates, four of them women, including Tina Wingfield, who gained 671 votes (1.4 per cent). Emphasising again the greater strength of Tyndall's organisation, where half of the BNP candidates had gained more than 1 per cent, the majority of the smaller National Democrat contingent had not. (Big Flame 1991: 20; *Elle* July 1992; *Spearhead* 166, August 1982; 167, September; 149, March 1981; 171, January; 173, March; 176, June 1983; *British Nationalist* 32, October 1983; 91, June 1989; *New Frontier* 5, June 1981; *Daily Telegraph* 4 May 1994; *Searchlight* May 1992, March, June 1997.)

At times, the BNP has sought especially to mobilise women. In 1982 women in its Leicester branch picketed and distributed leaflets outside a meeting of the National Housewives' Register which was discussing racially mixed marriages. In 1993 what was described as the 'first all women's event by the British National Party' took place when 'More than 20 women made history by demonstrating against an eviction of a White family' in East London. In addition, some individual women have been particularly visible in the party. One, Isabel Hernon, described in *Spearhead* as a 'first class candidate' when she stood for a council seat in Epping Forest, is a long-time activist whom we will discuss later (p. 117). Another, Christine Yianni, who we have already encountered (p. 113), was much involved in BNP activity during the 1980s but was later removed from a party rally for attempting to disrupt it. This did not, however, mark the end of her political involvement. A militant supporter of the Church of the Creator, an American-based organisation which claimed Christianity to be a Jewish device for weakening the white race, she was subsequently active in support of Lady Jane Birdwood during a court case in 1991 concerning the distribution of anti-Semitic material. (*Spearhead* 170, December 1982; 316, June 1995; *Rune* 8, n.d. (1993); *Searchlight* February, December 1991; *Guardian* 17 October 1991; *Independent* 19 October 1991.)

Other women, for instance, have run as BNP candidates in council elections. As we will have further cause to observe, it is perhaps more surprising that women join the BNP at all. None the less, Tyndall has expressed concern at the low numbers of women within the organisation. 'Our women', he declared in *Spearhead* in 1986, were 'generally feminine and attractive, though as yet too thin in numbers – possibly a product of their conviction that their role is to run the home while their menfolk are out fighting for hearth and homeland!' The previous year he had noted that the BNP had not yet 'achieved the balance of sexes in its membership that is the ideal'. Men would always be more likely to be active politically than women, he held:

> particularly in our sector of politics where traditional attitudes towards women's role are stronger than elsewhere and domestic duties are liable to command greater female priority. Nevertheless, we should have more women members and activists than we do, and every encouragement should be given to women to join and participate with their menfolk in branch work.

Spearhead also published an extract from a speech by a woman activist, Christine Ryan, to the BNP's Stoke-on-Trent branch. Having received a letter from Tyndall about the BNP's weakness among women, she declared, she had decided to address the topic of 'the role of women in the party'. As a mother of three, she recognised that bearing and rearing 'healthy offspring' was women's most important contribution – but not their only one. 'Whether a woman works outside the home for purely financial reasons or because she desires a career', it did not mean, she argued, that she had abandoned her duty to the family. Indeed, more women would vote BNP, she suggested, 'if we could prove ourselves to be a party of roughly equal rights'. (*Spearhead* 212, June 1986; 198, April; 197, March 1985; for women BNP council candidates, see e.g. *Searchlight* June 1994.)

Reportedly pleased that at the party's 1991 rally as many as sixty of the 450 in attendance were women, Tyndall continued to be concerned with the question, and the issue was to come to particular prominence in early 1995 when *Spearhead* reported that the editor had agreed to plans to improve the magazine. As part of this, it had been agreed that 'There should be more items of interest to women' and the report also called for better articles including 'as mentioned above, issues of interest to women – preferably written by women'. Later in the same issue, a report on a recent gathering of officials to plan the party's future development noted that it had been agreed that 'the party must do more to attract women'. (*Searchlight* December 1991; *Spearhead* 313, March 1995.)

The British extreme right has found real problems in achieving greater support from women. This has applied to both voters and members. Studies carried out during the 1970s, when voting support was at its peak, found a degree of female support, but one exceeded by that among males. In a sample survey conducted in a number of localities during the latter part of the decade, Husbands found that 20 per cent of males and 16 per cent of females were strong NF sympathisers, and a further 17 per cent of males and 13 per cent of females weaker sympathisers. It was the female unemployed, he suggested, who were the most sympathetic (and only a little less sympathetic than men in the same position) while women in work were considerably less likely to support the NF. (Husbands 1983: 149, 100, 132–3.)

These figures are particularly high, far outstripping those who actually voted for the NF. Surveys conducted in England between 1971 and 1978 found only 0.7 per cent of respondents intending to vote for the National Front, of whom 71 per cent were male. But other studies also show considerable sympathy. A survey in South Hackney and Shoreditch in 1978 found 15 per cent of young whites highly sympathetic to the NF and a further 12 per cent somewhat sympathetic; 73 per cent of the first group and 63 per cent of the second were male. Finally, in 1979, a survey of 885 adolescents in West Midlands schools found 55 (6.2 per cent) were NF sympathisers; of these, 40 were male, 15 female. (Harrop *et al.*, 1980: 273–5; Weir 1978: 189–91; Cochrane and Billig 1982: 87–8, 93.)

To most of the minority of a minority who made up the female support base for the National Front, voting NF might never occur as an option and certainly membership would not. On occasion, however, the organisation has found it useful not only to draw attention to its women members but to quote some of them on their reasons for belonging to the movement. In the early 1970s, for instance, *Spearhead* published an article in which six people explained why they supported the NF. The one woman among them, a former Labour voter was described as a 'Housewife with 2 grown up sons and 3 grand-children'. Having decided to join after hearing the NF's candidate for the North Islington constituency at an election meeting, she emphasised immigration while also referring to patriotism, communism and the Common Market as factors in her support for a movement which spoke out, she believed, 'for what ordinary people believe but can't always express'. Similarly, a leaflet produced in the late 1970s quoted members on why they had joined including a Wandsworth woman pensioner who declared that her neighbourhood had been 'a nice clean place' but now was 'filthy' and crime-ridden. 'I'm in the NF because I want this to become a fit place to live in again . . . I say Britain ought to be for the British people.' (*Spearhead* 49, January–February 1972; NF leaflet n.d. (c. 1978).)

Other NF publications emphasised other factors. In 1978 *Bulldog* quoted one young female member as saying 'I didn't think it was right that I couldn't get a job when there were blacks doing the jobs I wanted to do. In Britain we should come first.' A later issue reported on two pupils at a Westminster girls' school who had joined Central London YNF after walking out of a lesson in protest against being taught about Asian religions, while in 1983 Tina Dalton, soon to be a prominent NF activist, was quoted attacking Thatcher for supporting the rich 'while people like me and my mates rot on the dole'. But this was not her only grievance. Rather than her getting a job, she complained, it was 'the Blacks' who were getting 'the jobs I could be doing'. (*Bulldog* 9, August 1978; 16, n.d.; 35, September 1983.)

The BNP has not found it so important to produce literature in which individual women members explain why they joined the party. It has, however, found it useful for some of them to give interviews to the press or television. Interviewed in the early 1990s for a programme on women on the extreme right, 35-year-old BNP activist Angela Barr declared that she had become involved after moving into an area that was preponderantly black. The granddaughter of an Italian who had been interned in the war and daughter of an RAF family, she was 'petrified about decline of the white race'. One final example spans both the NF and the BNP. Isabel Hernon, who left school at 16 with no qualifications to become an accounts clerk, had joined the NF in 1974 because, she believed, Glasgow was being 'overrun by Asians'. Subsequently moving to Essex, where she sold the BNP paper most Saturdays, she had been highly active – 'I spoke at a National Front rally in Scotland . . . I have given newspaper interviews, I have rallied, I have canvassed. I was the BNP candidate for Epping Forest in 1989.' Despite this level of activity, she holds that 'the highest role a woman has in life is to have children . . . I'm having the future white race.' (*Spearhead* 132, October 1979; *Cosmopolitan* September 1978; Barr interview 1994; *Elle* July 1992; *Sunday Telegraph* 3 June 1990; *Independent* 13 October 1993.)

All these women were united by racism. But few other common factors drew them to the extreme right. NF material emphasised their women members' patriotism, their concerns about crime and their economic grievances. The two BNP interviewees gave more extended accounts, in which not only their individual autobiography but their commitment to a particularly virulent form of extreme right politics is brought to the fore. Hernon, who categorised herself as a National Socialist, described immigration as brought about by Jewish bankers 'in order to wipe out the Aryan race', while Barr declared that the Holocaust was the 'biggest con of the twentieth century'. (*Elle* July 1992; Barr interview 1994.) All of them had chosen to join parties that are overwhelmingly male not only in their leadership but in the ethos that suffuses their activities. For women to be selected to lead a march or appear on the cover of a magazine because of their looks, or for John Tyndall to emphasise their role as guardians of the hearth are some of the most noticeable characteristics of a movement which is and is likely to remain highly male. There are other factors too – the gender balance of such parties' leadership, the emphasis on men as fighters for the race. This is not to say, as we have seen, that women cannot play a visible role in the NF or even the BNP. More importantly, some women clearly want to play a greater role and some male leaders, for their own reasons, would support such a development. But if the BUF should surprise us in the part women played in its activities, the NF – and certainly the BNP – has proved less of a shock. A study of women's role in such parties suggests the need for a more nuanced account than they customarily receive. But it is not yet clear to what degree the NF and the BNP might diverge from our stereotypes of extreme right parties. Women appear to play a less than prominent role in their ranks. If we turn to their policies, will we have cause to modify our judgement?

6 Breeding more Britons

As we have seen, the British Union of Fascists said far less about population than we might have expected. For the post-war British extreme right, however, this has been a central question. Indeed, of all the NF's (and, even more, the BNP's) policies, one of its greatest concerns and the one that most affects women as a group is its position on population. It is appropriate, then, that we should start our discussion of the modern British extreme right here before turning our attention to a question which in recent decades has become a particularly important issue for those who seek to fight for race and nation – abortion.

In its election manifesto for October 1974, the National Front called for an end to 'the growing frenzy of "population control" and "family planning"'. What was needed, it declared, was a 'vigorous birth-rate' and any problems of overpopulation in Britain would be solved by emigration abroad, preferably within the Commonwealth. In its 1979 manifesto, this theme was reprised. Family size, it insisted, would not be the subject of state pressure, but by the removal of 'economic discouragements' those who wished to have large families could do so. 'Alone among parties', it declared, 'the National Front is also concerned to reverse those trends which make for a decline in our population qualitatively as well as quantitatively.' At present, punitive taxation, lowered standards in schools and racial mixing all contributed to 'a tremendous totalitarian-style pressure to lower our population in qualitative terms'. In its place, the National Front would bring about 'the preservation and improvement of the British people as a whole and the encouragement of the best among them of all classes'. (National Front 1974: 12; 1979a: 57.)

Where the first of these manifestos had called for a high birth-rate, the second argued not just a pro-natalist policy, but a eugenic one. At first sight, there would appear to be little to explain in the adoption of such a policy by the National Front. Surely, it might be argued, since we have already noted the influence of National Socialism on many of those who came together to form the NF, its adoption of a eugenic population policy was inevitable. In the early 1960s, the British National Party, when it still included those who would subsequently create the rival National Socialist Movement and Greater Britain Movement, had declared that the role of education in the future 'Racial Nationalist Folk State' would include 'eugenic instruction to encourage racial betterment in marriage'. A commitment to a selective population policy persisted both among those who would later join the NF and those who did not. Significantly, John Tyndall's Greater Britain Movement was particularly virulent in this regard. Its programme advocated both laws against racial intermarriage and the prevention of 'procreation on the part of all those who have hereditary defects, either racial, mental or physical'. Nor were such views restricted to the GBM programme. In 1965, *Spearhead* claimed that Aryans had prospered because they were the fittest to do so. Other races, it declared, were predominantly worthless and rather than provide them with foreign aid, it should be left to nature to ensure that they did not multiply. The following year, the magazine returned to the subject, this time in terms of the pernicious effects of welfare provision on 'the lowest elements in our own indigenous British population'. It was argued that they were responsible for much of the brutal crime not usually seen among 'Nordic' peoples. While they were pampered and having large families, the industrious were persecuted by crippling taxation and being restricted to one or two children. Only by introducing a policy whereby 'the best are encouraged to multiply and the lowest are prevented from doing so', it was concluded, could the natural order be restored. As we will see, such views, if not in such overtly National Socialist language, would be strongly espoused within the NF. Yet it is important to recognise that not all those who came into the organisation in its early years shared such views. As we noted in discussing the BUF, eugenics had been much criticised by the Distributist G. K. Chesterton. This stance appears to have been carried over into the grouping led by his cousin (and former BUF official), A. K. Chesterton, and in the mid-1950s *Candour* published an article by a Distributist and future NF National Directorate member arguing that if eugenics were to prove feasible ('which, thank God, is extremely doubtful') it would be people with the lowest incomes who would suffer its attentions. Furthermore, it was not only class-discriminatory but anti-Christian. How, the author enquired, was procreation by the supposedly unsuitable to be prevented? 'By mass-sterilization? Or by merely declaring them ineligible for employment cards, health benefits, family allowances and breathing licences?' A government pursuing such policies as these, it was suggested, would not allow the continuation of a religion that believed in 'the value of human life' and 'the sanctity of marriage'. While this article was, in part, concerned that eugenics could be used by the opponents of nationalism in order to eliminate separate races, it was clearly arguing against eugenics as such. Its author, Aidan Mackey, would leave the NF at the beginning of the 1970s, but this would not be the last time such arguments would be heard on the extreme right. Nor, as we will see, would they be the only source of doubt about population policy. Under Chesterton's leadership, the NF did not prioritise population and it was not until Tyndall's rise to leadership that either pro-natalism or eugenics became a crucial part of NF policy. The stance he had long espoused, however, would never win over all of those who adhered to the NF or its successor organisations. (*Combat* 15, January–February 1962; Walker 1977: 47; *Spearhead* February 1965; 11, June 1966; *Candour* 28 January 1955; on Distributism and the League of Empire Loyalists, see *Candour* May 1982.)

The existence of disagreements within the organisation was evident from soon after Tyndall's admission into the NF. In a three-page article which appeared in *Spearhead* in late 1968, he set out what would, in time, become the NF's policy. For so-called progressive thinkers, he declared, birth control was seen as an unquestioned good. Yet if we examined different families, we found some who were intelligent and industrious, others who were indolent or criminal. In a normal society, the first would prosper and we would 'get an abundant breeding of the best and most productive elements of the population' while the less desirable families would prove unable to sustain large numbers. Left alone, 'the better stocks' would increase but in a society where contraception was widely available, it is they who would use it, while the more ignorant would not. Furthermore, Tyndall observed, taxation penalised the most productive and there were even proposals to target family allowances to those families supposedly more deserving. Not only were the unfit multiplying while more useful citizens were receiving no support to 'increase their kind', the Pill was also being espoused as a solution to the problem of unmarried motherhood. But the stigma attached to motherhood outside of marriage was something to be defended rather than decried. 'The ignominy of illegitimate birth, brutal though it undoubtedly is to the child concerned, has at least had the virtue of serving as an agent of restraint to those tempted by the attractions of illicit intercourse.' Without it, sexual licence would prevail and marriage and the family would be undermined.

There was, the article continued, one remaining argument that could be deployed by advocates of birth control – that Britain and the world were overpopulated. The latter might well be true yet birth control was not stemming the population explosion. In some countries – the Soviet Union, De Gaulle's France and, in the past, Germany – state policy favoured not restricting population but expanding it, for the right question was not how to stop the global population explosion, but who would survive it. Britain, while overpopulated in relation to its natural resources, was not overpopulated in comparison with China or Russia or America, and by distributing its population between Britain and the white Commonwealth, 'a vigorous birth-rate among Britons' could be sustained. How could this be brought about? 'We have no right', Tyndall declared, 'to dictate to husbands and wives that they should have large families.' Nor should they be condemned 'for practising birth-control within the present social context'. But through a change in social values and social benefits, the industrious could be encouraged to increase their numbers. An increase in quantity would be accompanied by an increase in quality, and to these aims 'all ephemeral social considerations should be subordinated'. (*Spearhead* 21, November–December 1968.)

In the following issue of the magazine, a letter appeared challenging Tyndall's argument, defending the Pill for allowing 'efficient planning of a family' and saving women from the anguish of bringing children they could not afford into the world. Both in order to protect women in situations where they would be risking their lives in childbirth and to enable parents with congenital defects to have happy marriages with no fears of passing the defect on, the Pill, it was suggested, was 'a godsend'. Not only did the writer, a member of the NF, support contraception, he opposed Tyndall's call for increased numbers. The country could not feed an increasing population and it was 'brains and not brawn that make a nation great'. Tyndall, in reply, made clear he was unimpressed by such doubts. He had not argued that what was needed was an increased population in Britain, he declared, but had called for a high birth-rate and its distribution to Canada, Australia and other white Dominions. As for the social problems his critic had noted, these, he snapped, were 'nothing more than a potpourri of the standardised Hampstead-Leftist views' one could find in any paper. Only on one point could there be agreement, that in exceptional cases of illness or congenital factors, 'some form of contraception (not necessarily the Pill) is justified'. (*Spearhead* 22, January–February 1969.)

Each of the groupings that joined the infant NF had brought their own publications with them. The BNP's paper, *Combat*, did not long survive but where *Spearhead* continued under the control of Tyndall, former Empire Loyalists continued to produce *Candour*. *Spearhead* had published an article in defence of eugenics and then a reply. Immediately after the former, *Candour* also published an article on the subject, this time by Tyndall's former Greater Britain Movement colleague, Martin Webster. But, in what was unlikely to have been a coincidence, Webster's views appeared less an endorsement of Tyndall's views than a critique. Nationalists were right, he suggested, to be concerned over 'the debilitating effect which contraception is having on the White World'. However, any suggestion of legislative compulsion to increase the birth-rate was not the answer. Given the undermining of patriotic values by 'Marxist-orientated internationalists', he claimed, it was thoroughly understandable that British people had become obsessed with material possessions and no longer wanted to have large families. But 'moralising cant, from whatever quarter' was irrelevant and impertinent. 'The individuals who compose our population will only adopt a healthy attitude to ensuring the survival of their species when they are living in a healthy environment' and when they had a proper leadership. Such a leadership would enable the problem of 'the abuse of contraceptive technique' to solve itself but to 'attempt to impose . . . any sort of specific pressure on married couples with regard to how they conduct their intimate relationships is an unthinkable tyranny. Our womenfolk must not be condemned to the status of baby-producing cattle' and the state had 'no business in the bedrooms of the nation'. Any politician who thought that it did was 'treading the dangerous road towards artificial incubation units and baby hatcheries' and in attacking the rights of the family they were admitting an 'inability to create the atmosphere' in which people would voluntarily take on the responsibilities needed to secure the future. (*Candour* January 1969.)

If Webster (and *Candour*) were indicating reservations about Tyndall's stance on population, they were not alone. The following year Tyndall was to complain of *Spearhead* receiving 'a series of letters from NF university members' criticising what they saw as its 'reactionary attitude' on such questions as contraception. But if, from early on, there were signs of dissent from Tyndall's views, it was also evident that he did not stand alone. Even before the appearance of Tyndall's article, the former BNP leader John Bean had written in *Spearhead* on the subject of birth control, decrying attempts to restrict Britain's birth-rate. Returning to the issue at the beginning of 1970, he argued that it was the disparity in racial birth-rate, 'and also the swamping of the talented by the untalented', that was the problem. Arguing along different lines from Tyndall, Bean not only insisted that it was in all mankind's interest that the talented, who had 'given us all the improved living standards we now enjoy', should increase in numbers but he linked an argument against indiscriminate population increase with the rising movement against 'man's poisoning of his environment'. Both, he argued, were responses to threats to the balance of nature. (*Spearhead* 31, March 1970; 20, September–October 1968; 29, January 1970.)

The possibility of linking concern over population with the growing popularity of environmentalism was taken up by Tyndall himself later in the year. Only by controlling economic forces, it was argued, could the nation find 'a sounder ecological balance between urban and rural society'. Instead of there being too many Britons, they were wrongly distributed into tightly packed urban areas while vast areas of Britain and the Dominions were almost empty. A nationalist approach to population would be 'much more in accordance with the rhythm and harmony of the universe' than an approach which favoured providing aid to countries that could not feed themselves. For such areas, the answer lay in natural selection, an approach that trusted 'the eternal wisdom of the Creator rather than the meddlesome intellectualism and emotionalism of man'. (*Spearhead* 46, September 1971.)

If key figures in the NF were committed to the need for a pro-natalist population policy, they were even more convinced that the enemies of the race were to be found conspiring against it. It is not surprising, then, that an anonymous article in early 1972 should claim that 'the powers-that-be' were 'urgently promoting population control among the White races' in order to eliminate 'the one element that has the intelligence and the will to resist the oncoming of the collectivist, communist world-state'. It was ironic, however, that an article on the very next page by Chesterton's successor as NF chairman, John O'Brien, was to argue for a reduction in Britain's population. Admittedly, this concern for 'an already overcrowded island' was put forward as grounds for the expulsion of black immigrants and their descendants, and O'Brien further argued for sending Britons to the white Commonwealth to assist in resistance 'to the threat of submersion by the teeming millions of Africa and Asia'. But in describing England as 'the most densely populated major country in the world' and regretting that political expediency would stop government from 'taxing those who produce more than two offspring . . . thus adding to the ecological burden of future years', O'Brien's argument was pointing in a very different direction from Tyndall's. Successive governments, he charged, were guilty of promoting 'the breeding of large families by automatic additional State hand-out for each new arrival . . . A massive increase of population is the last thing this overcrowded and polluted island needs'. (*Spearhead* 50, March 1972.)

The issue continued to trouble the NF leadership, and in 1973 *Spearhead* gave particular prominence to an article on 'The Population Plot'. Sinister moves were afoot, the author suggested, to promote population control. The Commons Select Committee on Science and Technology had called for a minister responsible for population, the 800-strong Doctors and Overpopulation Group (which included David Owen) advocated liberal abortion and increased sterilisation and the project director of a panel chaired by John D. Rockefeller III had proposed that childbearing should be discouraged by discouraging marriage. While part of the enthusiasm for decreasing population, the author suggested, lay in a perverted hostility to 'normal procreative sex', attention also had to be given to the vast array of interlocking organisations funded by international finance. 'The fear of a population explosion', he concluded, 'is quite clearly being used as yet another means to destroy the family basis of Western civilisation and stampede us into World Government.' (*Spearhead* 64, May 1973.)

In making such arguments, National Front writers could not but be aware of the political traditions from which they drew, and in 1974, in response to the Labour government's announcement of contraceptive provision through the National Health Service, *Spearhead* reproduced an extract from the pre-war German radical rightist Oswald Spengler's book, *Decline of the West*. Modernity, Spengler argued, had brought sterility and where the peasant believed in eternal land and eternal blood, continuing a blood-line was no longer seen as a duty. 'When the ordinary thought of a cultivated people begins to regard "having children" as a question of *pros* and *cons*, the great turning-point has come.' Two years later an extract from another of his works appeared, bewailing 'the decay of the white family'. Amid the increase of both 'the coloured races' and, Spengler declared, of 'abnormal people of every description' within the white race, the battle for the planet had begun. But where his account attributed birth-rate decline to the effects of urbanisation, an exhaustion of the spirit, *Spearhead* inclined to a more conspiratorial explanation. Thus, after the appearance of the first Spengler extract, the magazine published 'The Real Conspiracy', in which attention was drawn to a 'sinister' population control industry which sought 'contraception legislation of a most objectionable nature' and which wilfully misinterpreted the 'abortion act, which in itself, is a perfectly adequate piece of legislation' to secure virtual abortion on demand and to launch a smear campaign against its critics. 'Already, in the wake of vast government-assisted propaganda, it is becoming almost a social stigma for couples to have children.' The author did not advocate, he declared, that 'government should deliberately encourage people to have large families', along pre-war German or Italian lines. 'Nor am I adopting the attitude of certain churches toward contraception. Encouraging too many births as a kind of political "cannon-fodder" is as morally wrong as encouraging an anti-family concept.' Today, however, 'some people even boast how they are doing their bit by *not* having a family'. (*Spearhead* 75, May 1974; 98, October 1976; 79, September–October 1974.)

This article, as we will see, held a significantly different view of abortion legislation than did others in the organisation and in the next few years it would be the issue that would attract controversy within NF ranks. On population policy itself, however, O'Brien's 1972 article appears to have marked the end of an argument, rather than its beginning. O'Brien himself broke with the NF shortly after and for the remainder of the decade what was at stake was not whether the NF would champion more (white) births, but whether it would argue for eugenics too. There were several dangers with taking this path. First, to espouse the policy that the Third Reich had adopted and that Tyndall had once championed in openly National Socialist terms would make it even harder to deny claims that the National Front was really a Nazi front. Second, to call for a selective population policy posed the dangerous question of which groups among white Britons the NF wished to see increase and which it wished to decline. Third, the NF did not want to alienate Christians in general or Catholics in particular. Each of these concerns was relevant not only to the party's future growth, both electorally and in membership, but in retaining those members it had. Already before the NF's creation, *Candour* had sought to warn against the adoption of an approach to population that it saw as opposed to the family, Christianity and the least well off. Subsequently, Martin Webster had used its columns to warn against the temptation of too intrusive a stance towards the family. In putting forward a population policy, the NF's October 1974 election manifesto declared that it was up to parents, not the state, to decide 'how many children they should have'. Here it both repeated Tyndall's assurance in his 1968 article and anticipated what the 1979 manifesto would declare. But, unlike both of those, the 1974 manifesto took a simply pro-natalist stance. As yet, the NF had not adopted a eugenic policy although the outline of something more than pro-natalism was already to be seen in a pamphlet published by the NF Policy Committee in 1974. Predominantly the work of Tyndall, the pamphlet sought to show the feasibility of a new 'policy for British survival'. Towards the end, it turned its attention to 'the absolutely insane policy of discouraging a high birth-rate'. There was no movement more dangerous to Britain's future, it declared, than that which called for family planning. Instead of reducing numbers while other races multiplied, what was needed was 'a high birth-rate coupled with high incentives to emigration' to 'populate the great empty acres that our ancestors won for us'. A passing reference, however, to 'the reproduction of our best stocks' indicated that the argument was not simply concerned with the quantity of births and an article which appeared in *Spearhead* made this clearer still. Reprinted from *Mankind Quarterly*, a journal 'dealing with race and inheritance', the article lamented the lagging of 'the fertility of the educated, the intelligent and the successful' behind that of 'the masses'. In recent times, it went on, the situation had worsened as higher education, which should produce an aristocracy of intelligence, was instead being subordinated to the pressures of egalitarianism. Rather than 'assortative mating', the coming together of 'the best', what we were now seeing was the multiplication of incompetents, bringing into existence 'future generations so mediocre and spiritless that they will serve as pliant instruments of the gargantuan state'. (National Front 1974: 12; n.d. (1974): unnumbered page, 2, 26; *Spearhead* 99, November 1976; for a discussion of *Mankind Quarterly*, see Billig 1979.)

For an organisation seeking both voters and members from among the masses, such an overt way of arguing the social implications of a eugenic policy was, to say the least, unwise. The appearance of the article did, however, confirm how important the issue was to some in the NF and shortly after an article by one of its leading figures, Richard Verrall, made it clear that it was not seen as merely a subject for discussion. Amid 'the rising tide of colour', he argued, the low fertility level among whites indicated either the existence of a death wish or the work of 'forces which are deliberately promoting the progressive reduction of White peoples throughout the world as a dominant racial factor'. Not only was white reproduction falling, but 'the racial quality' of whites was falling too, 'both as a result of deliberately promoted racial integration' and the erosion of 'sexual mating for intelligence inspired by the mania for "equality"'. What was needed, then, was a Nationalist policy, the first element of which should be 'an education programme which will eliminate the moral and political sensitivity which has surrounded population policy, and has inhibited governments from taking the necessary action'. This did not mean forcing a change in fertility. 'It simply means that Government should *positively encourage*, by every means possible, the raising of large families.' Abortion should be restricted or even banned, contraception should cease to be encouraged and government policy reorientated to encourage the building of families. Instead of seeing the nation as 'a sea of individuals' and viewing a population policy as an interference with women's rights, the nation should be seen as 'an organic whole and an ethnic entity', the survival of which stood higher than "freedom". Generous financial incentives should be provided for young couples, more resources channelled into child welfare services and an end should be put to 'the contemporary derision of maternity and domesticity'. Instead, Britain would be a society 'that respected and cherished the feminine role as principally one of wife, mother and home maker'. (*Spearhead* 101, January 1977.)

Returning to some of these themes later in the year, Verrall cited an entry on eugenics in an unnamed medical encyclopaedia in order to decry the use of birth control by the intelligent when instead it was the ignorant who should be using it. In modern society, he declared, 'equalitarian non-selective schooling breaks down the natural pattern of assortative sexual mating of the best types', birth control was 'lowering national fertility alarmingly' and even physical fitness was decried. 'What is happening, in fact, is that the elite, both in terms of the Race as a group and within the group, is being remorselessly eradicated . . . Only by a total rejection of liberal values can we create a society which allows the best, the superior to flourish.' (*Spearhead* 108, August 1977.)

In 1979, as we have seen, the NF's election manifesto adopted an overtly eugenic stance. Writing on 'The Creed of a Nationalist' at the end of the previous year, Tyndall contrasted the 'national and race ethic' with liberalism in their thinking about 'the field of procreation'. Liberalism, he argued, encouraged birth control because 'in the spiritual wasteland that is the modern West families must be kept down to a size that will not endanger our enjoyment of . . . cars, colour TV sets and washing machines'. Sex was merely a pleasure, birth an inconvenience. For the nationalist, however, the pleasure of sex was at the same time 'a means to the creation of new life . . . the continuance of family and race'. But if this was simply a pro-natalist argument, it should not be taken as suggesting that Tyndall had retreated from the eugenic stance he had long championed. Shortly after the 1979 election, he returned to the theme with a language that almost revelled in its harshness. Discussing a book by an American racist, *Which Way, Western Man?*, Tyndall praised the author's argument that caring for 'human wreckage – millions of morons, feeble-minded, insane, criminals and all sorts of the hopelessly incurable' was a dysgenic endeavour. 'This could be demonstrated', Tyndall noted, 'by the simple example of a healthy intelligent woman who sacrifices the opportunities of marriage and motherhood of sound offspring in order to devote herself to work in a home for mental defectives.' The same mentality, he suggested, could be seen in fears of overpopulation and the encouragement of birth control. The latter served 'as a propaganda weapon aimed at driving the White peoples to racial suicide through limitation of births'. As for overpopulation, if it ever did become a problem, the key question would be '*Who is going to do the dying?*' (*Spearhead* 124, December 1978; 135, January 1980.)

We have so far traced the development of NF thinking on population predominantly through articles in *Spearhead*. In early 1980, *Spearhead* (and John Tyndall) would cease to support the National Front. How did the extreme right deal with population in the 1980s and 1990s? The NF, as we have seen, would split again in 1986, but a debate published shortly before already showed some of the tensions between NF radicals. Writing in a short-lived NF journal in 1984, Steve Brady, at one time a prominent figure in the ill-fated National Party breakaway and later a leading figure in the *Flag* group, took issue with the Christian assumption that 'all men' (as he put it) are equal and separated from all other creatures by the possession of a soul. The result of this view, he argued, was the creation of an economic system which, following the Biblical command to 'Be fruitful and multiply', treated nature as something to be subdued. Western capitalism, he declared:

> hacks down the forests, slaughters the wildlife, spreads the concrete cancer of giant cities ever wider across the land, encourages the dusky hordes to proliferate ever faster and gobble up ever more food and resources, and pollutes and fouls the sky, the sea and the land.

Communism too endangered 'the global ecology' and 'the survival of the Race' and it was only racial nationalism which saw humans not as above nature but as part of it, 'bound by the . . . laws of biological evolution . . . with its ethnocentricities, inequalities, dominance hierarchies and territorialities'. In a world without God, Brady argued, nationalists could create a race of virtual Gods. 'Through a gradual, scientific and humane programme of eugenics we can direct our own evolution towards higher orders of physical beauty and fitness and mental nobility of character and intelligence.' (*New Nation* 6, Winter 1984.)

In the following issue, Paul Matthews, a political soldier (and Catholic), replied. Nationalism, he insisted, was not antithetical to Christianity nor grounded in evolutionary theory. Indeed, Darwinism's belief in the survival of the fittest would subordinate the weak to the strong, the poor to the rich, and Brady's 'grim' notion of a scientific programme of eugenics would result in abortion, euthanasia and the rule of an elite empowered to define who was fit and who was unfit. Man lived in nature but transcended it and it was the spiritual ideas of Christianity that would create a society which reunited him with the land, obeying God's instruction not to ravage the earth, but to replenish it. (*New Nation* 7, Summer 1985.)

Both Matthews, who cited Chesterton's Distributism in arguing that traditional Christianity was anti-capitalist, and Brady, who believed that materialism not religion was the basis of a coherent nationalism, believed that the NF should take a radical stance. But they could not agree on whether a eugenic population policy would be part of that radicalism and what is noticeable in the period following the NF split is how weak the support for eugenics was. While Brady was plainly concerned with the issue, neither the *Flag* group nor the political soldiers took it up. Both wings, however, were sympathetic to a family policy that would encourage an increased birth-rate. The pre-split *National Front News* had called for 'encouraging a healthier birth-rate amongst the White people' and in 1987 the political soldiers praised the French government for paying mothers to have extra children. Shortly afterwards, as part of a detailed discussion of family policy, they alluded to the need to introduce incentives for large families. (*National Front News* 58, July 1984; 93, August 1987; *Nationalism Today* 44, n.d. (1989); for Brady's continued concern with 'higher birthrates among those of lower innate intelligence', see *Vanguard* 27, September–October 1989.)

In 1988, for its part, a council candidate for the *Flag* group declared in his election leaflet that the poll tax was 'anti-family' and that it should be repealed 'because it penalised large families. Children make family life and every encouragement should be given to young couples to have children.' A number of articles appeared in the group's press on the subject. In 1990 an anonymous article in the *Flag* warned that the white race was dying out. 'Thanks to the easy availability of contraception and abortion, together with the decline in the family and soaring divorce rates', the birth-rate had plummeted while every day there were more and more non-whites. Only, it declared, by 'an all-out commitment to racial survival' by an NF government could this be averted. In *Vanguard* the following year, Brady praised proposals by the Italian government for economic measures to encourage marriage and increase the birth-rate in Europe. 'The only hope for civilization', he declared, was for the white world and Japan to 'batten down the hatches and prepare to ride out the storm' while nature reasserted its control of Third World numbers, a reassertion in which most of the Third World would die. Writing later in the year in the *Flag*, he attacked the materialism engendered by capitalism and 'the widespread availability of the technology to prevent babies' which together, he argued, were causing the fall in the white birth-rate. 'Across Europe, millions of babies that do get conceived are murdered by abortionists', while inflation and high interest rates had undermined the traditional family and made it necessary for wives to go out to work. Fertility had to be restored by measures such as those that had been introduced in Sweden – the granting of well-paid leave from work for mothers 'if a second child is born within 30 months of the first' and improved financial allowances for child care. 'We need more babies, for in their tiny hands they hold our future and that of our ancient nations and peoples.' (NF 1988; *Flag* 44, July 1990; 59, October 1991; *Vanguard* 33, January–March 1991.)

The NF's concern with population policy has varied considerably, and in its 1992 election manifesto, for instance, it urged increased family allowances, not to encourage large families but to save parents from 'financial strain' and the resulting marital instability (National Front 1992: 15). But if elements within both wings of the NF were concerned with population, it would not be inaccurate to say that the group led by John Tyndall was obsessed with it.

An issue of *Spearhead*, produced shortly before the New National Front's transformation into the BNP, illustrates this particularly well. In one article, Tyndall was at pains to claim that Britain contained large numbers of 'low grade human material'. Rather than assuming that the nation's problems were a matter of black immigration, he suggested, one should look also at the existence of 'inferior strains within the indigenous races of the British Isles'. These groups had 'tended to congregate in certain city areas . . . since the industrial revolution' and as a result of a combination of 'religious background' and welfare provision frequently had a high birth-rate. Medical opinion should decide which of these should be sterilised to stop their reproduction, while for the majority all that could be done would be to lower welfare benefits 'so as to discourage higher fertility'. The issue also contained an article reprinted from the American racist magazine *National*

Vanguard in which the contemporary West was criticised for exalting 'the botched' and believing that 'everything which walks upright on two legs and talks is precious and ought to be preserved'. Modern morality, the author declared, condemned the German people for 'attempting to rid themselves of a pernicious infestation which was stifling their national life'. The Holocaust, however, had to be judged on the basis of a higher morality. Until this was grasped, those who refused 'to share everything we have – our land, our food, our women' would not secure 'a White future'. (*Spearhead* 161, March 1982.)

In the years that followed, a eugenic approach to population was repeatedly urged in the BNP press. In 1987, for instance, a discussion of inner city problems included the suggestion that among the necessary policies was one which recognised the impact of 'the proliferation of very low-grade white people made possible by an undiscriminating welfare state'. A key objective, *British Nationalist* readers were told the following year, was population quality. There should be 'policies for genetic cleansing and progress', in which the 'breeding' of undesirable stocks – criminals, 'the feeble-minded . . . the lazy', should be discouraged, while the strongest and most industrious should be encouraged. (*British Nationalist* 72, October 1987; 85, December 1988.)

While such ideas were usually merely outlined in BNP publications, in 1989 *Spearhead* published a three-part essay on 'Genetics And Culture In A Racial Nationalist State'. Written by prominent activist Tony Wells, it was accompanied by an editor's note making clear that Wells' view was neither the party's nor Tyndall's. But regarding the latter, it noted, the difference was one of 'detail' over how a eugenic programme could be pursued. On the 'broad objectives' Wells had set out, there was no disagreement. Coyly citing an unnamed (but, no doubt, identifiable) 'European leader during the earlier part of this century', Wells declared that this figure had urged the centrality of racial improvement, a 'truth' that had 'prompted the writing of this essay'. Racial nationalists had too often concentrated on race while ignoring genetics, but after 'our racial house' had been 'put in order' by the removal of aliens a policy of genetic improvement should be pursued. The 'strongest possible inducements', he declared, had to be provided for the racially sound majority 'to breed' and a positive eugenic programme would include a massive scheme of in vitro fertilisation in which superior genes would be introduced into the wombs of less gifted women. Couples 'deemed unsuitable for breeding' would also be able to adopt children from the higher groups, thus spreading the economic cost of bringing up gifted offspring. For the less gifted, 'sterilisation would be the primary weapon', although specially created ministries would have to decide which physical or mental defects should preclude procreation and which not. (*Spearhead* 240, February; 241, March 1989.)

Beyond eugenics, Wells envisaged more ambitious intervention still. A positive genetic programme would include compulsory amniocentesis (with obligatory abortion in the event of a defective foetus) and the selection of genetic characteristics to match a distribution pattern decided on for a particular year. Thus, for instance, IQ, already raised by 'breeding the next generation from the top half', could be raised yet further. Finally, through a genetic engineering programme, human DNA itself could be altered, perhaps to decrease 'emotionally impulsive behaviour', certainly to increase intelligence. Genetic material could be stored in the event of a nuclear war; a gene could even be developed which could be added to whites to make them able to procreate only with their own race. (*Spearhead* 242, April 1989.)

Where Tyndall had expressed disagreement with 'detail', such views, however, did not meet with universal agreement among *Spearhead* readers. Indeed, the response to them is reminiscent of the earlier arguments on the extreme right we discussed at the beginning of this chapter. Wells' article was criticised both in the magazine's correspondence columns and in an article written in reply, in which the author argued that the possible benefits of Wells' proposed genetic engineering were outstripped by the definite dangers. The creatures he envisaged could turn on their creators, terrible mistakes could be made, the scheme could be utilised not by nationalists but by their enemies. Nor was this the first time such disputes had broken out since the break with the NF. In 1981, *Spearhead* had criticised a court for stopping a couple from allowing 'their mongol child to die' by refusing permission for medical treatment. At the least, the magazine suggested, parents should be able to decide on euthanasia, but such a decision might be a matter not for parents alone but for society. The next issue contained a letter which argued that a reduction of taxation would enable parents and charities to care for 'the handicapped'. *Spearhead*, it was suggested, should not 'wallow in the murkier realms of eugenics' and should withdraw its 'hateful paragraph'. Tyndall, in reply, declined to do so, despite his 'high regard' for the letter's author. The critic was former Empire Loyalist (and one-time member of the NF National Council) Leslie Von Goetz. (*Spearhead* 243, May 1989; 155, September; 156, October 1981.)

If some on the extreme right continued to be critical of the morality of eugenics, this was not the only source for concern. In 1984, a frequent *Spearhead* writer, Noel A. Hunt, criticised a decision by the

European Parliament to examine how Europe's birth-rate could be increased. As a result of the high taxation needed for health services and child allowances, he argued, the prudent, 'who should be breeding', were economically discouraged from doing so, while the 'stupid and the feckless' were encouraged 'to continue to breed recklessly'. What was needed was 'not more babies, but more babies of the highest possible quality' and the deliberate creation of an elite. What the enemies of the race sought, however, was 'a mindless, brainless proletariat such as the welfare state is so admirably designed to produce'. Two issues later, BNP activist Eric Brand expressed his concern 'that such Tory arguments were allowed space in a Nationalist journal'. To imply that the low paid and the unemployed were all inferior and the prudent superior, Brand declared, was to blame the masses for a situation that their supposed superiors had brought about. (*Spearhead* 189, July; 191, September 1984.)

If even within the extreme right, eugenics came under fire, its adoption by the Third Reich has driven it to the margins of respectability in post-war society more generally. Furthermore, a large number of voters might be calculated to be highly resistant to the suggestion that those with disabilities should be eliminated or the proletariat discouraged from procreating. None the less, the BNP has remained committed, and publicly so, to a strongly eugenic policy. Writing in the late 1980s, Tyndall argued that while the state should not 'put pressure on people to have large families', they should be encouraged. In a healthy society, he declared, 'the best' would 'tend to proliferate and the worst not . . . through the sensible and just provision of incentives and rewards at one end of the social scale and the correct imposition of penalties and deterrents at the other'. It was precisely such views that appeared in the party's general election manifestos. In the manifesto for 1983, the BNP declared that 'choice of family size' was 'a private matter to be decided by parents themselves' but called for the removal of 'all present economic discouragements' of the growth of large families among 'intelligent, healthy and industrious stock'. The 1992 manifesto suggested that social benefits had encouraged 'the breeding of the least responsible', lowering 'the quality of the population', and proposed instead that they should be altered to encourage larger families among 'our most valuable people (the majority)' and discourage them among 'our least valuable people (a minority)'. (Tyndall 1988: 313, 400–1; British National Party 1983: 17; 1992: 11.)

This description of those fit to have children as the majority was, no doubt, intended to assure BNP supporters that they would not be excluded from that happy band. The 1997 manifesto, in its treatment of the subject, did not attempt to quantify who exactly was to be found in the 'underclass' which, it suggested, a carefully created system of child allowances should avoid encouraging in its 'breeding'. The alienation of potential supporters may also have been lessened by the party's linking of its stance on eugenics with that on law and order. While the 1992 manifesto declared that it would deal with 'the breeding of criminal types', in 1997 the party promised to 'do everything possible to discourage the breeding of hereditary criminal classes'. But that eugenics should appear in the manifestos at all is a marker of its central role in the party's world-view (British National Party 1992: 19; 1997: 20, 35.)

As we have seen, for both the National Front and the British National Party, population has been a vital concern. Within mainstream British parties, however, arguments about the birth-rate, let alone about eugenics, have been little evident. But there has been considerable debate around a number of developments concerning reproduction. Of these, the most important, both for society in general and the British extreme right in particular, is abortion, and it is to that issue that the remainder of this chapter will be devoted.

Originating as a bill put forward by the Liberal MP David Steel and enjoying the support of the then Labour government, the 1967 Abortion Act allowed a woman to terminate her pregnancy if two doctors were agreed that its continuance involved a greater risk to her life or her physical or mental health or if there was a substantial risk that the child would be 'seriously handicapped'. In the years that followed a number of attempts to amend the Act were made, some seeking to change the grounds on which abortion might be obtained, others attempting to lower the time limit after which an abortion would no longer be permissible. While the 1967 Act was to remain substantially in place (there was a nominal lowering of the time limit in 1990) the issue has remained highly controversial, both for those who believe that the most important factor was a woman's right to choose and those who hold instead that the central question is the right to life of 'the unborn child'. If, for the pro-choice camp, the 1967 Act goes part (but not all) of the way in recognising a woman's right to abortion, for pro-life activists abortion is to be opposed on principle. It is an opposition that is often misunderstood. Although disproportionately Catholic, the anti-abortion movement contains evangelical Christians, Muslims and others and is much more likely to use secular than religious arguments in its campaigning. Although more likely to be supported by Conservative MPs than those of other parties, the movement has supporters of different political persuasions and even contains some who define themselves as feminists. Finally, in arguing that abortion is wrong, it is not arguing that it is British or white abortions that are at issue. It is an argument it applies universally, in opposition to the very eugenics to which many on the extreme right are drawn. As I have argued elsewhere, to use the term 'right wing' to describe the Society for the Protection of Unborn Children or LIFE, the two main pro-life organisations, is more likely to obscure our understanding of them than illuminate it. (See Marsh and Chambers 1981: 17; Durham 1991: 16–38, 161–78.) This is even more the case when we consider the relationship between the anti-abortion movement and the extreme right. Yet, as we have seen, both before the war and since, the extreme right has often vociferously opposed abortion. In examining the stance that the National Front and the British National Party have taken towards the issue, we will be particularly concerned to explore two questions. First, on what basis has the extreme right opposed abortion? Second, if it has often opposed it, why has it not always done so?

Despite the passing of the 1967 Abortion Act, in the first year of its existence, the National Front, somewhat surprisingly, initially paid almost no attention to the issue. *Spearhead* had opposed the introduction of the Abortion Bill and continued to oppose the Act after it was passed, while in 1971 the party paper attacked 'the vile practice of abortion'. It was not, however, until 1974 that the NF was to take up the issue. Although absent from its manifesto, the decision was taken to include opposition to abortion in the NF's election address for the October 1974 general election. The result was a dispute within the organisation which was to lead to what *Spearhead* called 'very passionate exchanges' at the NF's subsequent Annual General Meeting. While it was ultimately agreed that the NF was opposed to abortion on demand, the meeting also voted to allow terminations 'if special medical grounds required', and in a subsequent article, Martin Webster declared that the AGM had not only rejected the stance on abortion which had been put forward during the election but recognised that it was not the function of a political party to 'adopt official policies on questions pertaining to private morality'. (*Britain First* 25 March–7 April (1972); NF election address 1974; *Spearhead* 17, November–December 1967; 27, November 1969; 81, February; 82, March 1975.)

Such a view was not likely to pass without comment either within the NF or within the pages of *Spearhead* and, shortly after, a letter from Malcolm Skeggs, like Webster and Tyndall a veteran of the 1960s, appeared arguing that while Webster was right that the NF should not 'promote policies on issues affecting private morality', this did not apply to abortion. The taking of human life, he argued, could not be seen as a private matter and it was legitimate for a political party to seek to do something about it. For another correspondent, shortly afterwards, however, it was Skeggs' view that was unacceptable. Instead of opposing legal abortion, Joan Sandland argued, activists should

> work within the framework of the party to fight for the sort of conditions in this country that will stop our young couples being driven to the despair of the necessity of an abortion, when they would much prefer to have a child. The answer to the high number of abortions, is to withdraw the need, not to drive women back to the back street butcher.

(*Spearhead* 84, May; 88, October 1975; for Skeggs, see *Spearhead* 103, March 1977.)

While Sandland, as we have seen, was soon to leave the organisation, the issue was not to go away. In one article in late 1977, Tyndall criticised not the Abortion Act as such but its 'flagrant abuse'. More importantly, the following year *Spearhead* published an article that noted that while most members were 'opposed to mass abortion . . . there are a number who disagree'. Consequently, the author suggested, the arguments against abortion needed to be looked at again. The Abortion Act, he declared, was 'the logical offspring of the Permissive Society', whereby the denial of 'life to hundreds of thousands of babies a year' was portrayed as essential to the liberation of women and the advancement of human dignity. 'For nationalists', he added, 'there are even more cogent arguments to put forward.' For the white race to resort to abortion was to be driven by a death wish at a time when 'the already disproportionately high coloured birthrate' threatened racial survival. Those who favoured abortion, he claimed, were seeking to destroy Western society by destroying the family. Spengler had seen that a civilisation declined when 'the having of children became a matter of debate'. But abortion was not only a failure of nerve. 'Above all, it is a calculated weapon in the hands of the nation-wreckers'. (*Spearhead* 112, December 1977; 120, August 1978.)

Six months later, reporting on the next NF AGM, *Spearhead* noted that 'Lively debate again surrounded the issue of abortion' as Richard Verrall, seconded by Melanie Dixon of the Young National Front, defended a resolution calling for the repeal of the Abortion Act and for abortion to be allowed only on genuine medical grounds. The meeting, it noted, had been told that abortion 'could not be considered a matter of private morality' and the motion was carried. The Abortion

Act, the resolution argued, was 'immoral and disastrous' and provided abortion on demand. Party policy should only allow abortion 'when medical opinion deems it necessary to save the life or protect the health of the mother' and the NF 'should support the creation of a society in which British mothers have no economic fears of having children – through higher family allowances, cost of living-linked maternity grants and other such measures – rather than support the legalised murder of babies'. Such a policy, it was held, was not 'in conflict with previous resolutions which have regarded matters of private morality as falling outside the consideration of political policy. Killing unborn children is not a matter of private morality but of absolute morality, racial health and the sanctity of our children's life.' Within the NF's National Directorate, however, argument over abortion continued, with Tyndall's leading inner-party opponent, Andrew Fountaine, criticising the issuing of a leaflet describing NF policy as being against abortion on demand without the Directorate's approval and before the AGM had discussed the issue. He also attempted to have opposition to abortion removed from the party's proposed Statement of Policy. Neither move was successful, and the Statement called for the repeal of the Abortion Act and the granting of 'abortion rights only on genuine medical grounds'. Similarly, the NF's election manifesto for the 1979 general election called for the repeal of the Abortion Act. Abortion would only be legal, it declared, in cases where 'it was judged by a qualified medical practitioner to be necessary to the health of the woman concerned'. (*Spearhead* 126, February 1979; NF 1979 AGM Agenda; NF National Directorate minutes, 28 January, 24 February 1979; National Front 1979b; 1979a: 56.)

Following the 1979 debacle, debate on abortion continued in Fountaine's short-lived breakaway NF Constitutional Movement. At the organisation's AGM in November 1980 the first motion for debate, proposed and seconded by two former NF activists, Susan McKenzie and Jean White, was to resolve 'that the issue of abortion is purely a matter of individual conscience' rather than policy and to repudiate 'any purported previous decision' on the issue. The motion was carried, the conference report claiming that it had been argued that the vote was not 'on the moral issue' but only on its irrelevance when a nationalist government's need to consider the issue was a distant proposition. A critical letter in a subsequent issue of the NFCM magazine, however, complained that the motion had favoured the provision of 'abortion as and when it suits the mother'. (*Excalibur* November 1980, January 1981.)

Within the NF itself during this period, there appeared to be little concern with the issue, although its 1983 election manifesto declared that an NF government would 'only tolerate abortions' in cases of rape, serious damage or malformation of the foetus or 'where medical opinion asserts that there is a genuine and serious danger to the health or life of the mother'. After the 1986 split, however, the political soldier wing became particularly animated on the question. In 1987, *National Front News* published 'Abortion: The Nationalist View'. Abortion, it claimed, was 'the greatest and most fundamentally evil holocaust that the world has ever seen', a slaughter which was 'against Natural Law' and had to be 'opposed vigorously'. Partly in a question and answer format, the article held that abortion was 'the destruction of a genetically unique individual', a being which possessed 'a soul from the moment of conception' and which women had no right to kill. What of cases of rape or 'massive deformity' of the foetus, it asked, replying that 'Most Nationalists believe that abortion must be permitted under these extreme circumstances.' As for what could be done to stop abortion, two groups that took a pro-life stance, LIFE and the Society for the Protection of Unborn Children, existed throughout the country, but support for abortion was 'firmly entrenched within today's materialist system' and could only be defeated by a revolution, based on natural laws. 'The only political and social movement in these islands which fully embraces this concept of total revolution is the National Front.' (National Front 1983: 21; *National Front News* 97, November 1987.)

As with Matthews's critique of eugenics before the 1986 split, we can see here how the particular form of radicalism espoused by the political soldiers was shaped not only by Distributism but by a broader Catholic social theory. Yet in the letters column of the paper in the following months, abortion proved to be a highly contentious issue. For one of those who wrote in, the problem was that the NF had not gone far enough. To recognise that life began at conception, it was argued, meant that abortion could 'never be allowed under any circumstances'. In the case of rape, 'the infant' should not be 'murdered for the vile actions of its father', while with 'regard to handicapped babies – who are we to judge what their quality of life is to be?' Another correspondent, however, complained that *National Front News* was marred by its 'excessive anti-abortion line'. It was a mother's right to choose abortion; under the present system, there would be many abortions while 'in the society we hope to build, things will be better and not too many will want abortions anyway'. The letter finished with an attack on the previous correspondent's 'disgusting' opposition to allowing abortions to rape victims, only to receive an immediate editorial reply which declared that the organisation was opposed to liberal individualism. 'The majority of NF members hold a spiritual view of life', it claimed, and believed the soul existed from conception. They accepted that 'abortion in the case of severe handicap, or after rape' was 'the lesser of two evils' but no true Nationalist could support abortion for selfish reasons, 'a brutal attack on the most helpless and innocent section of their community'. (*National Front News* 99, December 1987; 102, February 1988.)

But the subject of this reply was not the only defender of abortion, and soon after another letter-writer argued that a generalised opposition to abortion would alienate many potential women supporters. The foetus was not a child but part of a woman's body and it was the right of both the parents to decide if a termination should be carried out. The NF's anti-abortion policy, the writer suggested, discriminated against the poor and was incompatible with the need to reduce urban population and return to the land. Such a view received short shrift from other correspondents. For one, the heart and brain activity of the embryo confirmed its independent status and to defend life and the family was not class-discriminatory but a fundamental tenet of the NF's Third Position politics. For another, the paper had been at fault to publish a letter 'diametrically opposed to our position' or at least an editorial comment should have been attached. Far from 'putting women off from joining the NF', the writer suggested, 'there must be many women who long to have a family but who cannot' who believed in the intrinsic value of human life. Two further correspondents likewise objected to a defence of abortion, but in significantly different ways. To tell the poor to have an abortion, one claimed, was itself class-discriminatory, an 'evil Tory philosophy'; the answer to poverty, the other argued, was not abortion but the NF's policy of Distributism. Both, likewise, took the view that 'all good nationalists' should know that life began at conception. Where they differed, however, was in how they treated race. For one, an unborn child had the right to life 'whether it's Black, White or Yellow'. For the other, where the earlier correspondent had advocated reducing Britain's population, 'we need more European children if our race is to survive'. They had called 'the anti-abortion case "*reactionary*"', I call it the programme of preserving our Race, the principle purpose of the NF!' (*National Front News* 104, April; 105, June 1988; 106, n.d. (1988).)

The debate had revealed a wide array of views within NF circles, from support for abortion rights to an equally astonishing support for the right to life for all races. One later correspondent even argued that he and other 'comrades' believed the NF was right to oppose abortion but wrong to favour the death penalty. The movement, he declared, should take a consistent pro-life stance. But amid this array of views, an anti-abortion stance was clearly prevalent and it was that which continued to be espoused in the pages of *National Front News*. In 1989 the NF's Oldham unit reported on its local anti-abortion campaign, including the publication of a leaflet, 'Today My Mother Killed Me'. A new version of the leaflet was now planned, it announced, and 'those comrades who feel particularly strongly about the Life issue' were urged to send money. A subsequent issue called on NF supporters to 'join those societies dedicated to the preservation of life' and to distribute Oldham NF's 'excellent' leaflet. (Oldham members, indeed, not only attended local LIFE meetings but had even succeeded in getting the chairman of the Oldham LIFE group to address an NF meeting.) Increasingly, however, attention was being given to the 'effective pro-life direct action movement' which had emerged in the United States and now existed in Britain. It was a movement, the paper declared, that was 'reminiscent of the Rumanian Legion of St Michael Archangel – the Iron Guard, in its militancy, discipline, sacrifice and spiritual emphasis'. An account was published of the first national action of the Rescue-Pro-Life Action Network, in which twenty-three people were arrested after blocking the entrance to a London abortion clinic, and one correspondent contrasted the 'militant approach' of 'the dynamic new anti-abortion group' to that of other anti-abortion organisations. The message was clear, the correspondent wrote: 'Direct action on the streets to save the unborn child.' This increased emphasis on anti-abortion activity linked not only with NF militants' convictions but also with an important shift in strategy, with *Nationalism Today* calling for the setting up of 'a myriad of militant cells'. In organisations ranging 'from animal welfare to ecology and from racial separatists to pro-life groups', it declared, 'our networking influence must be brought to bear'. But if the NF was taking up abortion more strongly than ever before, it would have little impact. The letter calling for direct action appeared in the last issue of *National Front News*, the one which announced the organisation's dissolution. (*National Front News* 108, n.d. (1988); 118, n.d. (1989); 120, n.d. (1989); 102, February 1988; 121, n.d. (1989); 122, n.d. (1989); 126, n.d (1990); *Searchlight* October 1987, March, August 1988; *Nationalism Today* 46, n.d. (1989).)

If the political soldiers were predominantly opposed to abortion, what of the other two organisations? An early article in the *Flag*, entitled (and repeating as its concluding phrase) 'Abortion is Murder. Repeal the Abortion Act!', held that human life began when an egg was fertilised. There were, it declared, 'few medical reasons for abortions ... Many pregnancies are preventable and a lot of abortions are the result of promiscuity.' Yet in a subsequent issue of *Vanguard*, another article attacking abortion was published under the heading 'Debate'. 'The subject of abortion', it was suggested, had 'traditionally been a very controversial one within Nationalist circles, and debates on the subject have in the past generated more heat than light'. None the less, it argued, the subject was too important to be ignored and readers' comments would be welcome. The article held that in a society as 'advanced as ours in matters of contraception . . . and sexual education there should be no need for abortion'. Humans existed from the moment of conception and 'Every individual has the right to choose life'. Abortion, however, killed human beings, brutalised society and 'usually' injured the woman herself, either physically or psychologically. In the magazine's letters column two issues later, however, an East Midlands single parent (her letter ending 'Yours for Race and Nation') argued that while she had chosen to have her child, it had been a choice and that it was women who should make that choice. This in turn elicited a reply from 'a Nationalist and father' who insisted that there was no right to abortion ('Handicapped children have just as much right to life as the rest of us') and that childbirth, 'the continuation of the species', was the point of existence. (*Flag* 4, December 1986; *Vanguard* 20, July; 22, September; 23, October 1988.)

Despite such disagreement, the *Flag* group continued to oppose abortion. In 1990, denouncing leading politicians of all three major parties for their position on the question, it claimed that only 'a National Front Government would purge our Nation of this terrible scourge'. In its 1992 election manifesto, the exact language used in the pre-split NF was reiterated – abortion would only be allowed in cases of rape, 'genuine and serious danger' to the woman's health or life or serious damage or malformation of the foetus. Such a policy, Tina Wingfield proclaimed in the party paper, rested on a fundamental commitment to civil liberties. The liberties of an unborn child, she suggested, took precedence over those of a woman who, 'given that contraception is widely available', had chosen, by not using it, to run 'the risk of pregnancy'. In the case of rape, however, the pregnancy itself represented a denial of civil liberty. If the *Flag* group continued to adhere to the policy reached in the days of Tyndall's NF, unsurprisingly so did the BNP. In 1983 its general election manifesto declared that it was 'utterly opposed to Abortion on demand' and was 'pledged to amend the Abortion Act so as to make Abortion available only to women who can provide evidence of genuine medical need' while in its 1992 manifesto it argued that repeal of the abortion law would end 'the lawful murder of hundreds of thousands of mostly healthy and normal British children'. Only in cases of rape 'or when medical evidence indicates either that the child would be born with serious physical handicap or that childbirth might seriously endanger the life or health of the mother-to-be' would abortion be legal. (*Flag* 48, November 1990; 63, n.d. (1992); National Front 1992: 30; British National Party 1983: 17; British National Party 1992: 20–1.)

Other BNP literature has made clear the assumptions which lie behind such statements. In his book, *The Eleventh Hour*, Tyndall argued that one reason, although not the only one, for the repeal of the abortion law was to reverse the fall in the birth-rate. Liberal abortion encouraged 'a totally irresponsible attitude towards sexual relations' and those women who supported it were rejecting their 'duty to posterity, to the blood, to the task of continuance of family and race'. This emphasis on race was particularly evident in early 1988, when an attempt by the Liberal MP David Alton to restrict abortion was reported on the front page of *British Nationalist* under the headline, 'Abortion Means Race Suicide'. The attempt of the MP to lower the time limit for legal abortion from twenty-eight weeks to eighteen, it declared, had led to demonstrations by 'the scum of the political underworld' and had been opposed by all the major party leaders. Yet it had been 'a weak and flabby piece of legislation' put forward by a 'half-baked compromiser' whose refusal to attempt to ban abortion on demand seemed to indicate an acceptance that people could 'indulge in unrestricted irresponsible sex without having to worry about the consequences'. Birth control had been encouraged, abortion had stopped the births of 'good, healthy, Anglo-Saxon or Celtic stock' and no government, least of all Margaret Thatcher's, had done anything to stop it. Only the banning of abortion except under exceptional circumstances could restore morality and avert 'the eventual biological extinction of the British people'. (Tyndall 1988: 313, 605–6; *British Nationalist* 76, February 1988.)

When the debate over abortion became particularly prominent in Britain some years later, the BNP returned to the subject again. In doing so, however, it rejected the view that there were only two sides to the argument. Those who took the pro-choice side, it noted, were opposed by pro-lifers who argued 'against any abortion at all' and who, in the case of the leading figure in LIFE, took the view that 'nearly all contraception is a form of abortion and hence is wrong'.

The BNP, in contrast, 'occupies what may be termed the middle ground', rejecting abortion 'for convenience' but holding that in other cases 'there *is* a place for abortion'. The cases were described as 'almost entirely' consisting of rape, 'severe handicap' and risk to the mother's health. These exemptions, of course, were the familiar ones of BNP policy. In an accompanying article, however, another example was given, one which reminds us not only that the BNP takes a different view from that of the pro-life movement but why it should be described in rather different terms than 'middle ground'. The example the BNP decided to discuss was the much-publicised controversy surrounding a woman who was carrying eight embryos following fertility treatment. The woman, the article noted, was white, while her partner was black. 'Such a relationship is to be regretted at the best of times', and rather than merely selectively terminating some of the embryos so that some could survive, it would be best, the article suggested, for the woman to 'abort the pregnancy entirely for the good of society'. (*British Nationalist* 171, September 1996.)

For the National Front in the 1980s, the contradiction between a pro-life stance and racism had resulted in considerable ideological confusion. For the BNP, however, there was little doubt that racial purity stood paramount and that a politics which did not prioritise eugenics was one that was not to be accepted. But, as we have already seen, even here not everyone spoke with one voice. In 1990, an article appeared in *Spearhead* with the title, 'A Woman's Viewpoint on Embryo Research'. Most Christians, the author complained, failed to recognise the dangers of 'downbreeding' and consequently were opposed to research into human embryos through which we could discover how to eliminate genetic disorders and 'ensure that people could have healthy children'. For them, all human life was sacred and such research was seen as 'reminiscent of Nazi Germany'. This, she declared, was to adopt arguments which were ignorant and superstitious. Until more was known, genetic engineering was best avoided. But embryo research, like 'positive eugenics through taxation and by education and propaganda', deserved support. In part, the article was sounding a more cautious note than the nationalist Utopia (or, more accurately, dystopia) Tony Wells had portrayed in his extended cogitations on population the year before. But it was also a deliberate challenge to the pro-life movement, the leading opponents of embryo research, and in a reply two months later, a correspondent argued that such research could never be countenanced because it was God who brought about birth and endowed children with immortal souls. But this was not the only such disagreement among BNP supporters. The previous year, another writer's suggestion that 'aborting severely handicapped babies' should be compulsory had led to a sharp reply that there could be *'no* justification for killing an innocent Aryan'. The race could develop the technology to conquer handicap, and no-one, it was held, had the right to climb on a pedestal and decide which of the race should live and which should die. (*Spearhead* 255, May; 257, July 1990; 246, August; 248, October 1989.)

If there was dispute in the BNP press over eugenics, it also appears that the party itself was uncertain how important it was to oppose abortion and on what grounds termination might be permissible. In part, the latter may be noted in the difference between the 1983 manifesto's argument that only strict medical reasons could be justification for abortion and the inclusion of other grounds in the 1992 manifesto. There is even more suggestive evidence in the changing content of the regular 'What We Stand For' section of the party's paper. In the August–September 1989 issue, as it had done for some time, this included a call for the repeal of 'the laws permitting Abortion and Homosexuality' and a tightening up of legislation against obscenity in the media. The following issue, however, dropped explicit reference to abortion, calling instead for an 'effort to restore traditional moral values, aimed at strengthening the family and recreating the fabric for a sound and healthy social order'. Four months later, the column was changed again, urging 'Repeal of the laws permitting homosexuality and abortion (except where the latter is a result of rape or necessary on medical grounds)'. The new section went on to call for 'the wiping out of AIDS and a return to healthy moral values aimed at strengthening the family and community'. After yet another reformulation in March 1995, however, only the call for a return to healthy moral values had survived, the references to abortion, homosexuality and AIDS all disappearing. That the BNP should link together its opposition to abortion with an abhorrence of homosexuality and a call for the restoration of traditional moral values is not surprising. We have already touched on the extreme right's objections to sexual permissiveness and, in chapter 7, we will explore the question further. In the final chapter, in discussing how the extreme right's views of women are linked with its attitude towards men, we will address a question already raised with regard to the NF at the end of the 1970s – the question of homosexuality. Here, however, it is not the links between the BNP's opposition to abortion, permissiveness and homosexuality which should detain us but the inconsistency of that concern. In particular, if we are to assume that abortion is a major issue for the BNP, why does it sometimes disappear from the party's summary of its policy and why, come to that, does it at other times return? (*British Nationalist* 93, August–September; 94, October 1989; 98, February 1990; 153, March 1995.)

In the 1930s, when National Socialism was vigorously repressing abortion, the BUF, in ignoring the issue, may well have been influenced by the assumption that it was of little concern in Britain. For the BNP, however, the availability of abortion is both evident and abhorrent. But there are inconsistencies in both its policy and the significance that is attributed to it. One possibility is that it has been more successful than the National Front in concealing internal differences on the issue. Where the NF, in both the 1970s and 1980s, permitted open debate on abortion, the BNP, with its strong emphasis on a single leader, is likely to have been far more wary about showing disagreement. At first sight, it would appear to be intransigently opposed to abortion. Closer examination, however, suggests that even in the BNP, the types of disagreement that have surfaced in the NF (and, for instance, in Germany's Republikaner) may also be taking place. The modern extreme right is, indeed, drawn to pro-natalism, to eugenics and to a strongly anti-abortion stance. But in a situation in which many women object to restrictions on abortion, where the extreme right needs electoral support and where eugenics alienates both its potential targets and many religious believers, parties such as the National Front and even the British National Party do not always adopt the policies on abortion or on population that we might expect.

7 The home and the homeland

In chapter 6 we explored the modern British extreme right's stance on population and abortion. But these are not the only concerns that have entered into its policies towards women. One, the impact of sexual permissiveness, was touched on at the end of chapter 6. Two others have also been alluded to – its attitude towards the modern feminist movement and its violent objection to inter-racial sexual relationships. In addition to these, one other area is of particular importance – its attempt to respond to the decline of the 'traditional family'. In examining these four areas, feminism and the 'crisis of the family' will be discussed before permissiveness and, finally, race. In part, this order has been adopted because these issues fall into two different categories. For the groupings that came together to form the National Front, changing sexual values were already causing anxiety and their vehement objection to immigration was already entangled with feelings about sexual contact between racial groups. Feminism and concern about the state of the family, however, had not yet achieved the same prominence and would present the new organisation with problems that groups earlier in the 1960s had not had to encounter. By discussing the four areas we have selected in this particular order, we will be able to see where the NF was inheriting a view from its immediate predecessors and where it was forced to innovate. But it will also help us to better appreciate the ways in which the modern extreme right in Britain differs from the BUF. For Mosley's movement, the conflict between men and women over jobs was of greater importance than the issue of population. For the NF and the BNP, however, not only is population central to its battle for the nation, but it is profoundly shaped by an issue that almost passed the BUF by. For the BUF, there was little sense of the racial 'Other' as sexual rival. For the modern extreme right, it is crucial.

For the BUF, as we have seen, the existence of a feminist movement had had an impact on the forging of its policy towards women. But feminism was already weaker than it had been in the days of the suffrage movement, and it would weaken yet further in the decades that followed before it re-emerged again in the late 1960s. The extreme right groupings which had immediately preceded the inception of the NF had little need to consider the question (although, it should be noted, one article *Spearhead* published in 1966 had already managed to link the rise of sexual permissiveness to a conspiracy to encourage 'the power of the female . . . at the expense of the already debilitated male'). The NF, we might anticipate, would not welcome the revival of feminism. Initially, however, this was far from clear. In the early 1970s, when *Spearhead* published an imaginary Question and Answer session with potential NF voters, the question was asked, how it saw 'Women's Lib'. In some fields, it declared, it was right that full opportunities for women now existed but any legislation that assumed that women were 'cut out for the same roles in life as men' could not be supported. The issue was raised again shortly after. *Spearhead*, it was argued, could not give 'a straight answer of yes or no' to such a question. Like 'many other causes', it was 'neither wholly good nor wholly bad'. (*Spearhead* 13, November–December 1966; 62, March; 69, October 1973.)

But if the NF had been concerned that a simple denunciation of feminism might alienate voters, this moment appears to have passed and just as its October 1974 election address had opposed abortion, so too its manifesto declared its revulsion at the 'inversion of the age-old natural instinct of young men to aspire to masculinity and young women to femininity'. If this theme was to surface in election propaganda, it was even more prominent in other party literature. *Spearhead*, for instance, denounced a declaration by the National Union of Teachers that sexist books should no longer be available in schools. 'What conceivable point', it asked, 'could there be in eradicating the obvious truth that women are weaker than men, that male and female have biologically-based inclinations, the latter to childbirth and motherhood? What advantage is there in obscuring sexual differences and dehumanising the distinct qualities of manhood and womanhood?' It was communism, the magazine suggested, that stood to gain by undermining tradition and promoting division. In opposing feminism, NF writers sought to argue that they were in tune with new thinking among scientists. Recent developments in biology, Richard Verrall argued, showed racialists to be correct in holding that 'man is . . . the product of his genetic inheritance'. Sociobiologists were vindicating the arguments of such figures as Gobineau and Galton and for feminists to claim that sexual roles were socially constructed was nonsense. 'One has only to observe the degree to which male dominance and female passivity in sexual courtship obtains in the animal world, likewise qualities of male aggression and female domesticity, to understand their fundamental biological basis.' (National Front 1974:13; *Spearhead* 94, May 1976; 127, March 1979.)

Spearhead also published an abridged translation of an essay on 'The Feminine Condition', by Alain de Benoist, the founder of the French Nouvelle Droite. The essay drew widely for its claims. Endocrinology, it was argued, had established that there were physical differences between the male and female brain, with men having a natural urge to dominate, and women to submit. Psychoanalysis too was called on, with one of its pioneers, Carl Jung, being cited expressing concern at the trend for women 'to learn masculine callings, to become active in politics, to found and lead societies etc.' Some good had come from these efforts, Jung declared, but it was impossible to ignore that 'in taking up a masculine calling, studying, and working in a man's way', women were injuring their feminine nature. (*Spearhead* 113, January 1978.)

Such views continued to be expressed in the *Spearhead*'s pages following its defection from the NF. One article, drawing on sociobiology, claimed that men and women had different natures: 'in general males are competitive . . . and dominant over women; women are nurturant and home-loving'. The falling quality of the race, it was claimed, could be attributed partly to an 'excess of autonomy' on the part of women: 'When women are given the freedom to do so they will usually under-produce.' On another occasion, *Spearhead* published an extract from the writings of one of the most influential writers on the post-war extreme right, Francis Parker Yockey. Attacking liberalism, Yockey argued that it wanted 'every day to be a birthday, life to be a long party . . . Liberalism is an escape from hardness into softness, from masculinity into femininity.' What, he declared, was feminism but a means of feminising men? History was masculine, and liberal 'tampering with sexual polarity' was doomed to failure. The extract was accompanied by a commentary by Tyndall. It was, he argued, an 'eternal fact' that Yockey had spoken of when he described History as masculine, and when liberalism feminised the male it would inevitably mean that a society, unless it returned to masculinity, was doomed to succumb to stronger forces. (*Spearhead* 205, November 1985; 295, September 1993.)

If gender confusion was the danger, what part had feminism played in it? In 1989 the magazine published an article on 'the blight' affecting relationships between the sexes. In better days, it claimed, a 'sexual mystique' had prevailed. Now, however, the reproduction of the race was endangered as polarity turned to uniformity and feminism, divorce and materialism blurred 'the old lines of gender'. The 'writings of white nationalists', it was suggested, had almost completely failed to discuss sexuality, an omission which urgently needed to be repaired. The account that followed was not completely what we might expect. Women, it was claimed, had been right to oppose 'the man-centredness of the West' and nationalists should 'encourage the participation of women in daily life'. The overall tone, however, was far from favourable to what was described as 'extreme feminism'. Women, it was claimed, no longer sought complementarity but superiority and 'The dreadful spectre of the "career woman"' had arisen. In response, men had resisted encroachment and had lost 'their old respect', their 'sense of vague awe'. What was needed, then, was to build first within the BNP, and ultimately within the nation, a way of life in which men were once again men, and women women. (*Spearhead* 246, August 1989.)

The BNP's inclinations were made clearer still in an article which appeared the same year in its paper, *British Nationalist*. Under the headline, 'Women Turning Away From Feminism', it welcomed a newspaper report that women were beginning to reject the blurring of sexual differences. In the past, it was suggested, 'millions of women (and men)', had succumbed to the 'hoax' of feminism and the disparagement of domesticity and motherhood. But now there was an opportunity to break with the

> counsellors of decadence and recognise again the importance of . . . traditional biological roles. This did not mean that we have to close the career doors to those women who are determined on pursuing careers . . . If a few women want to make careers, let them. But let the majority be encouraged to be housewives and mothers first and foremost.

It was this view that the party would promote in the years that followed. With 'a sensible number of exceptions', another article declared the following year, young women should 'be encouraged to return to the proud and honourable profession of motherhood'. Nobody in their right mind, it claimed, 'would wish to deny careers to those women absolutely determined on them'. But only by encouraging women to be housewives and mothers could 'generations of young men' be available to the nation. (*British Nationalist* 96, December 1989; 99, March 1990.)

So crucial were such views to the party that they were to be found in its 1992 election manifesto, which argued that there needed to be 'a very basic review' of the role of women. 'We have no wish', it claimed, 'to withdraw from women those fundamental rights under the law' that they had won in the twentieth century. But they were not suited to the same roles as men. If given the chance, the majority of women, 'would naturally and voluntarily choose to be mothers and home-makers . . . Those women who are determined to make careers for themselves should have no legal barriers placed in their way' except when they sought to enter such unsuitable roles as combat positions in the armed forces. But 'the concept of the career woman' could not be a 'national and social ideal' and instead the BNP would 'encourage our womenfolk to regard home – and family-making' as their 'highest vocation'. (British National Party 1992: 11–12.)

In the mid-1980s, it will be recalled, a BNP woman activist had suggested that the BNP should avoid antagonising women who worked. By taking the view it did, however, the party seems to have decided that emphasising women's domestic role is not only crucial but unlikely to alienate potential voters. Such views, however, were not even universally well received among readers of *Spearhead*. The BNP's 1995 decision to attempt to attract more women resulted in several letters in the magazine, one of which accused it of publishing 'directly insulting' articles suggesting 'that women do not qualify as human beings capable of having legitimate interests'. Nor did the writer, the former NF candidate for Canterbury in the 1979 general election, Joan White, confine her comments to *Spearhead*. 'I am', she wrote, 'surprised that there is any aim to recruit women into the BNP; I really thought they were being intentionally excluded.' Yet, for some women, the party's stance was attractive rather than abhorrent. In the same issue in which White's letter appeared, a woman writer argued that only the BNP was committed to protecting women's rights. Establishment politicians, she declared, claimed to oppose pornography because it degraded women yet had brought about the permissiveness which had led to pornography's increase. They had presided over increased attacks on women, and where today sex offenders received short sentences or even fines, the BNP was committed to tougher punishment. As for rights at work, she suggested, the BNP had 'always believed that women should be free to pursue the career of their choice'. But it also believed that women who wanted to raise families should be able to do so and, she went on, 'I personally believe women should be paid a state wage (*not* a "benefit") for choosing to fulfil their social responsibilities.' Such a policy would 'restore to young children' the full-time care they often lacked and would take women out of the labour market while increasing consumer spending. It would be voluntary – women could 'select to return to work after childbearing' – but would no longer 'be compelled to compete' with men in the marketplace. If British women wanted less crime, a strong family and economic support for motherhood, she concluded, then the BNP was 'the only logical choice'. (*Spearhead* 314, April 1995.)

In the general election that followed, however, few women were to draw such a conclusion. The BNP's manifesto, as we would expect, emphasised Britain's economic decline and called for the creation of a wholly white society. But it did not forget to put forward also its views on gender. It was those who were most intelligent, it lamented, who had been persuaded by 'propaganda for female careers' to go 'in droves into the professions and into business, placing family and children second'. In familiar tones, the manifesto linked this to a lowering of fertility among the 'most favourably endowed families', but this was not its only complaint. 'At a more general level', it claimed, the '"working woman" has resulted in the fewer children that are being born growing up in a domestic environment in which adequate parental love, care and supervision are often sadly lacking.' Feminism was to blame, and instead of promoting careers, it was the task of education to 'idealise traditional womanhood in all its beauty and glory, with the function of mother constituting the pinnacle of female achievement'. (British National Party 1997: 19.)

As such quotations richly illustrate, the BNP and, to a substantial degree, the NF before it, has been strongly anti-feminist. Yet we should not be led by this to conclude that extreme rightists always take this stance. Other groups have been considerably more hesitant, as was particularly evident in a ferociously anti-Semitic – but not anti-feminist – article which appeared in the political soldiers' magazine, *Nationalism Today*, in the mid-1980s. Written by a prominent NF activist, John Field, it criticised a failure to discuss women's rights in Nationalist publications. This, he declared, was wrong and if it was assumed that 'the heavy involvement of Jews, Lesbians and communists' in the women's movement condemned it, this ignored the fact that 'our goal is to protect and advance the whole White race – not just the 50 per-cent of it which happens to be male'. Early supporters of women's rights, he declared, had sought to gain justice for women and if, today, the women's movement was 'under Jewish control, it is simply another example where our Race has surrendered control of its own affairs'. Nationalists should not believe women's place was in the home. Certainly, in the society they sought, mothers would not be forced to work outside the home by economic necessity and motherhood would be the highest aspiration of white women. But women would not be stopped from working outside the home and, furthermore, in present-day society they faced real problems of job discrimination, sexual harassment and unequal pay. Nationalists, he concluded, should oppose attempts to divide white men and white women and support the fight for women's rights. (*Nationalism Today* 25, November 1984.)

In the event, as we will see, Field's faction of the NF would move away from this view. At the time, however, a letter by another party activist was published congratulating Field for putting forward 'the Movement's stance' concerning women's issues. So-called feminists, he claimed, were 'merely using the very real and genuine problems women face' as a way of advancing an 'alien-inspired' course. Instead, Nationalists should champion 'the cause of women'. (*Nationalism Today* 28, April 1985.)

If for one wing of the NF it was possible to envisage claiming feminism for a white nationalist movement, then within the other a debate soon afterwards between two of its leading activists brought to light disagreement about the women's movement not of today but of the past. The initial impulse came from former *Bulldog* editor Joe Pearce, who was reviewing a book by the radical feminist writer Andrea Dworkin. Attacking 'the folly of feminism', he quoted extensively from G. K. Chesterton on the importance of motherhood, sexual difference and how demands for women's emancipation had led to their entry into the same 'rat race' as men. Replying the next month, Tina Denny made it clear that she was not impressed by Pearce's (or Chesterton's) treatment of the 'struggle for the emancipation of women'. Women, she declared, had fought for 'political equality, education and the right to be the friend, not the humble dependent, of their husband' and the courage and determination of the Suffragette movement deserved 'more than a sneering paragraph in our magazine'. The modern feminist movement could not be supported. 'They are fighting for an absolute equality which Nationalists know to be illusory because human nature itself is inherently unequal.' But this should not mean that Nationalists should dismiss the movement which had secured equal citizenship for women earlier in the century. (*Vanguard* 12, September; 13, October 1987.)

Such views were not the settled policies of either wing of the movement. In the early 1990s, *Vanguard* published an article arguing that Nationalists should accept that the nature of society had changed and that women no longer played their traditional role. In an age in which strenuous manual labour was in decline and where families needed both partners to be in employment, then women should not be confined to the home. The nation would be weakened if it did not make full use of the talents of all its people and, indeed, when the NF's repatriation policy was implemented, women should take up many of the positions that fell vacant. But such an argument was untypical. *National Front News* in the late 1980s looked forward, it declared, 'to the birth of true women's groups who will promote the beauty of femininity and the sacred role of motherhood'. *Vanguard*, less poetically, was to publish an article which not only called for the restoration of traditional sex roles but declared that women should stop complaining about the supposed drudgery of housework! 'In the past', the writer declared, 'the men instinctively and unselfishly turned a protective shield around the family group. Nowadays in return for their trouble men get complaints from their womenfolk.' (*Vanguard* 40, n.d. (1993); 37, n.d. (1992); *National Front News* 105, June 1988.)

While both groups had published sympathetic comments on feminism, it was clearly not the dominant response. In part, the anti-feminism so evident in the movement linked effortlessly to an enthusiastic defence of the 'traditional' family. This had already been apparent in the late 1970s, when the same issue of *Spearhead* which had published de Benoist's musings on 'The Feminine Condition' had also included an article which began: 'The huge rise in juvenile delinquency is to a large degree the inevitable result of a growing number of mothers going out to work.' But it is perhaps most evident in a two-part article on the family which appeared a decade later in *Nationalism Today*. For the Tories, it claimed, the family was a matter of chasing votes but for the NF it was central. It enabled absolute values to be passed from generation to generation, yet in contemporary society 'the very *idea* of Family risks being extinguished by the malignant forces of the modern world'. The Industrial Revolution had seen 'a major assault on the family' in its elimination as an economic unit. People had been herded into cities and factories and 'a new class came into being: the working mother'. The mother's natural role of rearing children, building the home and supporting the breadwinner had crumbled and the family had come under even more attack from the rise of 'the so-called "Women's Liberation Movement", a movement less concerned with rectifying the genuine grievances of women . . . as with promoting an essential antipathy between Man and Woman'. On both left and right women were encouraged to pursue careers or to take such jobs as navvies or hod carriers, and with the sexes no longer recognising their essential difference there had arisen surrogate motherhood, genetic engineering and lesbians having children through artificial insemination. The family was facing eclipse and only by re-establishing it as the basis of Nationalist Revolution could 'the dream of National Revolution' ever become reality. (*Spearhead* 113, January 1978; *Nationalism Today* 43, n.d. (1988).)

It was the pre-eminent task of militants, the magazine argued, to espouse a 'pro-family' attitude. A future order would promote healthy values through the media, drawing particularly on the energies of traditionalists within the Church. The Distributist revolution would not only encourage small businesses and co-operatives but, by taking over the banks, would free families from the need to pay life-long mortgages. Women's 'social equality before the law' would be ensured and while they would usually aspire to motherhood, it could be combined with a profession. Finally, new legislation would deal with social ills. Compulsory pre-marriage counselling could be introduced to reduce the epidemic divorce rate, 'all public expression of deviancy' would be outlawed and the 'abolition of abortion, more widespread adoption counselling and tax incentives to raise large, healthy families' would avert the decline of the nation. The Movement of the Future, it declared, would be the Movement of the Family. (*Nationalism Today* 44, n.d. (1989).)

In the early 1980s, Joe Pearce declared in the same magazine that family life had 'been crumbling amid the perpetual onslaught of Jewish decadence' and that both capitalism and communism opposed strong Nordic families. Shortly after, it had denounced the increasing divorce rate as an 'encroachment upon the traditional British way of life by the alien forces of liberalism and capitalism'. The 'New Order', it pledged, would ensure that 'undue pressure is not put upon married couples' and 'strong families' would 'once more flourish'. (See *Nationalism Today* 4, n.d. (c. 1980); 11, n.d. (c. 1982).) In later years the political soldier wing of the NF took this approach, minus the somewhat Germanic imagery, and developed what it saw as a comprehensive family policy. But what of the other groups on the extreme right?

Just as earlier it had been argued that sociobiology supported the NF's views on sex roles, so, subsequently, the writings of the American conservative Charles Murray have been cited in support of the *Flag* group's views on the family. Nationalist support for 'the healthy two-parent family', one leading figure declared, was backed by the 'scientific research' of such figures as Murray. Rising crime, he had shown, was linked to the 'collapse of the traditional family' and the rise in births outside marriage – 'the fewer fathers in a community the more children ran wild'. The 1992 election manifesto, describing the family as 'the ideal social unit', criticised both rising divorce and the increased numbers of single-parent families. Increased family allowances and preferential housing policies, it argued, would strengthen family life and there should be an end to the pressures on 'girls to follow a profession rather than to have and rear children'. (*Vanguard* 31, July–September 1990; National Front 1992: 15–16.)

As for the BNP, we have already seen how in early 1995 *Spearhead* had published an article on why it was the only party which offered a 'genuine commitment to protect women's rights'. The previous month its author, Christine Stevenson, had been responsible for another article, this time arguing that the BNP was alone in having 'a coherent package of policies directed towards restoring and protecting the family unit'. Almost effortlessly, the article linked the BNP's concern with the family with the racism that gave it its purpose. The other parties, she declared, had attacked the family, and today the high divorce rate was creating a rapid rise in single-parent families while many young people lived alone, unable even to form a family relationship. Every form of degradation, from lesbianism to interracial marriage, was treated by the media as part of normal life, while immigration and the destruction of British industry had brought about mass unemployment and an obsession with consumer goods led to an unwillingness to have more than one child. The BNP, however, would turn television into a means of improving moral standards, remove immigrants from Britain and revive the economy, British families would be assured of employment and housing, mothers would be paid a wage to stay at home and look after their children and homosexuality and 'the more obscene forms of pornography' would be banned. The result, it was claimed, would be the creation of a country with 'stable, happy families . . . able to achieve their full reproductive potential'. (*Spearhead* 313, March 1995.)

In thus claiming to champion the family, the British extreme right has also sought to identify itself with the concerns of movements that have emerged from the early 1960s onwards in support of 'traditional' morality. The first such group, the Clean-Up TV Campaign (subsequently the National Viewers' and Listeners' Association) had been set up by Mary Whitehouse and others in protest at the 'disbelief, doubt and dirt' being transmitted into British homes. Subsequently, just as groups were established to oppose abortion, others came into existence to oppose the whole array of legislative and cultural changes that have been involved in the creation of the permissive society. (For a fuller discussion of campaigns against sexual permissiveness, see Durham 1991.) We saw earlier the extent to which the extreme right and the pro-life movement agree and the degree to which they diverge. Is there greater concurrence between racial nationalists and opponents of sexual permissiveness?

What the NF stood for, it declared in 1971, was the cleaning up of Britain: 'Put an end to filth and pornography. Replace the "Permissive Society" by a Responsible Society.' Already in the late 1960s it had described permissiveness as a symptom of national degeneracy, while in 1970 election literature had called for the protection of 'family life and decency' and 'the re-introduction of censorship of books, theatres, T.V. and radio'. Such views were elaborated in its publications. In 1971, for instance, *Spearhead* reprinted an article by a South African racist, Ivor Benson, on 'Permissiveness and Revolution'. Lenin, Benson implausibly claimed, had once declared 'We will undermine the youth of the West with sex and drugs' and what we had set in motion ever since had been 'a massive campaign of cultural subversion' intended to make society 'amenable to alien manipulation and control'. Another article, published towards the end of the previous decade, had summoned up a picture of a sinister-looking stranger being allowed into a family's house.

> It is the wife who is the subject of his first questions. He demands intimate details of her sexual life, speaks freely of abortion and perversions, tells her of the pleasures of 'free-love', and derides the institution of the family. His attention is then directed towards the young daughter and he points out to her the advantages of marriage with the coloured races . . . It is suggested that when she is older she should experience the delights of a lesbian relationship.

Having pressed on the son the delights of drug-taking and rebellion, the visitor 'produces photographs of masturbating men and women and claims that these are works of high cultural value'. He leaves, promising to return, and the writer brings the story to a close. 'What man', he asks, 'would invite such a monster into his home and expose his family to filth and sedition?' The answer, of course, is that many do, for the vile visitor is the television set and the answer to the danger it represents is to make the transmission of material 'which perverts public morals... a punishable offence'. (*Britain First* 11, 2–15 October 1971; Scott 1972: 552–3; *Spearhead* 27, November 1969; 44, July 1971; 20, September–October 1968.)

Some of these arguments echoed those of Mary Whitehouse's campaign to clean up television. But as the references to 'marriage with the coloured races' and 'alien manipulation' should remind us, the NF's views are not the same as those of Whitehouse. This is even more obvious if we examine the extreme right before the NF's inception. In part, what we are seeing here is the origin of the NF's views on the subject. Thus, as early as 1965, the BNP paper, *Combat*, was attacking 'the debauchery of our youth' by television, magazines and cinema, attributing it not only to alien 'money-grabbers' but to a communist conspiracy. If, as we saw earlier, the NF's treatment of population used a different vocabulary than had some of the organisations that preceded it, this was also true when it addressed the subject of permissiveness. Thus while the BNP was relatively cautious in its language, the Greater Britain Movement was not. Less than two years before the NF's inception, *Spearhead* could be found denouncing 'the promotion of dirt' on television as 'Jewish filth' and declaring that both Soho's pornography and 'the most depraved works of stage and screen' were the creations of Jews. (*Combat* 26, January–March 1964; 33, June 1965; *Spearhead* March; April 1965; for a Greater Britain Movement sticker linking anti-Semitism with a call for a boycott of 'Pornography; Sex Plays' and 'T.V. Smut', see *Searchlight* December 1982.)

While the NF sought to avoid such language, it was still undeniably a racist organisation where other groups opposed to the permissive society were not. None the less, the NF consciously sought the support of those who saw moral standards as under attack. In 1968, *Spearhead* reported that an NF member had addressed a meeting of the National Viewers' and Listeners' Association while in 1977, in an open letter to clerical critics of the NF, Tyndall accused the churches of failing to condemn single parenthood, abortion or 'depravity and perversion' in the arts. It was the National Front, he declared, that stood for Christian values, that condemned illegitimacy, and that was 'pledged to attack all those menaces at work in our literature, in our theatre and film... which undermine family life'. (*Spearhead* 18, February–March 1968; 112, December 1977.)

Tyndall had made similar points at a rally earlier in the year and they were to appear again in a leaflet in the same period accusing Church leaders of attacking the very party that stood for family life, moral discipline, opposition to abortion on demand and 'the defence of the

Christian West'. Given such views, it is hardly surprising that NF activists in this period were to be found campaigning against prostitution. In 1974, for instance, the chairman of the Bristol branch attracted attention in the local press after complaining to the chief constable about prostitution in the St Paul's area of the city. Six years later, a local Campaign Against Prostitution wrote to the *Guardian* from the Hillfields area of Coventry complaining that prostitutes were engaged in 'general slaggish behaviour' while 'local womenfolk' could not go out in safety. What was needed, it declared, was the strengthening of the law concerning prostitution so that children could be brought up 'in a good moral atmosphere'. Subsequent correspondence, rejecting the picture of the area painted by the Campaign, was to point out that one of the signatories was an NF activist. It is unlikely, however, that hostility to prostitution as such was the only motivation of such campaigns. In 1975 *Spearhead* had called upon NF prospective council candidates to take up local issues such as vandalism, parking – and prostitution. Furthermore, not only could taking up the concerns of local residents be potentially fruitful but opposition to commercialised sexuality could also be seen as helping the organisation in its efforts to escape its association with violent confrontation and an apparent single-issue obsession with immigration. As one member of its National Directorate somewhat hopefully declared in 1978, to take up a national campaign against pornography, would 'push more the acceptable face of the NF'. (*Camerawork* November 1977; NF leaflet, n.d. (c. 1979); *Western Daily Press* 5 June 1974; *Guardian* 26, 30 April 1980; *Spearhead* 87, September 1975; NF National Directorate minutes, 26 November 1978.)

But while other factors should be borne in mind, the National Front in the 1960s and 1970s was certainly concerned with sexual morality and this was to continue to be true for the extreme right subsequently. Before the 1986 split, one NF writer, Margaret Ballard, attacked the 'spiritual and cultural waste land' brought about by 'the so-called permissive society' while at the end of the decade, the *Flag* decried the 'promiscuity' of the 'Swinging Sixties' as an attack on family life. But it was to be the political soldier wing of the NF and the BNP who would be most vociferous against permissiveness, particularly around obscenity in the media. (*New Nation* 6, Winter 1984; *Flag* 34, September 1989.)

In the late 1980s, an editorial in *National Front News* declared that the movement, in discussing the family, had neglected to consider the issue of pornography. Such material, it was argued, was 'morally wrong and extremely damaging' and men should not continue to see 'the sick fantasy world of pornography as an escape from the harshness and pain of modern life'. Pornography was contrary to the ideal of the family and could be men's 'first step to betraying their wives, as spiritual adultery can eventually lead to the material version'. Rather than being based on lust, it declared, nationalist society would be based on love and the sooner that 'we can stamp out this mindless filth', the better it would be. (*National Front News* 109, n.d. (1988).)

The following year, the final issue of *Nationalism Today* took up the question. In the recent past, it remarked, it had been 'considered scandalous for a decent woman to show her knees in public'. Now, however, 'gynaecological explicitness' and child pornography had followed in the trail of the supposedly harmless 'Page 3' girl. The men who consumed pornography were led to believe that they could totally control women, and the result was rape, 'wife beating' and child abuse. Pornography could drive 'a wedge between the sexes' and unless men were freed from its delusions, it would be impossible for them to forge committed relationships and recognise 'the natural balance and relationship' between men and women. (*Nationalism Today* 46, n.d. (1989).)

But if the political soldiers' opposition to permissiveness had led them to take up the issue of pornography only shortly before their demise, the BNP had been concerned with both for a considerable time. In the mid-1980s, for instance, *Spearhead* had published an article claiming that the same conspirators who had produced the *Communist Manifesto* and the *Protocols of the Learned Elders of Zion* were also responsible for attempts 'to break down the sexual morality of our race', while subsequently it reprinted an article from a right-wing Conservative publication suggesting that Thatcherism's infatuation with free market liberalism implicated it in the sexual permissiveness it sometimes verbally opposed. Nor was it only in *Spearhead* that the BNP offered its views on the subject. Its 1983 manifesto included a commitment to 'a considerable tightening' of the laws concerning obscenity in 'the theatre, films and publishing' while in its 1992 manifesto, under the heading 'Cleaning Up Britain', it declared that it was committed to the family, 'the sanctity of marriage and the need to discourage the breeding of children out of wedlock'. Divorce should be made more difficult, homosexuality banned, abortion severely restricted and media obscenity should fall under 'the full force of the state'. Unlike Mary Whitehouse, the manifesto claimed, the BNP would not merely appeal 'to the more worthier aspects of "public opinion"', but would give the 'pedlars of this filth . . . the criminal status that they deserve'. This concern with pornography has linked up in turn with the BNP's enthusiasm for stricter punishment for sexual assault. In one article in 1994, for instance, it argued that 'the sick trade in pornography' was a factor in the rising number of sex attacks on 'British women and children' and in 'A message to the women of Britain', which appeared on the same page, it called for the castration of rapists. (*Spearhead* 196, February 1985; 260, October 1990; British National Party 1983: 19; British National Party 1992: 20–1; *British Nationalist* 143, May 1994.)

If the extreme right's views of rape are linked with opposition to pornography, they are also linked to race. In 1979, for instance, the Young National Front organised a march in West Bromwich against rape, and the placards the marchers carried included such slogans as 'Capital Punishment Must Be Restored For Rape and Muggings', '75% of Rapings Are Done By Immigrants' and 'No More Rapes Against Our White Ladies'. But such slogans, of course, did not mean that it was only coerced sex the extreme right opposed. In part, NF antagonism to sex between black and white is rooted in its conviction that the nation is under attack from conspiratorial forces. It was these sinister forces, Martin Webster declared in 1971, who were seeking to encourage 'racial inter-breeding' in order to eliminate racial difference and impose world government. Similarly, the first issue of *Nationalism Today* claimed that racial integration was calculated to destroy nation states. 'In effect', it declared, 'your granddaughter's marriage to a Black has already been planned. What are you doing to stop it?' Such views, of course, had long existed on the extreme right, and in far more blatant language. Writing for *Combat* in the late 1950s, John Tyndall had claimed that 'the Jew' realised that the mixing of races would lead to the destruction of white civilisation. Similarly for the National Socialist Movement, shortly before Tyndall's break with it, black immigration into Britain had been engineered by Britain's Jewish rulers so that the nation's 'Anglo-Saxon stock' could be diluted and destroyed. (*Searchlight* December 1979; *Spearhead* 42, April 1971; *Nationalism Today* 1, March 1980; *Combat* 4, Autumn 1959; *National Socialist* 6, n.d. (1962).)

As with sexual permissiveness, sexual contact across racial lines is seen through a conspiratorial lens. But to speak of sex and race is to invoke a whole series of other interconnections, as a 1969 *Spearhead* article well demonstrates. Illustrated with a photo of black comedian Sammy Davis Jr embracing a blonde white woman, the article claimed, somewhat implausibly, that 'sexual relationships between . . . a white woman and a black man' were 'rarely discussed by Nationalists'. It might be thought, it suggested, that the existence of inter-racial sex undermined the racialist case. In fact, it claimed, white women who were attracted to black men were really motivated by psychological motives of guilt and rebellion. Surprisingly, the National Front press did not always attack inter-racial relationships. In the late 1970s, a veteran extreme rightist, Peter Peel, who had once been a BUF member and would end his days as a supporter of the BNP, was cheerfully to 'admit that I find women of all races desirable... Knowing this of myself, I can hardly justify moral indignation at a woman of my own race who... is attracted to a healthy male of some other race.' But this 'generosity' was not echoed elsewhere in the NF. Thus, one issue of *Bulldog* which declared on its front page, 'Black Pimps Force White Girls into Prostitution', also contained an editorial which claimed that some young women deserved to be ill-treated. 'White Girls Who Mix with Blacks Are Traitors to Their Race. We Have No Sympathy for Them.' (*Spearhead* 25, September 1969; 133, November 1979; 237, November 1988; *Bulldog* 35, September 1983.)

In many ways, hostility to inter-racial sex was seen through a construction of women as contested territory. 'The enemy within', *Spearhead* claimed in 1974, had taken 'our houses, our jobs, our women'. Likewise, *National Front News* in the following decade was to claim that whites resented immigrants 'taking their jobs and houses' but 'above all they detest immigrants taking the women-folk of their race'. This element of rivalry is particularly well illustrated in a report in *Bulldog* that 'race war' had spread to East Anglia. 'The fighting is centred around Norwich's night spots. Blacks converge on these night spots from miles around in order to pick up White girls. This, understandably, has met with a hostile reaction from local White youths.' (*Spearhead* 78, August 1974; *National Front News* 79, n.d. (1986); *Bulldog* 13, July 1979.)

But it was also linked with the NF's constant pressing of the law and order issue. Thus the Croydon branch in the early 1970s issued a leaflet which was headed 'WARNING! ATTACKS ON WHITE WOMEN ARE ON THE INCREASE IN THE SOUTH LONDON AREA.' 'Coloured Thugs', it declared, were responsible for 'savage attacks on White women' and unless the police dealt with it, 'then *White Vigilante Groups* may be the only answer'. At national level, such rhetoric played a central role in the party paper. The cover of its second issue, in May 1976, declared 'White Women Are Muggers' Main Target.' Marauding 'savages', it claimed, were 'seeking out White women to assault and rob' and were 'as happy to batter to the ground the elderly and frail for the sake of their pensions as they are to snatch the handbags of young secretaries on Underground stations'. At this point, no attempt was made to link street crime with sexual attack. By the following year, however, stories such as 'Muggers Rampage' were being put next to 'Big Increase in Multiple Rape' and a montage of newspaper clippings placed a report of street violence in Peckham above one on 'street sex attacks' in Birmingham. One year on, the link the NF sought to make was even more explicit. On one part of a page, a story entitled '"A Rape A Day in London" – Police' brought together reports from several localities. Immediately below, under the headline '"Schoolgirls" and Nude Black Men = Multi-Racial "Fun"', consent and coercion were blurred as the paper attacked the much-publicised dance group Hot Gossip for an obsession with 'schoolgirls and sado-masochism . . . in which *all* the females are White and *all* the males Black'. (NF Croydon, leaflet, n.d.; *National Front News* 2, May 1976; 8, March–April 1977; 16, December 1978.)

Following the splits at the end of the 1970s, the theme continued to surface in NF publications. One *National Front News* front page declared 'It's Our Women Under Attack!' while in *Nationalism Today* a horrific account of a white American girl's gang-rape concluded with the comment: 'if we do not want the blood of British schoolgirls staining the floor of British schoolrooms, we must act now'. But it was the British National Party that most determinedly returned again to the theme of inter-racial sex. In 1982, for instance, it published an article, 'Media Jews behind race-mix poison', which once again attacked the overt sexuality of television dance groups. In particular, it complained, Hot Gossip promoted 'the idea of black/white sexual encounter, with the black men usually dominating the white girls'. This, it claimed, 'set the most dangerous model-example for national decadence' in a society in which it was 'a deplorably *common* sight to see white girls not with white boyfriends but with blacks'. But while this article was written by a British author, it was from the most virulent sections of the extreme right in the United States, in particular, that *Spearhead* drew such material. In 1983, it reprinted an article from the American racist magazine, *National Vanguard*. Western males, it claimed, had been demoralised and were no longer capable of 'supporting and protecting a mate'. Demasculinised by working women, no longer able to exert authority over wife or daughter, they were seeking out Asian mates for their 'reputed docility and submissiveness'. White women, for their part, were turning to black men. 'The hurt felt by the woman who needs a strong man and cannot find one surpasses all' and while 'the Jews' were using the feminist movement as a weapon against Gentile society, feminism was as much a result as a cause of today's sexual confusion. The sexual crisis had deep roots. Urbanisation had fundamentally changed the role of the sexes and, further back still, the 'Asiatic sexual notions' of Christianity had been imposed on pagan sexuality. While the past could not be restored, a solution had to be found, and quickly, 'for the corruption of our women is proceeding more rapidly with each passing day' and while some young men were growing into 'something less than men . . . a blind rage is building in others'. (*National Front News* 60, October 1984; *Nationalism Today* 2, n.d. (1980); *Spearhead* 172, February 1983; 164, June 1982.)

As we have seen, *Spearhead* had been particularly inclined to link inter-racial sex with the influence of the media. Once again, it was American material that it particularly drew on. Thus, in 1993, it reprinted an extract from an American racist book *Which Way, Western Man?* There was an endless succession of plays, the author complained, in which 'the Negro males make love to White women' while television 'brazenly pictures comely, young, blonde White women' in black men's embrace. The result of this 'Unrelenting propaganda', he declared, was white confusion, and 'our women' now believed that 'affairs with Negroes are the vogue', making them 'open game for Negro males'. But if *Spearhead* attributed inter-racial sex to the pernicious effects of the media, it was also keen to link it with the impact of feminism. In 1992 it reprinted an article from the American racist magazine *Instauration*. The sight of white women with non-white men, it declared, was 'the most galling to white males, probably because racial memories tell us that women are a kind of property'. Their possession by a male outside the tribe was 'a visible sign of our defeat and dispossession . . . Our most treasured property has been seized. And the comelier the female the greater our distress and sense of loss.' A 'decline in male self-mastery', it lamented, had led to the rise of feminism and weak white men, unable to 'display the virtues of the hunter' with women of their own race, were ending in 'the arms of non-white females'. They feared 'the hard-edged modern white woman'. But if white men regained self-esteem, the hard qualities of white women would disappear. 'Like a violet after the first spring, the truly feminine will emerge.' (*Spearhead* 290, April 1993; 278, April 1992.)

8 Fascism and gender

The preceding chapters have sought to explore the relationship between women and fascism, and establish in what way it matches our expectations and in what ways it subverts them. The work has given particular attention to developments in Britain but has sought to place them in a broader context. Through a discussion first of German National Socialism, Italian Fascism and the British Union of Fascists before the Second World War, then of the post-war extreme right in France, Italy and Germany and finally of the main strands of the British extreme right since the late 1960s, it has become possible to understand the diversity of extreme right politics. Fascism is not always anti-Semitic nor agreed on economic policy nor, come to that, comfortable with the term fascist. Such differences are, in part, evidence of distinct strands or sub-types of the extreme right which exist across countries. But they are also linked with national differences between countries – appropriately, nationalism is differently constructed within different nations. Who might be seen as part of the nation, whether a movement identifies with a particular form of Christianity (or, indeed, rejects it altogether), the degree to which activists see themselves as part of the right or as beyond both left and right are each vitally linked with the history and current circumstances of the particular nations in which political forces emerge and by which they are shaped. If we can accept a diversity of fascisms, why then should we still believe that there is only one possible relationship between fascism and women?

Such a relationship, furthermore, is unlikely to be straightforward since it involves more than one question. It is concerned not only with the policy that fascism espouses towards women but with what role they play in fascist movements, both as members and as voters. How fascism deals with these different questions would need to be carefully explicated even if fascist ideology did have a necessary and invariant place for women within its logic. As we might expect, fascism has much to say about women, and discussions of the extreme right are woefully incomplete if they do not make this crystal clear. But to argue against omission or neglect is only part of what a study of fascism and women needs to do.

Much recent writing on the extreme right does, indeed, acknowledge the significance of the relationship between women and fascism. Discussing the inter-war movements, Stanley Payne has described fascism as displaying an 'extreme insistence on what is now termed male chauvinism' while Herbert Kitschelt has characterised it as involving 'a deeply antifeminist thrust that glorified decisive male action . . . and condemned gender equality' (Payne 1995: 13; Kitschelt 1995: 30). In the post-war period, Michael Minkenberg sees a new form of extreme right emerging in opposition to the movements that have developed from the 1960s onwards around a number of issues, including the equality of women. Kitschelt, likewise an advocate of the novelty of the modern extreme right, at the same time emphasises the continued importance of an 'authoritarian antifeminist thrust' (Minkenberg 1992: 55–9; Kitschelt 1995: 76). These studies, among the most important work on the extreme right that has emerged in recent years, come in the aftermath of a plethora of feminist scholarship which has done much to put women at the centre of our gaze. In one such work, written at the beginning of the modern women's movement, Kate Millett argued that Nazism's stance towards women derived not from economic factors or a concern with population but from male psychology. Drawing its 'most consistent support' from embittered male war veterans, National Socialism sought to regress to a quasi-tribal society where men 'could play master' over women. For another feminist writer, Sheila Rowbotham, writing in the same period, the British Fascism of the 1930s was an extreme manifestation of a shift in attitudes that had arisen as the feminist consciousness of the early twentieth century had receded (Millett 1971: 159, 163; Rowbotham 1974: 126–7). Each of these accounts drew on anti-fascist writers of the 1930s – in Millett's case, the radical psychoanalyst Wilhelm Reich, in Rowbotham's the feminist Winifred Holtby – to make an argument that fascism was not only a reaction to communism or an expression of an inflamed nationalism but was centrally concerned with asserting male supremacy. In the 1930s, however, those who argued such a case were often overshadowed by those who remained persuaded by more traditional interpretations. In contrast, Millett and Rowbotham were among the first of a later generation in setting out an argument that has been elaborated by other feminists and has come to influence subsequent accounts of the extreme right.

It is hard now (although, unfortunately, not impossible) to envisage an account of the extreme right that does not take the importance of gender seriously. Instead, the greater danger now may be that studies will recognise the importance of the relationship between the extreme right and women but in such a way as to obscure its complexity.

If we were to turn first to the pre-war movements, each of the examples we have considered is more problematic than might at first have been anticipated. As Lesley Caldwell has noted, Italian Fascism's 'sustained anti-feminism' can 'be fairly easily demonstrated'. Yet Italian Fascism did not originate as an anti-feminist movement. Of the elements which came together to create the new movement in 1919, Futurism is often seen as spectacularly patriarchal, having famously declared its 'contempt for women' in its 1909 manifesto. Yet later Futurist writings, while never losing that contempt, advocated women's suffrage and denounced women's enslavement to men. As for D'Annunzio's movement, in part a rival to fascism, in part a source of converts to it, it not only included prominent women but the Statute of Carnaro enacted during the occupation of Fiume advocated women's equal rights. (This links in turn to another strand of the infant fascist movement, the former leftist current of national syndicalism, leading figures of which wrote the Carnaro Statute.) Such views were reflected, as we have seen, in the founding programme of the fascist movement. Nor did they disappear with the influx of more conservative elements into the movement or in the immediate aftermath of its coming to power. Mussolini's 1925 speech to fascist members of the Chamber of Deputies, calling on them to recognise women's right to the vote, was framed in part by the 'stack of telegrams' he had received from fascist women's groups seeking 'this modest right'. But he also argued that women had entered factories and offices because of necessity and that fascists should recognise that the modern world was one where women went out to work. This speech is considerably less well known than either the Duce's later pronouncements on population or his article on the supposed incompatibility of women and machines. But an adequate account of fascism's policy towards women needs to be able to encompass them all and see policy as fluid and the object of contestation within the party. Ultimately, the desire for a higher birthrate combined with pressures from job-hungry war veterans and the ideological assumptions of both the Nationalists and the Catholic Church of the time to take the regime in a certain direction. The economic problems of later years reinforced this decision in favour of a particular kind of male pre-eminence. What did not decide it was the inherent nature of fascism itself. (Caldwell 1986: 135; Mercer 1986:

232–3; Gregor 1979: 281–91; Spackman 1990: 89–95; Meyer 1989: 27–32; De Grazia 1992: 35.)

If Italy is not to be seen as demonstrating the simple equivalence of fascismo and machismo, even Nazism is not to be understood as the uncomplicated expression of patriarchal power. Hitler's propaganda chief, Josef Goebbels, did, indeed, describe National Socialism as 'in its nature a masculine movement'. The decision at the party's first meeting to refuse to run women as electoral candidates undoubtedly marked it out as unashamedly chauvinist. (It is worth noting here, however, that just as fascist women students were critical of the Italian regime's discrimination towards women in the 1930s, for a time National Socialist women students ignored party rules and ran candidates for elected office in the late 1920s.) But while Nazism systematically excluded women from decision-making roles within both party and state, it consciously sought to recruit them to its ranks and, rather than shamelessly call for their removal into the home, was so desirous of their votes as to promise in 1932 that it would not deprive them of their jobs. Certainly, despite the protestations of male ideologues that their earlier comments had been misunderstood, we would be wise to be sceptical about the motives behind this aspect of the Nazi effort to win women's support. But any account of the Nazi rise to power that ignores this attempt will mislead us as to the nature of the party's appeal. One influential interpretation has argued that women abandoned the Weimar Republic and turned to the Nazis because their unashamed traditionalism was ultimately more attractive if the only alternative was to be devalued at work and exhausted at home. This may well explain why some women voted Nazi. But to argue that the Nazis felt no 'need to pay lip service to women's equality' and told women they 'should be honoured in their homes, not exploited in the factory' is to conflate what leading Nazis declared and what Nazi election strategy chose instead to promise. Nor, contrary to myth, did the Third Reich engage in a systematic campaign to remove women from employment or ban birth control shortly after coming into existence. Instead, as we have seen, while some women were sacked and others gave up employment as a condition of their marriage loan, women's labour remained of key importance for the economy throughout the Third Reich's early years and became so important that from 1937 the loan was granted without reference to women's position in the labour market. As for birth control, while the regime made access to it difficult, it was not until the war that the regime sought to ban it. (Millett 1971: 165; De Grand 1976: 962–3; Evans 1976: 155; Bridenthal and Koonz 1984: 56.)

Certainly, it is on issues of reproduction that National Socialism accords most closely with our expectations. Once in power, National Socialism pursued a population policy that sought to maximise the production of children by those it considered fit to breed and to minimise procreation among those it saw as unfit. Similar in many ways to the Italian drive for an increased population, it differed because it was not simply pro-natalist but eugenic, utilising propaganda, economic incentives and restrictions on abortion in an attempt to raise the birth-rate alongside the deliberate use of sterilisation to selectively lower it. The Holocaust came as the culminating point of a virulent anti-Semitism that portrayed Jews as vermin and the racial enemy of good Germans. Sterilisation policy, as Quine and others have noted, was not unique to Nazi Germany. 'Inspiration for it came from the United States', where thirty-two states practised it and, as we have recently learned, it was also widespread in Scandinavia. But in scale and in motivation, it represented, if not a terrible innovation, certainly a terrible development. That Nazis in the 1920s and 1930s debated women's role in society, and that Nazi feminists opposed government policy, after the party came to power, deserves to be better known. In power, National Socialism neither drove women from public life nor reduced them to mere breeding-machines. But if it is not to be seen as patriarchal by definition, from its very beginning it was powerfully drawn in that direction. For its leaders, only a male elite was fit to rule, and it was they who would decide which women were fit to reproduce. (Quine 1996: 116–21.)

If the German case is closest to our expectations as to what the extreme right must believe about the rightful place of women, then the British Union of Fascists is furthest away. Unlike either the Nazis or Italian Fascism, the BUF did not give a central role to the need to raise the birth-rate. Indeed, as we have seen, its attitude towards birth control came under criticism in a number of publications with strong views against contraception. Opponents of birth control were equally worried by the movement's sympathy for sterilisation. In Germany, while Catholics were critical of National Socialism's stance on 'the unfit', there was at least the compensation of its restrictions on contraception. In the British case, however, fascism appeared lax on the latter but on the former potentially Draconian. Yet, in general, the BUF appears to have been as little interested in pressing for compulsory sterilisation as it was in campaigning against contraception. Instead of issues of population, it was work and, in later years, war, that dominated its frequent pronouncements on the role of women. We will return to the latter question later. On work,

Lewis has argued that the movement espoused 'a doctrine of profound anti-feminism' which sought to consign women to 'the nether regions of domesticity' as mothers and housewives. As for its declared support for equal pay, he argues, in the absence of explicit measures against sexual discrimination it would lead to the women being sacked. This study has taken a very different approach. We have noted the ambiguity in the BUF's stance on equal pay, sometimes advocated as securing women's rights, sometimes as ending the situation where women, as cheaper labour, were performing tasks that rightly belonged to men. What is important to emphasise, however, is the conscious attempt by the BUF not to position itself as a bulwark against feminism, but, remarkably, as perfectly compatible with it. This is not to argue that the movement took a consistent egalitarian stance towards women's participation in either politics or the labour market. As Holtby noted at the time, in *The Greater Britain*, Mosley had declared that fascism would support the 'normal wife and mother' as distinct from the 'professional spinster politicians' with their desire to escape 'the normal sphere of woman'. Indeed, she was to use this quotation on more than one occasion during the period. In one article, referred to at the beginning of our earlier discussion of the BUF (p. 29), she drew too on an article in the *Fascist Week* in which Mosley had claimed that 'the interests of the normal woman' played little role in parliament. For the BUF's leader, women's 'normal' place was as wife and mother. But this does not say what else they might be or make his argument the same as that which shaped Goebbels' characterisation of National Socialism. Women, the Nazi propaganda chief declared, should be removed from public life. If, in Germany, women were excluded from running as candidates, in Britain they were not, and in the future Corporate State, women were not to be confined to the Domestic Corporation. (Lewis 1987: 53–4; Holtby 1934: 161; Berry and Bishop 1985: 84–6; Millett 1971: 165.)

Despite defeat, fascism survived the Second World War. Between different strands of the extreme right there continued to be considerable debate as to biological racism or economic policy. For many militants, it is likely that a particular notion of gender continued to be important, in which women's place – even if it had never actually been true even of the Third Reich – was ideally in the home. In Britain, the remnants of Mosleyism continued to espouse women's equality in the movement and in the labour market (see e.g. Mosley 1961: 229, 253, 278–9). But it is probable that the kind of pronouncements that we quoted from German parties of the 1950s and 1960s were typical of the extreme right of the time. Such views have continued to the present day, with the British National Party being a particularly striking example. But this is no more the only position on the extreme right than it was before the war. Nor, more importantly, should we draw an unbroken line from National Socialism and fascism to all the different movements of recent years. This, of course, takes us into one of the most contentious areas of discussion about the modern extreme right. Not only do such parties as the Front National or the (British) National Front deny that they are fascist, but so too do a number of scholars who insist on the novelty of what they see as new radical right or new right-wing populist parties. Some of the most useful definitions of fascism, for instance Griffin's, do encompass both pre-war and post-war movements. Furthermore, it can prove particularly illuminating to explore the overtly fascist political formation of a number of key figures in the modern extreme right or, as Billig has done, to trace ideological continuities between groups that defend the Third Reich and others that disassociate themselves from it (Griffin 1993: 32–36; Billig 1978). But this is not to deny that the more significant parties that have emerged from the 1960s onwards usually have not defined themselves as neo-Nazi (as many smaller groups have) nor as neo-fascist (as the MSI did) but as parties that wish to be seen, and are seen by many of their members, as nothing to do with the politics of the 1930s. As such, while recognising that those of its activists who were formed by earlier traditions will be bringing considerable ideological baggage with them, we should understand FN or Republikaner or National Front policy not as a simple revival of pre-war movements but as a distinctively post-war extreme right that has emerged after the division of Europe, after the end of empire, in reaction to large-scale immigration – and in response to changes in the family, in women's role and in sexual mores. We will find it fruitful to compare the policies of modern parties to those of the inter-war period, but both the circumstances and the self-definition of the two are crucially different.

In examining Western European extreme right parties, we have found considerable continuity with their pre-war counterparts. The display of photos of women in fascist Italy at the MSI women's convention is a particularly striking example of this. In Germany, for Kühnen's group to launch a German Girls' League in the 1980s (the Nazis had organised a League of German Girls) is another pointer to conscious emulation. But we should not expect to find such obvious connections in groups which eschew support for the movements of the 1920s and 1930s. For the FN or the REPs, or for the National Front, accusations of reviving those movements are indignantly denied (although the political soldier wing of the NF, it will be recalled, was to express a particular affinity for the inter-war Romanian movement, the Iron Guard). The British National Party, in turn, represents yet another variation, in which strong continuities with earlier movements are evident (including even support for a future occupational franchise for housewives) even if they are not too loudly proclaimed. (Mushaben 1995: 24; Stephenson 1981: 84; Tyndall 1988: 278.)

Amid these different forms of extreme right, we have already uncovered important common ground both with each other and with their predecessors. Often, the parties we have examined do, after all, come close to our assumptions. But if there are important areas of continuity around abortion, the birth-rate and woman's domestic role, we also need to emphasise that the social developments that, in part, the movements of the inter-war period were reacting against, have now advanced considerably further. Feminism, or, more precisely, an acceptance of feminist assumptions, is much stronger than it was in the 1920s or 1930s. The labour market from which attempts were made to expel women is now one in which women are massively represented. The 'permissive' sexual morality that National Socialists opposed in Weimar Germany has now become the ruling value system of much of the West. And the falling birth-rate that so horrified Nazis and fascists is now lower still. In short, what in the 1920s or 1930s appeared new – and reversible – is now far more deeply embedded. Even then, National Socialism was forced to make concessions to women voters or to accept that women's employment remained crucial. Today, that is even more the case. Hence, just as British extreme rightists tell voters that they do not advocate banning birth control, so the Front National declares that 'contraception is a choice made in the private sphere into which the state should not enter'. Similarly, just as even the BNP claims that it will not expel women from their jobs, so Le Pen is careful not to appear opposed to women's rights. The FN leader, Betz observes, has argued that while women have a 'fundamental mission' to bear and educate children, it is unrealistic to prevent them from pursuing careers and thus contributing to society. (Simmons 1996: 250; Betz 1994: 132.)

In asking why the extreme right takes this approach, we need to consider two groups who are affected by the changes we have noted and in turn have an impact on the construction of party policy. The first group is the voters for these parties, both those who support them already and those who might do so. Such voters would, of course, have different reasons for supporting such parties (nationalism, opposition to immigration, anti-communism etc.) and need not have the same views on women nor decide their vote on that basis. To the extent that an extreme right party takes an anti-feminist stance, it might not mean that its voters agree with it. In turn, that its voters might not accept such a stance could affect how vigorously the party argues it. Both of these may be at play, for instance, when we consider how, in the early 1980s, voters for the Front National and the two conservative parties in France were surveyed; while a majority of conservative supporters disagreed that the liberalisation of abortion represented progress, 53 per cent of FN voters believed it did. Indeed, one writer has suggested that the Front National has consciously recognised that its potential supporters hold different views on women, and targets those nostalgic for the familial certainties of the Vichy regime with a far tougher policy than it does those who fear immigrants but do not seek to restore the gender order of the past. (Schain 1987: 247–8; Méricourt 1990: 5–8.)

But if one factor is electoral, another is concerned with membership. Both Italian Fascism and German National Socialism engaged in internal debate concerning their views on women and this has been the case with post-war parties too. Mushaben found that women on the German extreme right were far from happy with the traditionalist stance they experienced in their organisations while in Britain, women on the NF National Directorate expressed criticisms of their party just as Alessandra Mussolini was critical of hers. If we should not assume that women members of such parties have stereotypical extreme right views on women, we should also not assume that all women members will agree with each other or that all men in the movement will hold a unified view. We have discussed elsewhere how women in the BUF expressed contrary views on women's role in society, some arguing a traditionalist view, others taking a more modernist stance. But quite surprising differences (and not only among women) are well documented for post-war movements too. In a survey of delegates at the MSI's 1990 National Congress, only 29 per cent agreed with abortion being legal under special circumstances. But not only did a further 23 per cent come into the 'don't know' category, when asked if they believed that men and women deserved equal rights, 71 per cent said yes and only 15 per cent no. (Asked if the man should be the authority in the home, 43 per cent said no, while only 24 per cent said yes.) In a survey conducted at the previous Congress, in 1987, a higher percentage supported the limited legalisation of abortion (39 per cent) and once again 71 per cent agreed with women's equal rights. Ignazi suggests that, while opposition to abortion had grown between 1987 and 1990, 'MSI cadres (who are overwhelmingly male) show a libertarian approach' towards relationships between the genders. Three points need to be made here. First, as we have seen in discussing its propaganda, it is probable that MSI activists see equal rights in terms of different roles rather than as interchangeability of roles. Second, they none the less do not adhere to a view of male domination that we might expect. Finally, and here we need to bear in mind our discussion in chapter 6, opposition to abortion needs to be understood in the context of views about human life – it is neither adhered to by all extreme rightists nor connected by definition to a hostile view to women's equality. Furthermore, while the MSI appears to be particularly disruptive of our expectations, it is not alone. Between 1978 and 1980, a survey was conducted at a number of European party conferences, including those of the FN, the MSI and the NPD (the Republikaner did not yet exist). On a scale in which 1 equalled strongly in favour and 5 strongly opposed, the delegates at each of the named parties' gatherings were found to be opposed to women deciding when to have abortions. While the FN's figure of 4.18 and the NPD's of 3.87 were noticeably high, the MSI's of 3.10 was almost exactly in the middle of the scale. But while here there was an important difference between extreme right parties, on another question, which might be expected to be directly correlated to the first, there was not. When asked about equal opportunities for women, the FN scored 2.58, the NPD 2.15 and the MSI 1.93. Not only were each of the parties far more favourable to equal opportunities for women than to abortion, suggesting the separability of views on the two issues, they were all nowhere near to strongly opposing equal opportunities. Certainly, as Merkl has pointed out, by comparison with supporters of other parties, extreme right delegates were more hostile to abortion and to women's equality. But that is not the same as saying they were strongly opposed to the first or that they were just as opposed to the second. (Durham 1990: 8; 1992: 517–19; Ignazi 1993: 86–91; Kitschelt 1995: 68–9; Merkl 1997: 35.)

In each of the countries with which we have been concerned, the extreme right should not be seen as defined by a total opposition to feminism. Some movements come close to this – particularly National Socialism and, more recently, the British National Party. Others (for instance, Italian Fascism or the National Front) were slower in adopting an anti-feminist stance. But these were not the only possible responses. The BUF, for example, claimed not to oppose feminism at all while the MSI has attempted to extend the notion of a Third Way from its customary meaning of going beyond capitalism and communism to an attempt to forge an alternative to both modern feminism and traditional male chauvinism. But in every case, even within the Nazi party, anti-feminist impulses have been confronted by other stances which, however unsettling it might seem, can legitimately be called egalitarian or even feminist. Rather than uniting to fight women's equality, parties of the extreme right have often been disunited in the face of feminism and should they declare their opposition to it, it is likely to be despite the inclinations and even the expressed dissent of at least some of their members and voters. If we concluded that the conventional wisdom was right, we would have had to explain why women, in some cases in large numbers, have been drawn to an openly anti-feminist movement. In denying that fascism can always be understood as anti-feminist, we have not escaped the problem of women's support but reframed how we might see it. What different reasons might there be, we should be asking, for women to adhere to an extreme right which, in different contexts, can give quite different answers to the question of women's role?

We noted earlier the influence of Wilhelm Reich and Winifred Holtby on later writers (p. 166). Reich, who argued that the patriarchal nature of the relationship between men and women in the middle-class family was central to understanding why men might support National Socialism, had surprisingly little to say about the support the movement received from women. To the degree that he did discuss it, he emphasised women's sexual repression, and the ways in which political and religious reaction manipulated their fear of 'sexual Bolshevism'. Particularly in the light of his belief that 'Hitler's party ... relied chiefly upon women's votes', it was a surprisingly underdeveloped argument. Just as Reich linked the appeal of fascism and the appeal of religion, Holtby too emphasised a connection between fascism and the opposition to birth control and female equality championed by the Catholic Church of the time. But here again, her analysis said relatively little about why women (rather than men) should turn to fascism. Indeed, when she actually encountered a woman Blackshirt striding towards BUF headquarters, her thoughts on why such a woman would join Mosley's movement turned to patriotism and, even, to a desire for social reform. As later interviews by Cullen were to demonstrate, women members of the BUF were indeed influenced by both factors. If the latter, at first sight, might appear perverse, it is worth noting that Holtby's suggestion that a woman might join the BUF to 'smash the foul slums and build a new Jerusalem' was almost exactly the reason given many years later by the movement's former women's organiser for Birmingham. (Reich 1975: 85–7, 64–6, 139–42; Holtby 1934:169–74; Berry and Bishop 1985: 170–71; Cullen 1996; Anon. 1986: 46–7.)

Perceptive as she was, Holtby could not find a way to link her analysis of the patriarchal nature of fascism to its appeal to women. A later writer, however, was to claim to make just such a link. For Maria-Antoinetta Macciocchi, writing in the 1970s, fascism in both Italy and Germany had been able to come to power through a particular appeal to women. It had not only addressed them as mothers of a future generation but had appealed to their submissiveness, utilising 'the martyred, baneful and necrophiliac femininity of the widows and mothers of men killed in the first world war'. In a particularly evocative passage, she describes Mussolini's declaration of a Day of Wedding Rings when women were called on to give what little gold they had to the nation following the declaration of the League of Nations sanctions over Italy's invasion of Ethiopia. In exchange for women's wedding rings, Macciocchi wrote, Mussolini gave them iron rings, as if he had become their new husband. (Macciocchi 1979: 68, 72.)

As Caplan argued, in introducing the essay to an English-speaking audience, Macciocchi's most important argument is that 'fascism enlists the support of women by addressing them in an ideological-sexual language through which they already familiar'. This is a language of sexual alienation, through which a woman who believes in 'the Holy Family' is permanently 'open to address as fascism's Fertile Mother'. Caplan raises problems with this account, particularly the tendency of Macciocchi's insistence that fascism received support from women towards an implication that women were morally responsible for its victory. Caplan is similarly concerned with Macciocchi's claim that women's support for Hitler is to be understood in terms of the unconscious and irrational adulation. On the contrary, Caplan argues, most women did not support Hitler while those who did can be understood without resorting to '"the irrational" as the ultimate in explanation'. The last point presents us with a number of problems. As the popular response to the death of public figures should remind us, the adulation of charismatic figures is not to be underestimated. But this is not to say that we should use notions such as the unconscious as the only or even necessarily the most likely explanation for fascism's appeal. Macciocchi's account remains both provocative and evocative, but, it should be suggested, poses a further problem. If, for Macciocchi (and, as we have seen, not only for her), Catholicism is central in understanding fascism's appeal to women, what of Catholics who were not drawn to fascism – or fascists (and, indeed, fascisms) not shaped by Catholicism? (Caplan 1979: 61–2, 64–5.)

Macciocchi was predominantly concerned with fascism in Italy. A number of writers have particularly sought to explore why women were drawn to National Socialism. In Stephenson's account, for instance, the Nazis' 'traditionalist' emphasis on women as wives and mothers was attractive to both men and women. There were also, however, 'a number of women with distinctly feminist views' and the party's women's groups developed in different ways both because leading men largely left them to their own devices and because the movement attracted 'different kinds of women'. While many, she suggests, joined because of a wish to support a husband or brother, the most important factor was National Socialism's opposition to the left, not least its denunciation of 'Bolshevist' immorality and irreligion. Hers is not the only account to emphasise the diversity of reasons for women to support Nazism. Koonz, for instance, suggests that one factor was generational conflict, in which girls defied their mothers, another was class resentment, a revolt against those in higher social strata who looked down on Nazi women as 'riff-raff'. But where Stephenson prioritises anti-socialism and sees Nazi women as predominantly (but not exclusively) 'traditionalist', Koonz holds that the movement attracted women who longed to escape 'male scrutiny'. Rather than expecting to retreat into the home, they are seen as taking the opportunity to behave in 'un-"ladylike" ways', marching, speaking and organising meetings. They were, she argues, pursuing a separate sphere of women's power in which 'an intensely communal vision of motherhood' involved female responsibility not only for the home but beyond. (Stephenson 1981: 13–14, 35–7; Koonz 1984: 212–13, 218–19; 1987: 5, 122.)

In the end, Koonz's argument has a tendency to overstate the importance of a particular aspect of the appeal of National Socialism to women, almost in compensation for its underestimation by others. But where Stephenson's account seems more persuasive, it is possible to draw on suggestions from both arguments. Stephenson's suggestion that women joined in order to support a husband or brother, for instance, should not be dismissed on a priori grounds of what it might say about women's agency. Leaving aside the arguable wisdom of preferring to see women as freely choosing fascism, we have already noted how Tina Wingfield, when elected to the NF National Directorate, commented on the frequency of women taking second place to their husbands or boyfriends in the organisation. But we should also expect to find cases where it might be the woman who joins first or who is most active. Furthermore, as our earlier references to *Bulldog* should also remind us, it is also common for individuals and single-sex peer groups to join and for one of the functions of a party to be to facilitate the very formation of couples. Our understanding of the extreme right's support among the young can also be linked to Koonz's suggestion about the attractions of rebellion and of 'un-ladylike' behaviour. We have already discussed female skinhead militancy in Germany but a particularly useful account in this regard has come from Norway. This study paints a portrait of a skinhead racist movement which does not accord with what we might expect of such a male-dominated youth culture. While the Norwegian movement included some males who believed that women should be excluded from political activity, it also included others who believed women should be more active. Women too did not agree on what role they should play, and this divergence of views was intertwined with sexual tensions around relationships between men and women in the movement. Over time, these conflicts led to the development of a women's group which organises some activities alongside and others separately from its male counterparts. (These activities range from classes on Viking history to weapons training.) This group, Valkyria, is in contact with similar extreme right women elsewhere. (Fangen 1997; Durham 1997.)

We might also think about other possible factors. One, for instance, is that of fascism's appeal to a sense of female endangerment. We have already seen this both with the British extreme right and with the Front National. As Ware has discussed, for instance, when Helena Steven stood as an NF by-election candidate in the late 1970s, she issued a leaflet which declared that 70 per cent of the victims of mugging were women and went on to link the figure with the NF's anti-immigration stance. But this need not be the only link that the extreme right can forge between women and violence. Macciocchi, we saw, suggested that fascism could appeal to women bereaved by war. In her account, these women were desperate to lash out at those they blamed for their loss and, as the Ethiopia war demonstrated, were willing to sacrifice again in another conflict. But we also discussed earlier (pp. 66–9) the somewhat disconcerting involvement of the British Union of Fascists in peace campaigning in which women were appealed to as mothers who naturally sought to protect their children from war. This appeal, usually associated with strands of the left or feminism, is considerably different from the bellicosity we would normally anticipate from fascism. But it is not unique. We have already noted the call by a woman NF member for women to work against nuclear war. What is even more surprising is that in the same period as the BUF organised against war in Britain the American extreme right was also involved in a women's anti-war movement. (Ware n.d. (1978): 14–15; Macciocchi 1979: 68, 70; Jeansonne 1996; Jenkins 1997: 207–9.)

The possible reasons for women's attraction to fascism vary considerably. But, as we have already seen, they cannot be fully understood without also thinking about men's relationship to both women and fascism. If, for women on the extreme right, racism is often linked with a feeling of threat, for men, as we have seen in Germany before the war and in Britain and France after the war, it can be deeply imbued with a dread – and an anticipation – of a life-and-death struggle not only for territory but for the right to possess 'our women'. Nor is this the only way in which the extreme right encodes notions of gender. Fixed notions of femininity are likely to exist in tandem with fixed views of masculinity, and we certainly see this in a number of the extreme right movements that we have discussed. One example is particularly striking. The nineteenth-century writer Gustave Le Bon, discussing the psychology of the crowd, declared that it was 'everywhere distinguished by feminine characteristics . . . Like women, it goes at once to extremes.' Such a gathering, he suggested, could be manipulated by orators willing to exaggerate and to express violent feelings. This notion of a relationship between the feminine mass and the masculine orator was to pass into the fascist movement. For Mussolini, who corresponded with Le Bon, both the crowd and women loved and at the same time feared strong men. For Hitler, writing in *Mein Kampf*, the masses were to be compared with a woman, moved less by reason than by an emotional longing to be dominated. (According to one early Nazi, Hitler took the argument a stage further, not only commenting on 'the intrinsically feminine character of the masses' but claiming that women in a crowd were the first to respond to the masculine power with which the gathering was addressed.) In time, this conception was to pass to later generations of extreme rightists. For Lincoln Rockwell, the founder of the American Nazi Party at the end of the 1950s, the masses were 'completely, hopelessly female'. 'When they say they reject National Socialism', he claimed, they were 'only the eternal female', who in saying no really meant yes. The notion of the masses as a sexually submissive female could only rarely be espoused either to 'the masses' or to women. To one, it would suggest cynicism and manipulation; to the other, it would not only make denials of male chauvinism sound somewhat hollow, it would also cast doubt on the movement's professed opposition to rape. None the less, notions of the feminine as weak (and of democracy as feminine) have persisted and, as we have seen, were espoused by Yockey in the late 1940s and, in turn, by Tyndall nearly fifty years later. (Le Bon 1909: 44, 56–7; Neocleous 1997: 98; Hitler 1969: 39; Nye 1975: 178–9; Koonz 1987: 66; Rockwell 1971: 23.)

Yet if, as we have suggested, there is far more fluidity than we might have thought in fascist notions of the feminine, is that also true for fascist notions of the masculine? The response of male MSI delegates to questions about gender relations should already have alerted us to this possibility. It is here possible only to begin to draw out the implications, but if there are grounds to challenge conventional wisdom on women and fascism, we also need to begin questioning existing accounts of men and fascism. The most striking, that of Klaus Theweleit, draws on the autobiographical and fictional writings of Freikorps veterans to argue that they saw women in one of three categories – the absent wife or fiancée, the pure battlefront nurse and the sexualised and evil 'Red Woman'. The last of these is identified in the fascist unconscious with the revolutionary crowd and just as the unconscious must be brutally subdued, so must both the rebellious woman and the insurrectionary mob. This brief summary cannot do justice to a rich and remarkable account. But, as Niethammer was to point out, a particular problem with Theweleit's account was that only some Freikorps veterans became National Socialists and only some National Socialists had been in the Freikorps. There are other problems too. In focusing on male fantasies, Segal has suggested, Theweleit is ultimately unable to explain a movement that involved both men and women. Furthermore, outside of the battlefield there are other male experiences (for instance, as Reich emphasised, in the middle-class family, or in certain modes of employment) that also might generate forms of consciousness (and of the unconscious) that could prove amenable to a movement such as National Socialism. Finally, and most crucial for us, we should not assume that an overtly misogynist form of masculinity can stand for all the different reasons why men might join the extreme right. (Theweleit 1987: xiii–xiv; 1989: 6; Niethammer 1979: 182–3; Segal 1989: 17.)

This insistence on a plurality of fascist masculinities has implications too for some of the most interesting material that has been written on National Socialism. Where Theweleit concentrated on the Freikorps, Mosse has written extensively on the German notion of male comradeship, the Männerbund. This was central, he has shown, in the early-twentieth-century Youth Movement, in which male middle-class youth reacted against the artificiality of bourgeois modernity by turning to the authenticity of heroic friendship and the German countryside. In the Youth Movement, in the trenches, in the Freikorps and in the Nazi party itself, the Männerbund had a powerful presence. Yet, as he and others have also noted, even National Socialism was not monolithic on the question. Thus, for Lydia Gottschewski, briefly leader of the NSF after the party came to power, the Männerbund deserved support as having saved Germany from the danger of communism. But, she argued, if carried to excess, it would present a danger to the right relationship between men and women in the new Reich. As against matriarchy and Männerbund, she declared, National Socialism stood for a 'new unity'. Himmler was also concerned about the Männerbund, not because it might reduce women's influence but because it might encourage homosexuality and the abandonment of the racial priority of procreation. (Mosse 1985: 45–6, 55–8, 153–80; Rupp 1978: 27; Vedder-Shults 1982: 218–19.)

The male band, beloved of Rosenberg and many other Nazis, lived in tension with the family as rival claimants to being the foundation of the *völkisch* state. It is arguable, too, if the high value National Socialism put on the Männerbund had equivalents in other countries. As I have argued elsewhere, if we look at the British Union of Fascists, for instance, we find occasional rhapsodies to the glories of manhood, but no developed sense of male solidarity as the basis of authority (Durham 1992: 522, 527). Yet, perhaps, it could be argued, we can be sure of one invariant in fascism. Surely, since we know of National Socialism's persecution of homosexuals, and we have also seen the BNP's stance on the issue, we can say that opposition to homosexuality is a defining feature of fascism?

Here, too, the answer has to be no. Already before it came to power, the Nazi party had declared that it was completely opposed to homosexuality, as weakening the *Volk*. In part, this was rooted in the drive for more children, in part it derived from a belief in the inherent value of clear sexual differentiation so, to use a phrase we have already encountered, we might have men who are men and women who are women. But in the British case, while leading figures in the NF vociferously opposed homosexuality, in the early 1970s some members wrote to *Spearhead* criticising the party's stance on the issue, while at the end of the decade the organisation was bitterly divided over the homosexuality of its national activities organiser, Martin Webster. Similarly, a central factor in the split in the German FAP in the 1980s was arguments over homosexuality. Finally, in the Nazi party itself, while the Night of the Long Knives marked the end of a toleration of homosexuality in the SA, in the period before the party came to power a gay publication had even published a letter from a stormtrooper declaring that sexual preference was irrelevant in National Socialism's fight for a new order. 'What two people do at home or in the hayloft', he declared, 'is nobody's business.' (Grau 1993: 25; *Spearhead* 29,

January; 31, March 1970; Husbands 1991: 95–7; Jensen 1993: 88, 94; Oosterhuis and Kennedy 1991: 251–2, 188–9.)

In examining women and fascism, the intention has been to show why we can no longer believe that fascism is to be seen as by definition a masculine movement pursuing a misogynist agenda. Certainly, it often shows such characteristics. But it is capable of winning over significant numbers of women and of being influenced by both electoral imperatives and internal dissent to take positions that are incompatible with our usual understanding. Much remains to be done in examining policies towards women across the range of fascisms that has emerged since the First World War. Much too is to be learned about what makes women vote for or even join such movements. But we also need to think again about fascism and masculinity. Both male bonding and heterosexual desire are crucial to understanding the extreme right, and the relationship between them is far more diverse than has often been suggested. If much has been written in recent years about women's role in society, much too has been written on fascism. A third area, the study of masculinities, has also begun to develop. All three would gain from the development of a new approach to gender and the fascist agenda.

References

Because some of the post-war extreme right publications are somewhat irregular in appearance, where possible I have given both the issue number and the date. In the case of the regular BUF publications, I have used the date only. Some material, such as the minutes of the NF National Directorate, are clearly indicated in the text. Public Record Office material is listed in the text as PRO HO, followed by the appropriate number.

Alberti, J. (1994) 'British Feminists and Anti-Fascism in the 1930s' in S. Oldfield (ed.), *This Working-Day World. Women's Lives and Culture(s) in Britain 1914–1945*, London: Taylor & Francis.
Allen, M. S. and Heyneman, J. H. (1934) *Woman at the Cross Roads*, London: Unicorn Press.
Anderson, I. (n.d., 1987) *100 Questions and Answers about the National Front*, London: Freedom Books.
Anon. (n.d., 1938) *Britain and Jewry*, London: Greater Britain Publications.
—— (1986) *Mosley's Blackshirts. The Inside Story of The British Union of Fascists 1932–1940*, London: Sanctuary Press.
Banister, J. (n.d., c. 1923) *Jews and the White Slave Traffic*, London: 'The Britons' Publishing Society.
Barr, A. (1994) interview for S. Cleary, *Rise of a New Eve*, Spectacle (video).
Bell, S. G. and Offen, K. M. (1983) *Women, the Family and Freedom. The Debate in Documents. Volume Two, 1880–1950*, Stanford: Stanford University Press.
Bellamy, R. (n.d.) *We Marched with Mosley*, unpublished manuscript.
Benewick, R. (1972) *The Fascist Movement in Britain*, London: Allen Lane: The Penguin Press.
Berry, P. and Bishop, A. (1985) *Testament of a Generation. The Journalism of Vera Brittain and Winifred Holtby*, London: Virago.
Betz, H.-G. (1990) 'Post-Modern Anti-Modernism: the West German Republikaner', *Politics and Society in Germany, Austria and Switzerland*, 2, 3: 1–22.
—— (1991) *Postmodern Politics in Germany. The Politics of Resentment*, London: Macmillan.

—— (1994) *Radical Right-Wing Populism in Western Europe*, London: Macmillan.
Biehl, J. and Staudenmaier, P. (1995) *Ecofascism. Lessons from the German Experience*, Edinburgh: AK Press.
Big Flame (1991) *Sexuality and Fascism*, London: 121 Bookshop.
Billig, M. (1978) *Fascists. A Social Psychological View of the National Front*, London: Harcourt Brace Jovanovitch.
—— (1979) *Psychology, Racism and Fascism*, Birmingham: A. F. & R. Publications.
Billig, M. and Bell, A. (1980) 'Fascist Parties in Post-War Britain', *Race Relations Abstracts*, 5, 1: 1–30.
Bleuel, H. P. (1973) *Sex and Society in Nazi Germany*, Philadelphia: J. B. Lippincott.
Boak, H. (1990) 'Women in Weimar Politics', *European History Quarterly*, 20, 3: 369–99.
Bock, G. (1984) 'Racism and Sexism in Nazi Germany: Motherhood, Compulsory Sterilization and the State' in R. Bridenthal, A. Grossman and M. Kaplan (eds), *When Biology Became Destiny*, New York: Monthly Review Press.
—— (1991) 'Antinatalism, Maternity and Paternity in National Socialist Racism' in G. Bock and P. Thane (eds), *Maternity and Gender Policies. Women and the Rise of the European Welfare States, 1880s–1950s*, London: Routledge.
Bridenthal, R. and Koonz, C. (1984) 'Beyond *Kinder, Küche, Kirche*: Weimar Women in Politics and Work' in R. Bridenthal, A. Grossman and M. Kaplan (eds), *When Biology Became Destiny. Women in Weimar and Nazi Germany*, New York: Monthly Review Press.
British National Party (1983) *Vote for Britain*, Hove: Albion Press.
—— (1992) *Fight Back! The Election Manifesto of the British National Party*, Welling: Albion Press.
—— (1997) *Britain Reborn. A Programme for the New Century*, Welling: Albion Press.
Bruley, S. (1986) *Leninism, Stalinism and the Women's Movement in Britain, 1920–1939*, London: Garland Press.
BUF (n.d.) 'London County Council Elections 1937' (leaflet).
Caldwell, L. (1986) 'Reproducers of the Nation: Women and the Family in Fascist Policy' in D. Forgacs (ed.), *Rethinking Italian Fascism. Capitalism, Populism and Culture*, London: Lawrence and Wishart.
Camus, J.-Y. (1992) 'Political Cultures within the Front National: The Emergence of a Counter-Ideology on the French Far-Right', *Patterns of Prejudice*, 26, 1/2: 5–16.
Caplan, J. (1979) 'Introduction to Female Sexuality in Fascist Ideology', *Feminist Review*, 1: 59–66.
Carioti, A. (1996) 'From the Ghetto to *Palazzo Chigi*: The Ascent of the

National Alliance' in R. S. Katz and P. Ignazi (eds), *Italian Politics. The Year of the Tycoon*, Oxford: Westview Press.

Cheles, L. (1991) '*Dolce Stil Nero?* Images of Women in the Graphic Propaganda of the Italian Neo-fascist Party' in Z. G. Baranski and S. W. Vinall (eds), *Women and Italy. Essays on Gender, Culture and History*, London: Macmillan.

—— (1995a) '"Nostalgia dell'avvenire". The Propaganda of the Italian Far Right between Tradition and Innovation' in L. Cheles, R. Ferguson and M. Vaughan (eds), *The Far Right in Western and Eastern Europe*, London: Longman.

—— (1995b) 'The Italian Far Right: Nationalist Attitudes and Views on Ethnicity and Immigration' in A. G. Hargreaves and J. Leaman (eds), *Racism, Ethnicity and Politics in Contemporary Europe*, Aldershot: Edward Elgar.

—— Ferguson, R. and Vaughan, M. (eds), (1995) *The Far Right in Western and Eastern Europe*, London: Longman.

Chiarini, R. (1995) 'The Italian Far Right: The Search for Legitimacy' in L. Cheles, R. Ferguson and M. Vaughan (eds), *The Far Right in Western and Eastern Europe*, London: Longman.

Childs, D. (1995) 'The Far Right in Germany since 1945' in L. Cheles, R. Ferguson and M. Vaughan (eds), *The Far Right in Western and Eastern Europe*, London: Longman.

Clark, M., Hine, D. and Irving, R. E. M. (1974) 'Divorce – Italian Style', *Parliamentary Affairs*, 27, 4: 333–58.

Cleary, S. (1994) *Rise of a New Eve*, Spectacle (video).

CNFE (1989) *Programme du CNFE*, Paris: CNFE.

Cochrane, R. and Billig, M. (1982) 'Adolescent Support for the National Front: A Test of Three Models of Political Extremism', *New Community*, 10, 1: 86–94.

Codreanu, C. Z. (1987) *The Nest Leader's Manual*, Madrid: Editorial 'Libertatea'.

Copsey, N. (1994) 'Fascism: the Ideology of the British National Party', *Politics*, 14, 3: 101–8.

Craig, F. W. S. (1984) *British Parliamentary Election Results 1974–1983*, Chichester: Parliamentary Research Services.

Cronin, M. (ed.) (1996) *The Failure of British Fascism*, London: Macmillan.

Cross, C. (1961) *The Fascists in Britain*, London: Barrie and Rockcliffe.

Cullen, S. (1987) 'The Development of the Ideas and Policy of the British Union of Fascists, 1932-40', *Journal of Contemporary History*, 22, 1: 115–36.

—— (1996) 'Four Women for Mosley: Women in the British Union of Fascists, 1932–40', *Oral History*, 24, 1: 49–59.

De Grand, A. (1976) 'Women Under Italian Fascism', *Historical Journal*, 19, 4: 947–68.

De Grazia, V. (1992) *How Fascism Ruled Women. Italy, 1922–1945*, Berkeley: University of California Press.

Detragiache, D. (1983) 'Il fascismo femminile da San Sepolcro all'affare Matteotti (1919–1925)', *Storia Contemporanea*, 14, 2: 211–51.

Drake, R. (1989) *The Revolutionary Mystique and Terrorism in Contemporary Italy*, Bloomington: Indiana University Press.

Driver, N. (n.d.) 'From the Shadows of Exile', unpublished manuscript.

Dupont, G. (1988) 'FN, GRECE: Deux Discours Sur La Femme', *Article 31*, 36: 18–20.

Durham, M. (1990) 'Women and the British Union of Fascists, 1932–1940' in T. Kushner and K. Lunn (eds), *The Politics of Marginality. Race, the Radical Right and Minorities in Twentieth Century Britain*, London: Frank Cass.

—— (1991) *Sex and Politics. The Family and Morality in the Thatcher Years*, London: Macmillan.

—— (1992) 'Gender and the British Union of Fascists', *Journal of Contemporary History*, 27, 3: 513–29.

—— (1996) 'The Conservative Party, the British Extreme Right and the Problem of Political Space, 1967–1983' in M. Cronin (ed.), *The Failure of British Fascism*, London: Macmillan.

—— (1997) 'Women and the Extreme Right: A Comment', *Terrorism and Political Violence*, 9, 3: 165–8.

Dutt, R. P. (1934) *Fascism and Social Revolution*, London: Martin Lawrence.

Eatwell, R. (1992) 'Why Has the Extreme Right Failed in Britain?' in P. Hainsworth (ed.), *The Extreme Right in Europe and the USA*, London: Pinter.

—— (1996a) *Fascism. A History*, London: Vintage.

—— (1996b) 'The Esoteric Ideology of the National Front in the 1980s' in M. Cronin (ed.), *The Failure of British Fascism*, London: Macmillan.

—— (1996c) 'On Defining the "Fascist Minimum": the Centrality of Ideology', *Journal of Political Ideologies*, 1, 3: 303–19.

Eglin, J. (1987) 'Women and Peace' in R. Taylor and N. Young (eds), *Campaigns for Peace: British Peace Movements in the Twentieth Century*, Manchester: Manchester University Press.

Empire Loyalists (1964) 'To the Electors' (leaflet).

—— (1964) 'Empire Loyalists Enter Election Fray' (leaflet).

Evans, R. (1976) 'German Women and the Triumph of Hitler', *Journal of Modern History*, 48, 1: 123–75.

—— (1987) *Comrades and Sisters. Feminism, Socialism and Pacifism in Europe 1870–1945*, Brighton: Wheatsheaf Books.

Fangen, K. (1997) 'Separate or Equal? The Emergence of an All-Female Group in the Rightist Underground in Norway', *Terrorism and Political Violence*, 9, 3: 122–64.

Farris, E. (1975) 'Takeoff Point for the National Socialist Party: the Landtag Election in Baden, 1929', *Central European History*, 8: 140–71.

Ferraresi, F. (1987) 'Julius Evola: Tradition, Reaction and the Radical Right', *Archives Européennes de Sociologie*, 28: 107–51.

—— (1988) 'The Radical Right in Postwar Italy', *Politics and Society*, 16, 1: 71–119.

Fielding, N. (1981) *The National Front*, London: Routledge and Kegan Paul.
Fischer, C. (1995) *The Rise of the Nazis*, Manchester: Manchester University Press.
Flood, C. (1997) 'National Populism' in C. Flood and L. Bell (eds), *Political Ideologies in Contemporary France*, London: Pinter.
Forgacs, D. (ed.) (1986) *Rethinking Italian Fascism. Capitalism, Populism and Culture*, London: Lawrence and Wishart.
Foucault, F. (1990) 'Le circle des femmes d' Europe. Maréchale nous voilà', *Les Cahiers du Féminisme* 54: 9–11.
Freeman, A. (1936) *We Fight For Freedom*, London: BUF Publications.
Frevert, U. (1989) *Women in German History. From Bourgeois Emancipation to Sexual Liberation*, Oxford: Berg.
Gable, G. (1991) 'The Far Right in Contemporary Britain' in L. Cheles, R. Ferguson and M. Vaughan (eds), *Neo-Fascism in Europe*, London: Longman.
—— (1995) 'Britain's Nazi underground' in L. Cheles, R. Ferguson and M. Vaughan (eds), *The Far Right in Western and Eastern Europe*, London: Longman.
Glass, D. V. (1967) *Population Policies and Movements in Europe*, London: Frank Cass.
Grau, G. (1993) *Hidden Holocaust? Gay and Lesbian Persecution in Germany 1933–45*, London: Cassell.
Gregor, A. J. (1979) *Italian Fascism and Developmental Dictatorship*, Princeton: Princeton University Press.
Griffin, R. (1993) *The Nature of Fascism*, London: Routledge.
Griffin, R. (ed.), (1995) *Fascism*, Oxford: Oxford University Press.
—— (1996) 'The "Post-Fascism" of the Alleanza Nazionale: a Case Study in Ideological Morphology', *Journal of Political Ideologies*, 1, 2: 123–45.
Griggs, A. B. (n.d., 1935) *Women and Fascism*, London: BUF Publications.
Grunberger, R. (1974) *A Social History of the Third Reich*, Harmondsworth: Penguin.
Hainsworth, P. (1992a) 'The Extreme Right in Post-War France: The Emergence and Success of the Front National' in P. Hainsworth (ed.), *The Extreme Right in Europe and the USA*, London: Pinter.
Hainsworth, P. (ed.) (1992b) *The Extreme Right in Europe and the USA*, London: Pinter.
Hanna, M. (1974) 'The National Front and other Right-wing Organisations', *New Community*, 3, 1–2: 49–55.
Harrison, B. (1978) *Separate Spheres. The Opposition to Women's Suffrage in Britain*, London: Croom Helm.
—— (1987) *Prudent Revolutionaries. Portraits of British Feminists between the Wars*, Oxford: Clarendon Press.
Harrop, M., England, J. and Husbands, C. T. (1980) 'The Bases of National Front Support', *Political Studies*, 28, 2: 271–83.

Hawks, O. (n.d., 1939) *Women Fight for Britain and for Britain Alone*, London: Greater Britain Publications.

Herf, J. (1984) *Reactionary Modernism. Technology, Culture and Politics in Weimar and the Third Reich*, Cambridge: Cambridge University Press.

Hill, R. and Bell, A. (1988) *The Other Face of Terror. Inside Europe's Neo-Nazi Network*, London: Grafton Books.

Hitler, A. (1969) *Mein Kampf*, London: Hutchinson.

Hofmann-Göttig, J. (1989) 'Die Neue Rechte: Die Mannerparteien', *Aus Politik und Zeitgeschichte*, B41–2: 21–31.

Holtby, W. (1934) *Women and a Changing Civilisation*, London: John Lane The Bodley Head.

Husbands, C. (1983) *Racial Exclusionism and the City: The Urban Support of the National Front*, London: George Allen and Unwin.

—— (1988) 'Extreme Right-Wing Politics in Great Britain: The Recent Marginalisation of the National Front', *West European Politics*, 11, 2: 65–79.

—— (1991) 'Militant Neo-nazism in the Federal Republic of Germany in the 1980s' in L. Cheles, R. Ferguson and M. Vaughan (eds), *Neo-Fascism in Europe*, London: Longman.

—— (1995) 'Militant Neo-Nazism in the Federal Republic of Germany in the 1990s' in L. Cheles, R. Ferguson and M. Vaughan (eds), *The Far Right in Western and Eastern Europe*, London: Longman.

Ignazi, P. (1989) *Il Polo Escluso. Profilo del Movimento Sociale Italiano*, Bologna: Società Editrice Il Mulino.

—— (1993) 'The Changing Profile of the Italian Social Movement' in P. H. Merkl and L. Weinberg (eds), *Encounters With the Contemporary Radical Right*, Oxford: Westview Press.

—— (1994) *Postfascisti? Dal Movimento sociale italiano ad Alleanza nazionale*, Bologna: Società Editrice Il Mulino.

Jeansonne, G. (1996) *Women of the Far Right. The Mothers' Movement and World War II*, Chicago: University of Chicago Press.

Jenkins, P. (1997) *Hoods and Shirts. The Extreme Right in Pennsylvania, 1925–1950*, Chapel Hill: University of North Carolina Press.

Jensen, E. (1993) 'International Nazi Cooperation: A Terrorist-Oriented Network' in T. Bjorgo and R. Witte (eds), *Racist Violence in Europe*, London: Macmillan.

Johnson, D. (1995) 'The New Right in France' in L. Cheles, R. Ferguson and M. Vaughan (eds), *The Far Right in Western and Eastern Europe*, London: Longman.

Kater, M. H. (1983) *The Nazi Party. A Social Profile of Members and Leaders, 1919–1945*, Cambridge, MA: Harvard University Press.

Kean, H. (1994) 'Searching for the Past in Present Defeat: the Construction of Historical and Political Identity in British Feminism in the 1920s and 1930s', *Women's History Review*, 3, 1: 57–80.

Kirkpatrick, C. (1938) *Nazi Germany: its Women and Family Life*, Indianapolis: Bobbs-Merrill.

Kitschelt, H. (1995) *The Radical Right in Western Europe. A Comparative Analysis*, Ann Arbor: University of Michigan Press.

Kofman, E. (1993) 'National Identity and Sexual and Cultural Differences in France' in M. Kelly and R. Bock (eds), *France: Nation and Region*, Southampton: University of Southampton Press.

Kolinsky, E. (1992) 'A Future for Right Extremism in Germany?' in P. Hainsworth (ed.), *The Extreme Right in Europe and the USA*, London: Pinter.

Koonz, C. (1984) 'The Competition for Women's Lebensraum, 1928–1934' in R. Bridenthal, A. Grossman and M. Kaplan (eds), *When Biology Became Destiny. Women in Weimar and Nazi Germany*, New York: Monthly Review Press.

—— (1987) *Mothers in the Fatherland. Women, the Family and Nazi Politics*, London: Jonathan Cape.

Kushner, T. (1989) *The Persistence of Prejudice. Antisemitism in British Society during the Second World War*, Manchester: Manchester University Press.

—— (1990) 'Politics and Race, Gender and Class: Refugees, Fascists and Domestic Service in Britain, 1933–1940' in T. Kushner and K. Lunn (eds), *The Politics of Marginality. Race, the Radical Right and Minorities in Twentieth Century Britain*, London: Frank Cass.

Kushner, T. and Lunn, K. (eds) (1990) *The Politics of Marginality. Race, the Radical Right and Minorities in Twentieth Century Britain*, London: Frank Cass.

Lane, B. M. and Rupp, L. J. (1978) *Nazi Ideology before 1933. A Documentation*, Manchester: Manchester University Press.

Le Bon, G. (1909) *The Crowd. A Study of the Popular Mind*, London: T. Fisher Unwin.

Lee, M. (1997) *The Beast Reawakens*, London: Little, Brown and Company.

Lehideux, M. C. (1994) interview for S. Cleary, *Rise of a New Eve*, Spectacle (video).

Lesselier, C. (1991) 'De la Vierge Marie à Jeanne d'Arc: images de femmes à l'extrême droite', *L'Homme et la Société*, 99/100: 99–113.

—— (1992/3) 'Apocalypse Now', *WAF Journal*, 4: 15–17.

Levy, D. R. (1989) 'Women of the French National Front', *Parliamentary Affairs*, 42, 1: 102–11.

Lewis, D. S. (1987) *Illusions of Grandeur. Mosley, Fascism and British Society, 1931–81*, Manchester: Manchester University Press.

Liddington, J. (1984) *The Life and Times of a Respectable Rebel: Selina Cooper 1864–1946*, London: Virago.

Linehan, T. P. (1996) *East London for Mosley. The British Union of Fascists in East London and South-West Essex 1933–40*, London: Frank Cass.

Lunn, K. and Thurlow, R. C. (eds) (1980) *British Fascism. Essays on the Radical Right in Inter-War Britain*, London: Croom Helm.

Lyttelton, A. (1973) *The Seizure of Power. Fascism in Italy 1919–1929*, London: Weidenfeld and Nicolson.

Macciocchi, M.-A. (1979) 'Female Sexuality in Fascist Ideology', *Feminist Review* 1: 67–82.
Mandle, W. F. (1966) 'The Leadership of the British Union of Fascists', *Australian Journal of Politics and History*, 12, 3: 360–83.
—— (1968) *Anti-Semitism and the British Union of Fascists*, London: Longman.
Marcus, J. (1995) *The National Front and French Politics*, London: Macmillan.
Marsh, D. and Chambers, J. (1981) *Abortion Politics*, London: Junction Books.
Mason, T. (1976a) 'Women in Germany, 1925–1940: Family, Welfare and Work. Part I', *History Workshop*, 1: 74–113.
—— (1976b) 'Women in Germany, 1925–1940: Family, Welfare and Work. Part II', *History Workshop*, 2: 5–32.
Mayall, D. (1990) 'Rescued from the Shadows of Exile: Nellie Driver, Autobiography and the British Union of Fascists' in T. Kushner and K. Lunn (eds), *The Politics of Marginality. Race, the Radical Right and Minorities in Twentieth Century Britain*, London: Frank Cass.
Mayer, N. and Perrineau, P. (1992) 'Why Do They Vote for Le Pen?', *European Journal of Political Research*, 22, 1: 123–41.
Mercer, C. (1986) 'Fascist Ideology' in J. Donald and S. Hall (eds), *Politics and Ideology*, Milton Keynes: Open University Press.
Méricourt, O. (1990) 'L'Extreme droite en France. Enfants, cuisine, église (Kinder, Küche, Kirche)', *Les Cahiers du Féminisme*, 54: 5–8.
Merkl, P. H. (1997) 'Why Are They So Strong Now? Comparative Reflections on the Revival of the Radical Right in Europe' in P. H. Merkl and L. Weinberg (eds), *The Revival of Right-Wing Extremism in the Nineties*, London: Frank Cass.
Merkl, P. H. and Weinberg, L. (eds), (1993) *Encounters With the Contemporary Radical Right*, Oxford: Westview Press.
—— (1997) *The Revival of Right-Wing Extremism in the Nineties*, London: Frank Cass.
Meyer, D. (1989) *Sex and Power. The Rise of Women in America, Russia, Sweden and Italy*, Middletown: Wesleyan University Press.
Millett, K. (1971) *Sexual Politics*, London: Rupert Hart-Davis.
Minkenberg, M. (1992) 'The New Right in Germany. The Transformation of Conservatism and the Extreme Right', *European Journal of Political Research*, 22, 1: 55–81.
Montagu, I. (1967) *Germany's New Nazis*, London: Panther.
Mosley, N. (1983) *Beyond the Pale. Sir Oswald Mosley and Family 1933–1980*, London: Secker and Warburg.
Mosley, O. (1932) *The Greater Britain*, London: BUF.
—— (1936) *Fascism: 100 Questions Asked and Answered*, London: BUF Publications.
—— (1938) *Tomorrow We Live*, London: British Union.
—— (1961) *Mosley–Right or Wrong?*, London: Lion Books.
Mosse, G. L. (1964) *The Crisis of German Ideology. Intellectual Origins of the Third Reich*, New York: The Universal Library.

—— (1985) *Nationalism and Sexuality. Middle-Class Morality and Sexual Norms in Modern Europe*, Madison: University of Wisconsin Press.

Mushaben, J. M. (1995) 'The Rise of *Femi-Nazis*? Female Participation in Right-Extremist Movements in Unified Germany', paper prepared for presentation at the Annual Meeting of the American Political Science Association, Chicago.

Nagle, J. D. (1970) *The National Democratic Party. Right Radicalism in the Federal Republic of Germany*, Berkeley: University of California Press.

National Front (n.d.) 'Warning! Attacks on White Women Are on the Increase in the South London Area', Croydon: National Front (leaflet).

—— (n.d., 1974) *Britain: World Power or Pauper State?*, Croydon: National Front Policy Committee.

—— (1974) *For A New Britain. The Manifesto of the National Front*, Croydon: National Front.

—— (n.d., c. 1978) 'National Front: What is the Real Truth?' (leaflet).

—— (n.d., c. 1979) 'Church Leaders who've Forgotten their Duties' (leaflet).

—— (1979a) *It's Our Country – Let's Win It Back!*, London: National Front.

—— (1979b) *Statement of Policy*, London: National Front.

—— (1981) *We Are NF*, London: Newport Fotos.

—— (1983) *Let Britain Live! The Manifesto of the National Front For The General Election of 9th June 1983*, Croydon: National Front.

—— (1988) 'John Hill, 5 May 1988' (leaflet).

—— (1992) *Caring for Britain. The Manifesto of the National Front*, Worthing: National Front.

National Front opposition (1979) 'Election of Members to the National Directorate' (leaflet).

Nationalist Welfare Association (n.d., 1984) *Marching On With The National Front*, London: Nationalist Welfare Association.

Neocleous, M. (1997) *Fascism*, Buckingham: Open University Press.

Newell, J. L. and Bull, M. J. (1996) 'The April 1996 Italian General Election: The Left on Top or on Tap?', *Parliamentary Affairs*, 49, 4: 616–47.

Newitt, H. (1937) *Women Must Choose*, London: Victor Gollancz.

Niethammer, L. (1979) 'Male Fantasies: an Argument for and with an Important New Study in History and Psychoanalysis', *History Workshop*, 7: 176–86.

Noether, E. P. (1982) 'Italian Women and Fascism: A Reevaluation', *Italian Quarterly*, 22, 3: 69–80.

Nye, R. A. (1975) *The Origins of Crowd Psychology: Gustave LeBon and the Crisis of Mass Democracy in the Third Republic*, London: Sage.

O'Hara, L. (1993a) 'Notes From the Underground, Part 3: British Fascism 1983–6', *Lobster*, 25: 16–20, 26.

—— (1993b) 'Notes From the Underground, Part 4: British Fascism 1983–6 (II)', *Lobster*, 26: 13–18.

Ó Maoláin, C. (1987) *The Radical Right: A World Directory*, London: Longman.

Oosterhuis, H. and Kennedy, H. (1991) *Homosexuality and Male Bonding in Pre-Nazi Germany*, New York: Harrington Park Press.

Passmore, K. (1997) *From Liberalism to Fascism. The Right in a French Province, 1928–1939*, Cambridge: Cambridge University Press.

Payne, S. G. (1962) *Falange. A History of Spanish Fascism*, Stanford: Stanford University Press.

—— (1995) *A History of Fascism, 1914-1945*, London: UCL Press.

Preti, L. (1974) 'Fascist Imperialism and Racism' in R. Sarti (ed.), *The Ax Within. Italian Fascism in Action*, New York: New Viewpoints.

Quine, M. S. (1996) *Population Politics in Twentieth-Century Europe*, London: Routledge.

Rawnsley, S. J. (1981) 'Fascism and Fascists in Britain in the 1930s. A Case Study of Fascism in the North of England in a Period of Economic and Political Change', unpublished Ph.D. thesis, University of Bradford.

Reich, W. (1975) *The Mass Psychology of Fascism*, Harmondsworth: Penguin.

Revelli, M. (1987) 'Italy' in D. Mühlberger (ed.), *The Social Basis of European Fascist Movements*, London: Croom Helm.

Richardson, M. (n.d.) Unpublished letter, MSS 127/NU/GS/3/5D, Modern Records Centre, University of Warwick.

Richardson, M. R. (1953) *Laugh A Defiance*, London: George Weidenfeld and Nicolson.

Roberts, D. D. (1979) *The Syndicalist Tradition and Italian Fascism*, Manchester: Manchester University Press.

Rockwell, G. L. (1971) *In Hoc Signo Vinces*, Arlington: WUNS.

Roux, M. (1995) 'The FN: Twists and Turns of a Fascist Front', *Trotskyist International*, 16: 1, 5–10.

Rowbotham, S. (1974) *Hidden from History. 300 Years of Women's Oppression and the Fight Against It*, London: Pluto Press.

Rupp, L. J. (1978) *Mobilizing Women for War. German and American Propaganda*, Princeton: Princeton University Press.

Safran, W. (1993) 'The National Front in France: From Lunatic Fringe to Limited Respectability' in P. H. Merkl and L. Weinberg (eds), *Encounters With the Contemporary Radical Right*, Oxford: Westview Press.

Schain, M. (1987) 'The National Front in France and the Construction of Political Legitimacy', *West European Politics*, 10, 2: 229–52.

Scott, D. (1972) 'A Political Sociology of Minorities: the Impact of Coloured Immigrants on Local Politics', unpublished Ph.D. thesis, University of Bristol.

Searchlight (n.d., 1989) *From Ballots to Bombs. The Inside Story of the National Front's Political Soldiers*, London: Searchlight Publishing.

Segal, L. (1989) 'Slow Change or No Change? Feminism, Socialism and the Problem of Men', *Feminist Review*, 31: 5–21.

Showalter, D. E. (1982) *Little Man, What Now? Der Stürmer in the Weimar Republic*, Hamden: Archon Press.

Sidoti, F. (1992) 'The Extreme Right in Italy: Ideological Orphans and Countermobilization' in P. Hainsworth (ed.), *The Extreme Right in Europe and the USA*, London: Pinter.

Simmons H. G. (1996) *The French National Front. The Extremist Challenge to Democracy*, Oxford: Westview Press.

Simpson, A. W. B. (1992) *In the Highest Degree Odious. Detention Without Trial In Wartime Britain*, Oxford: Clarendon Press.

Six Point Group (1934–5) *Annual Report*, London: Six Point Group.

Skidelsky, R. (1975) *Oswald Mosley*, London: Macmillan.

Soloway, R. A. (1982) *Birth Control and the Population Question in England, 1877–1930*, London: University of North Carolina Press.

—— (1990) *Demography and Degeneration. Eugenics and the Declining Birthrate in Twentieth-Century Britain*, Chapel Hill: University of North Carolina Press.

Soucy, R. (1986) *French Fascism: The First Wave, 1924–1933*, London: Yale University Press.

—— (1995) *French Fascism: The Second Wave 1933–1939*, London: Yale University Press.

Spackman, B. (1990) 'The Fascist Rhetoric of Virility', *Stanford Italian Review*, 8, 1/2: 81–101.

Stephenson, J. (1975) *Women in Nazi Society*, London: Croom Helm.

—— (1981) *The Nazi Organisation of Women*, London: Croom Helm.

—— (1983) 'National Socialism and Women Before 1933' in P. D. Stachura (ed.), *The Nazi Machtergreifung*, London: George Allen and Unwin.

Stachura, P. D. (ed.) (1983) *The Nazi Machtergreifung*, London: George Allen and Unwin.

Sternhell, Z., Sznajder, M. and Asheri, M. (1994) *The Birth of Fascist Ideology*, Princeton: Princeton University Press.

Stirbois, M.-F. (1994) interview for S. Cleary, *Rise of a New Eve*, Spectacle (video).

Stöss, R. (1991) *Politics Against Democracy. Right-Wing Extremism in West Germany*, Oxford: Berg.

Strachey, J. (1933) *The Menace of Fascism*, Victor Gollancz.

Taguieff, P.-A. (1989) 'The Doctrine of the National Front in France (1972–1989): A Revolutionary Programme? Ideological Aspects of a National-Populist Mobilization', *New Political Science*, 16/17: 29–70.

—— (1993–4) 'From Race to Culture: The New Right's View of European Identity', *Telos*, 98–9: 99–125.

Tassani, G. (1990) 'The Italian Social Movement from Almirante to Fini' in R. Y. Nanetti and R. Catanzaro (eds), *Italian Politics: A Review, Volume 4*, London: Pinter.

Tauber, K. P. (1967) *Beyond Eagle and Swastika. German Nationalism Since 1945*, Middletown: Wesleyan University Press.

Taylor, S. (1983) *Germany 1918–1933. Revolution, Counter-Revolution and the Rise of Hitler*, London: Duckworth.

Taylor, S. (1982) *The National Front in English Politics*, London: Macmillan.
Theweleit, K. (1987) *Male Fantasies I. Women, Floods, Blood, History*, Cambridge: Polity Press.
—— (1989) *Male Fantasies II. Male Bodies: Psychoanalysing the White Terror*, Cambridge: Polity Press.
Thomson, A. R. (n.d., c. 1934) *The Corporate State*, London: B.U.F. Publications.
—— (n.d., c. 1937) *The Coming Corporate State*, London: Action Press.
—— (n.d., c. 1938) *The Coming Corporate State*, London: Greater Britain Publications.
Thurlow, R. (1987) *Fascism in Britain. A History, 1918–1985*, Oxford: Basil Blackwell.
Toczek, N. (1992) *The Bigger Tory Vote*, Stirling: AK Press.
Tyndall, J. (n.d., 1977) *The Spoken Word. A Guide to Public Speaking and the Presentation of Meetings*, Teddington: National Front.
—— (1988) *The Eleventh Hour. A Call for British Rebirth*, London: Albion Press.
Usborne, C. (1992) *The Politics of the Body in Weimar Germany*, London: Macmillan.
Vaughan, M. (1995) 'The Extreme Right in France: "Lepenisme" or the Politics of Fear' in L. Cheles, R. Ferguson and M. Vaughan (eds), *The Far Right in Western and Eastern Europe*, London: Longman.
Vedder-Shults, N. (1982) 'Motherhood for the Fatherland: The Portrayal of Women in Nazi Propaganda', unpublished Ph.D. thesis, University of Wisconsin-Madison.
Walker, M. (1977) *The National Front*, London: Fontana/Collins.
Ware, V. (n.d., 1978) *Women and the National Front*, Birmingham: A. F. & R. Publications.
Warner, G. (1981) 'France' in S. J. Woolf (ed.), *Fascism in Europe*, London: Methuen.
Webber, G. C. (1984) 'Patterns of Membership and Support for the British Union of Fascists', *Journal of Contemporary History*, 19, 4: 575–606.
Weinberg, L. B. (1979) *After Mussolini: Italian Neo-Fascism and the Nature of Fascism*, Washington DC: University Press of America.
Weindling, P. (1989) *Health, Race and German Politics between National Unification and Nazism, 1870–1945*, Cambridge: Cambridge University Press.
Weir, S. (1978) 'Youngsters in the Front Line', *New Society*, 27 April: 189–93.
Wolff, C. (1986) *Magnus Hirschfeld*, London: Quartet.
Zimmermann, E. and Saalfeld, T. (1993) 'The Three Waves of West German Right-Wing Extremism' in P. H. Merkl and L. Weinberg (eds), *Encounters With the Contemporary Radical Right*, Oxford: Westview Press.

Index

abortion 13, 23, 82, 86, 87, 88, 89, 90–1, 92, 93, 125–6, 128, 130, 131, 133, 135–44, 145, 146, 155, 158, 160, 173, 174
Action Front of National Socialists/National Activists (Germany) 77–8, 87
Aitken, M. 54, 55
Alleanza Nazionale (AN) (Italy) 80–1, 85, 90
Allen, M. 43–4, 69, 70
Anderson, I. 112–13
anti-Semitism 3, 9–10, 15–16, 17, 18, 24, 28, 29, 41–2, 43, 55, 58, 60, 75, 114, 118, 152–3, 161, 163, 169

Ballard, M. 159
Barr, A. 117–18
Bean, J. 123–4
Bell, D. 55
Benoist, A. de 82, 149
Betz, H.-G. 172
Billig, M. 171
Birdwood, Lady J. 98, 114
birth control 13, 18, 23, 38–41, 89, 121–31, 142, 143, 168, 172, 175
Booth, A. 37
Bortone, A. P. 88, 93
Bothwell, S. 102
Bounevialle, R. de 101
Brady, S. 129, 130, 131

Brakes, B. 103
Brand, E. 134
Britain: post-war 94–164 171–2; pre-war 1, 27–73, 166, 169–70
British Fascists (BFs) 27–8
British Mothers' Campaign to Keep Out the Boat People 110
British Movement 96, 99, 102, 112
British National Party (BNP): 1960s group of that name 95, 96, 120, 158; later group 98, 99, 100, 113–18, 131–5, 142–6, 149–52, 160–1, 163–4, 172, 174, 181
British Union *see* British Union of Fascists
British Union of Fascists (BUF) 27–73, 146, 147, 169–70, 173, 174, 175, 178, 181
Britons, the (anti-Jewish society) 42
Brons, A. 106, 110
Buckley, R. 103, 104

Caine, P. 105
Caldwell, L. 167
Caplan, J. 176
Carrington Wood, Mrs H. 64–5
Catholicism 8–9, 38–40, 90, 130, 139, 167, 169, 175, 176
Cecil, N. 108
CEDADE (Spain) 89
Cheles, L. 87–8

Index

Chesterton, A. K. 41, 95, 96, 98, 101, 103, 120
Chesterton, G. K. 39, 98, 120, 153
CNFE (France) 92, 93
Combat 18 (Britain) 99–100
Corderey, U. 52
Corporate State 8, 30–4, 37, 38
Cosgree, J. 109
Cossar, J. 70–1
Cullen, S. 175

Dalton, T. 106, 117
D'Annunzio, G. 7, 11–12, 167
Darré, W. 18
Davies, P. 54
Denny, T. 106, 109, 153
Deutsche Frauenfront (DFF) (Germany) 87
Deutscher Frauenorden (DFO) (Germany) 19
Deutsche Frauenschaft (Germany) 87
Diehl, G. 19–20
Distributism 98, 120–1, 130, 139, 140, 155
divorce 24, 87, 90, 130, 155, 156, 160
Dixon, M. 137
DNVP (Germany) 10, 11, 20
Donati, I. 12
Downe, Viscountess D. 70, 71
Driver, N. 71
Drummond, F. 46
DVU (Germany) 76, 77, 85, 93

Eatwell, R. 5
Elam, N. 45–6, 59, 69, 70
equal pay 25, 31, 32, 33, 34, 35, 37, 170
eugenics 16, 17, 18, 23, 24, 38, 39, 40, 75, 119–35, 144–5, 146, 152, 169
Evans, R. 20
Evola, J. 79, 89

Falange (Spain) 11

family: and the British National Party 115, 131–5, 145, 151, 156, 160; and the British Union of Fascists 31, 32, 34, 35, 36, 37, 38, 40, 41, 42, 48, 60, 147; and the Front National 91, 92; and Italian Fascism 13–14, 176; and the National Front 108, 119–23, 125–31, 137, 140, 147, 152, 154, 155, 156, 158, 159; and National Socialism 15, 16, 17, 22, 23, 24, 25, 26, 177, 181; and post-war Italy 87, 88, 89, 173
Fascism, Italian 1, 6–9, 11–15, 39, 74, 167, 171, 174, 176
fascism, problems of definition 1–3, 5–6, 74–6, 165, 171
Feder, G. 18, 21
feminism: and the British National Party 163–4; and the British Union of Fascists 29, 30, 31, 32, 37, 44–6, 53, 65, 147, 170; and fascism 166, 172, 174–5; and the Front National 93; and Italian Fascism 12, 15–16; and the National Front 147, 148–55; and National Socialism 19–20, 22, 177; and post-war Italy 88, 89
Field, J. 152–3
Fountaine, A. 138
France 1, 11, 81–3, 84, 85–6, 89, 90–3, 173, 174
Frauenbund (Germany) 86
Free German Workers' Party (FAP) (Germany) 78, 86, 87, 181
Freeman, Lady E. 101
Frick, W. 23
Front National (FN) (France) 2, 82–3, 85–6, 90–3, 171, 172, 173, 174
Futurism 7, 167

Galton, F. 16, 149
German Reich Party (DRP) 76, 86

Germany: post-war 2, 76–9, 84, 85, 89, 93, 170, 171, 174; pre-war 1, 2, 4, 5, 9–11, 16–26, 39, 43, 47, 48, 168–9, 174, 177, 180–1
Giles, C. 105
Gobineau, A. de 6, 149
Goebbels, J. 168, 170
Goold, G. 102
Gottschewski, L. 180–1
Greater Britain Movement 96, 120, 158
Greene, L. *see* Von Goetz, L.
Griffin, J. 111
Griffin, N. 100
Griffin, R. 5
Griggs, A. B. 33, 41, 47–8, 52, 53, 56, 57, 60, 62, 64, 65, 66, 67, 69

Hadlich, E. 21
Hawks, O. 34, 36, 66, 68, 69, 71
Hernon, I. 114, 117–18
Hess, R. 24
Himmler, H. 24, 181
Hitler, A. 10, 16–18, 21–2, 74, 176, 179
Holtby, W. 29, 166, 170, 175, 176
homosexuality 145, 156, 160, 181
Hunt, N. A. 133–4
Husbands, C. 116

Ignazi, P. 173
Iron Guard (Romania) 11, 98, 141, 172
Italy: post-war 79–81, 83–4, 85, 87–90, 98, 173–4; pre-war 1, 6–9, 11–16, 41, 46–8, 167, 176

James, M. 104
Jones, S. 103
Joyce, W. 27, 28, 59
Jung, C. 149

King, L. A. 71
Kitschelt, H. 166
Koonz, C. 177, 178

Kühnen, M. 78, 171
Kushner, T. 72

Le Bon, G. 6, 179
League of Empire Loyalists (Britain) 95, 96, 101, 121
League for National Life 39–40
Lehideux, M. C. 92–3
Le Pen, J.-M. 81, 82, 83, 85, 90, 91, 172
lesbianism 149, 152, 155, 156, 157
Lewis, D. S. 170
LIFE 136, 139, 141, 143
Loffredo, F. 15
Lyons, E. 47

Macciocchi, M.-A. 176, 178
Macdonald, C. 103
McKenzie, S. 104, 109, 138
Mackey, A. 120–1
Makgill, Lady E. 50, 60, 63, 66
Männerbund 180–1
marriage loans 14, 22, 26
Mason, T. 22
Matthews, B. 104
Matthews, P. 130
Mégret, B. 93
Merkl, P. H. 174
Millett, K. 166
Minkenberg, M. 166
Mitchell, B. 104, 105, 109
Morris, S. 59, 71
Mosley, Lady M. 52, 56, 63, 65, 66
Mosley, Sir O. 27, 28, 29, 30, 36, 38, 40, 41, 48, 49, 50, 58, 59, 60, 61, 63–4, 69, 70, 95, 170
Mosse, G. L. 180
motherhood: and the British National Party 132, 143, 150–1, 152, 156; and the British Union of Fascists 29, 31, 33–4, 35, 36, 38, 41, 42, 47, 170; and fascism 172; and the Front National 91, 93; and Italian Fascism 13–14, 15, 176, 178; and the National

Front 110, 111, 122, 123, 128, 129, 130, 131, 138, 140, 142, 149, 153, 154, 155; and National Socialism 18, 22, 23, 24, 169; and post-war Germany 86; and post-war Italy 88
MSI (Italy) 79–81, 85, 87–90, 171, 173–4
Munson, A. 101
Murray, C. 155–6
Mushaben, J. M. 86, 173
Mussolini, A. 90
Mussolini, B. 1, 7, 8, 12, 13, 15, 74, 167, 176, 179

National Action Party (Britain) 112
National Association of the Sisters of the Legionnaires of Fiume and Dalmatia 1–12
National Democratic Party (NPD) (Germany) 76, 77, 84, 86, 93, 174
National Democrats (Britain) 99, 106, 112, 114
National Front (NF) (Britain) 2, 96–113, 116–17, 118, 119–31, 136–42, 146, 147–9, 151, 152–6, 157–60, 161–3, 171, 174, 178, 181
National Front Constitutional Movement (Britain) 97, 104, 138
National Party (Britain) 97, 104, 129
National Socialism, German 1, 2, 3, 4, 5, 9–11, 16–26, 132, 146, 166, 168–9, 171, 174, 175, 177, 180, 181
National Socialist Alliance (Britain) 99
National Socialist League (Britain) 28, 59
National Socialist Movement (Britain) 96, 161
National Viewers' and Listeners' Association 156–7, 158

Nationalist Association (Italy) 7, 8, 12, 167
Nationalsozialistische Frauenschaft (NSF) (Germany) 19, 20, 21, 25
Neil, C. 105
New National Front (NNF) (Britain) 98, 113, 131
Newland Movement (Germany) 19–20
NF Women's Support Group (Britain) 109
Niehammer, L. 180
Norway 178
Nouvelle Droite (France) 81–2, 149
Nuova Destra (Italy) 80, 88

O'Brien, J. 96, 124–5, 126

Pankhurst, S. 46, 47
Parker, V. 113
Payne, S. 166
Pearce, J. 106, 153, 155
Pearson, Lady 70, 71, 72
Peel, P. 162
Piat, Y. 83
population 13–14, 16–18, 22–4, 31–5, 38–41, 75, 91, 92, 93, 119–35, 137, 140, 142, 169, 172
pornography 151, 156, 160–1
prostitution 16–17, 42, 159
Pullen, B. 72
Pye, M. 60

Quine, M. S. 169

racism 3, 15, 17, 109, 117, 119, 120, 127, 133, 137, 140–1, 144, 156, 161–4, 178; and immigration 77, 82, 84–5, 91, 92, 95, 96, 124, 132
Rayner, Mrs H. 70, 75
Reeve, L. M. 71
Reich, W. 166, 175, 180
Reid, J. 102

Republikaner (REPs) (Germany) 2, 77, 85, 86, 93, 171, 174
Rescue-Pro-Life Action Network 141
Richardson, M. 46, 54, 63–4
Rinaldi, A. B. 88
Rockwell, L. 179
Romania 11, 98, 141, 172
Rosenberg, A. 18, 21, 181
Rowbotham S. 166
Rupp, L. 24
Ryan, C. 115

Sandland, J. 104, 137
Scholtz-Klink, G. 25–6
Seelig-Thomann, A. 47
Segal, L. 180
sexual morality 16–17, 19, 23–4, 41–4, 86, 121, 136–8, 142, 145, 157–9, 160, 172, 177
Shore, O. F. C. 56–7, 66
Skeggs, M. 136–7
Skingirl Front Deutschland (SFD) (Germany) 87
Socialist Reich Party (SRP) (Germany) 76, 86
Society for the Protection of Unborn Children 136, 139
sociobiology 148–9
Sorel, G. 6, 45
Spain 1, 11, 88–9
Spengler, O. 10, 125, 137
Steele, M. 68, 69
Stephenson, J. 19, 25, 177
Steven, H. 103, 104, 105, 178
Stevenson, C. 156
Stirbois, M.-F. 83, 84, 91–2
Strasser, G. 10, 11, 20–1, 76
Strasser, O. 10, 76, 98
Streicher, J. 18
Suffragettes 44–6, 59, 63, 153

Taylor, C. 105–6, 111–12
Terza Posizione (Italy) 80, 98
Theweleit, K. 180

Thomson, A. R. 27, 30–2, 39
Tyndall, J. 96, 97, 98, 108, 113, 115, 120, 121–4, 126, 127, 128–9, 132, 133, 134, 137, 149, 161, 179
Tyndall, V. 113

Union Movement (Britain) 95, 112
USA 91, 114, 128–9, 131–2, 163–4, 178, 179

Valkyria (Norway) 178
Verrall, R. 106, 110, 127–8, 137, 148–9
Viking Youth (Germany) 78, 87
Von Goetz, L. 101, 133

Walters, A. 101
Ware, V. 178
Webster, M. 96, 97, 99, 105, 106, 108, 123, 136, 161, 181
Wells, T. 132–3
Whinfield, M. G. 70
White, Jean 104, 138
White, Joan 151
Whitehouse, M. 156, 158, 160
Wilkinson, E. 53
Winch, E. 35, 65
Wingfield, T. 106, 111–12, 114, 142
Wiltshire, M. 111
women and war 66–9, 111, 178
women and work 14–15, 19, 21, 22, 24–6, 31, 32, 33, 34–8, 47–8, 86, 88, 89, 91–2, 93, 115, 131, 150–2, 153–6, 168, 172
Women for Aryan Unity 87
Women's Guild of Empire 46
Wright, S. 102, 104

Yianni, C. 113, 114
Yockey, F. P. 95, 149, 179
Young National Front (YNF) (Britain) 109–10, 112, 137, 161
Young Nationalists (Britain) 113

Zander, E. 19, 20, 21